W9-DJE-200

TRAINING COUNSELLING SUPERVISORS

Counselling Supervision

The *Counselling Supervision* series, edited by Michael Carroll and Elizabeth Holloway, has a clearly defined focus on counselling supervision issues and emphasizes the actual practice of counselling supervision, drawing on up-to-date models of supervision to assist, inform and update trainee and practising counsellors, counselling psychologists and psychotherapists.

Titles in the series include:

Counselling Supervision in Context
edited by Michael Carroll and Elizabeth Holloway

Training Counselling Supervisors: Strategies, Models and Methods
edited by Elizabeth Holloway and Michael Carroll

TRAINING COUNSELLING SUPERVISORS

Strategies, Methods and Techniques

Edited by
Elizabeth Holloway and Michael Carroll

SAGE Publications
London • Thousand Oaks • New Delhi

First published 1999

SAGE Publications Ltd
6 Bonhill Street
London EC2A 4PU

SAGE Publications Inc
2455 Teller Road
Thousand Oaks, California 91320

SAGE Publications India Pvt Ltd
32, M-Block Market
Greater Kailash – I
New Delhi 110 048

British Library Cataloguing in Publication data

A catalogue record for this book is available from the British Library

ISBN 0-7619-5786-3
ISBN 0-7619-5787-1 (pbk)

Library of Congress catalog card number 98–61794

Typeset by Photoprint, Torquay, Devon
Printed in Great Britain by Biddles Ltd, Guildford, Surrey

Contents

Notes on Contributors

Michael Carroll, Ph.D. is a chartered counselling psychologist and Fellow of the BAC. He has been Director of Studies in Psychology and Counselling at Roehampton Institute London and Director of Counselling and Training at Right Cavendish, London. He is consultant to a number of organizations in both the public and private spheres.

Hardin Coleman, Ph.D. is an Associate Professor in the Department of Counseling Psychology at the University of Wisconsin-Madison. He received his Masters in Counseling Psychology from the University of Vermont and his doctorate in Counseling Psychology from Stanford University in 1992. His primary area of research is in multi-cultural counselling training for counsellors. He co-edited *Multicultural Counselling Competencies* with Donald B. Pope-Davis in 1997.

Maria C. Gilbert, MA (Clin Psych), has extensive experience in adult education and psychotherapy, as well as in the supervision and training of psychotherapists and psychotherapists' supervisors in Integrative, Transactional Analysis and Gestalt psychotherapy. She is a Teaching Member of both the Gestalt Psychotherapy Training Institute in the United Kingdom and of the International Transactional Analysis Association. Currently she is head of the Integrative Psychotherapy and the Supervision trainings at the Metanoia Institute in West London.

Shoshana Hellman, Ed.D, was born in Israel. She has a BA from Hebrew University in Jerusalem in English and French literature and a teaching certificate, an MA in linguistics from the Sorbonne in Paris and a doctorate from Columbia University, New York, in counselling psychology. Since 1980, she has worked as a supervisor for school counsellors for the Ministry of Education in Israel.

She also teaches courses in counselling and supervision at the university level.

Julie Hewson, BA (Hons) postgraduate, Cert. ED Dip SW, CQSW, TSTA, CTA, BAC Registered Supervisor and Assessor of Supervisors, registered with UKCP. She is the Director of the Iron Mill Centre in Devon and Cornwall providing Counselling, Psychotherapy and Supervision training and Management Consultancy Services. She is currently delivering the first Supervision Training in the Czech Republic and regularly works in Dublin and Zurich. Julie is pursuing a Ph.D. entitled 'Shame in the Supervisory Process'.

Elizabeth L. Holloway, Ph.D., is a professor in the Department of Counseling Psychology at the University of Wisconsin-Madison and has directed clinical training centres at the Universities of California, Oregon and Wisconsin. She is a Fellow of Division 17 (Counseling Psychology) of the American Psychological Association and holds a Diploma in Counseling Psychology of the American Board of Professional Psychology. Elizabeth is author of *Clinical Supervision* (1995, Sage).

Francesca Inskipp, is an Accredited Supervisor and Fellow of BAC. She is co-director of CASCADE, a training organization for supervisors. She has been involved in the training of counsellors and supervisors since 1973, and has published several books and audiotapes on supervision, counselling skills and on counsellor training.

Willem Lammers, is a clinical psychologist and psychotherapist with a specialization as a Teaching and Supervising Transactional Analyst in the field of psychotherapy. He is the founder and director of the IAS Institute for training in counselling and supervision in Maienfeld, Switzerland. Besides his tasks as a trainer, he runs a practice for supervision and organizational consulting.

Susan Allstetter Neufeldt, Ph.D., is training clinic director and lecturer in the Counseling/Clinical/school Psychology Program at the University of California, Santa Barbara. Author of *Supervision Strategies for the First Practicum*, she has written and lectured widely on the topic of reflectivity in the training of therapists and supervisors.

Charlotte Sills, MA, MSc (Psychotherapy), PGCE, Dip Syst Int. Psych. UKCP Registered Psychotherapist. She is a counsellor and psychotherapist in private practice and has worked as a trainer and consultant in a variety of settings. She is a qualified Transactional Analysis clinician and a Teaching and Supervising Transactional Analyst. She is author of a number of publications on counselling and psychotherapy. Charlotte is head of the Transactional Analysis Department at Metanoia Institute in West London.

Acknowledgements

Our thanks to the chapter authors – they have contributed generously from their experience and wisdom and put up gallantly with our editorial demands. To Susan Worsey, Melissa Dunlop and Kate Scott at Sage – our thanks for on-going support and patience throughout the project.

A special mention to Leo Canny, Josephine Murphy, Liam McCarthy and Margaret O'Shea and the supervisor trainees in Ireland who have brought a humour and groundedness to our ideas.

Chapter 1 adapted from E.H's chapter in C. Edward Watkins Jr. (1997), *Handbook of Psychotherapy Supervision*, pp. 249–76, reproduced by permission of John Wiley and Sons, Inc.

Introduction

Elizabeth Holloway and Michael Carroll

Throughout Britain, Europe and the United States trainers are using innovative programmes to teach the professional role and skills of supervision. Educating the supervisor, regardless of the supervisor's primary professional identification or setting, is linked intrinsically to the theoretical, empirical and practice knowledge of both counselling and teaching. The practice of supervision is nested in a dyadic relationship of committed fellowship, emotional challenge and strategic collaboration. From this multifaceted phenomenon, in the best of times, there emerge new knowledge and skills, increased professional confidence, and a sustained engagement in one's work. How, as trainers, do we explicate this knowledge, demonstrate these skills of supervision and judge competence?

Even though a number of articles and books have been used, very effectively, as training methodologies, as far as we know this is the first book specifically geared to methods for educating supervisors. It has taken supervision some time to reach this stage in its own development. The history of supervision has two strands, one emerging from the USA and the other from Britain. In the US supervision, there has been an emphasis on empirical work and the creation of supervision models. The work of supervising is concentrated in training environments for practicum, internships, and residencies. There are only a couple of organized and sustained training packages (Holloway, 1995; Neufeldt et al., 1995). Although training material has been available, more typically seasoned counselling practitioners were expected, without much formal training, to don the mantle of supervisor. Prior to the 1980s, counselling-bound models of supervision relied on the training methods used in their counsellor mode and worked on the principle that the same methods and skills that made the individual a good counsellor would now make them a good and effective supervisor. In the early 1980s, Bernard (1981) had translated her 'discrimination model' into a training event and Loganbill, Hardy and Delworth (1982) had introduced the developmental model of supervision later expanded by Stoltenberg and Delworth (1987). In the late 1980s, Holloway introduced a social role systems model. It was the advent of social and developmental role models of supervision which heralded more awareness of the need for specific training in supervision.

While the US supervisory scene relied on theory and research as a basis for any supervisory training, quite the opposite was true in Britain. From its earliest days within the counselling arena, supervision started as a training methodology and its literature and theory emerged from supervisory training. Proctor (1986) was one of the first trainers of counselling supervisors in Britain and formulated her three supervisory tasks (normative, formative, restorative) as training outlines in the first instance. Hawkins' and Shohet's (1989) seminal text on supervision emerged from their training work for supervisors and their process model, with an awareness of the organizational dimension, was primarily a training tool for supervisors. In the 1990s, the floodgates opened somewhat and an array of supervisory books emerged. It is probable that the majority of these were written by practitioners who were already training supervisors and used their books as the end-product of that process rather than the beginning (for example, Carroll, 1996; Inskipp and Proctor, 1993, 1995; Page and Wosket, 1994). Again, it is noticeable that this literature emerged from those who were using social role models of supervision. For those still using 'counselling-bound' models there continued to be a reaction to formal training in supervision. Bramley, for example, writes:

> No doubt supervision too is about to come under inspection in this regard and therapists will flock to 'recognised' training courses that will spring up all over the country to meet the demands. While welcoming any move to keep up standards and protect the public, I am worried about too much standardisation; too much concern about career prospects and making sure one is part of the professional 'in crowd' at the expense of the patient, who would benefit much more from his therapist's supervisor if she had been allowed to develop the art of supervision gradually, as her own expertise and knowledge as a practitioner increased, rather than in a rushed once and for all qualifying course. (1996: 182)

In spite of this debate, by the mid 1990s it was estimated that there were forty-three training courses in supervision in Britain – not just short courses, but programmes leading to Certificates (usually one year), Diplomas (two years) and at least two Masters programmes in Clinical Supervision.

The supervisory role, as a recognized function of counsellor training, led to the development of ethical codes and guidelines. In the US, the 1993 *Ethical Guidelines for Counseling Supervisors* from the Association for Counselor Education and Supervision (USA) is in no doubt about the importance of training for supervisors:

> Supervisors should have had training in supervision prior to initiating their role as supervisors. Supervisors should pursue professional and personal continuing education activities such as advanced courses, seminars and professional conferences, on a regular and on-going basis. These activities should include both counseling and supervision topics and skills. (Section 2.01/2.02)

The American Psychological Association in 1996 recognized supervision training as a required practice skill for psychologists and includes ethical guidelines for practice.

The BAC *Code of Ethics and Practice for the Supervision of Counsellors* (1990) is no less demanding. In the section on 'Issues of Competence' it stresses the requirement for supervisors to engage in 'specific training in the development of supervision skills . . . monitor[ing] their supervision work . . . monitor[ing] the limits of their competence . . . evaluating their supervision work' (Section B.3). The professional organizations in both the UK and USA have taken the position that supervision training is no longer not needed or a luxury, but a necessity and a requirement for those who choose or are chosen to become supervisors.

Mainland Europe, in the meantime, has taken a broader approach in the training of supervisors. They expanded the venue and relevance of supervision into a more generic professional role, no longer confining it to counselling, psychotherapy and social work. Supervision has become an inter-professional activity with the trained supervisor able to work across professions. The cross-professional model utilizes existing individual and organizational interventions. Supervisors become skilled at working not only with their own specialization, but with individuals, small groups and organizations inter-professionally. This movement, taking the skills and roles of supervisors and applying them in ever-widening contexts, is almost akin to seeing supervision as a profession in its own right. It may well be that professional, trained supervisors will become the new supporters of the people-workers of the future.

In recent years, there has been spirited collaboration among trainers from all of Britain, Europe and the United States. Four international conferences on supervision (held in London in 1992, 1997 and 1998; Hanover, Germany, in 1996) have brought together practitioners, supervisees, supervisors, trainers in supervision, researchers in supervision, and supervision theorists to present current work, to share ideas and to listen to differences.

This book is a celebration of these recent years of fruitful collaboration across different countries, training models and professions. These authors from the USA, Britain and Europe, all of whom actively engage in the training of supervisors, focus on aspects of supervisory training. There is a recognition that the trainer's challenge is multi-layered: identify those factors of supervision that are potentially influential to the process and outcome of supervision and then determine how to teach these factors. The emphasis on knowing not only 'what and how to do' supervision, but more importantly, what are the critical factors in supervision process that result in effective teaching of the supervisor, keep supervisors engaged in effective supervision of the therapist, and delivering efficacious service to the consumer.

This book is not a full curriculum in what could be a formal training course in supervision. A number of sources have outlined curricula for training supervisors (Bradley, 1989; Clarkson and Gilbert, 1991; American Association for Counseling and Development, 1988; Hawkins and Shohet, 1989). This book describes what trainers are doing to teach critical elements in the practice of supervision. It focuses on educating supervisors in crucial themes that are embedded in the core of the supervision process. Each of these authors has uncovered his or her understanding of one critical factor in the teaching of supervision. They have described their models for teaching within the context of their practice.

The text is organized to provide a continuity across the elements addressed by the authors and allow for their own creative ways of addressing the topic. Each chapter starts with a brief description of the author's focus in their work as trainers. The supervision topic of their interest is then discussed theoretically and is conceptually described. Finally, case studies and/or exercises for teaching are provided. We have designed this text to be a working document, one that we hope trainers will turn to in the design of their own teaching strategies and to stimulate their own creativity. The topics that have been chosen are by no means inclusive of the many different techniques and models being used to educate supervisors. We do hope, however, that we have given the reader a substantial 'helping' in the practice of educating the supervisor.

In Chapter 1, Elizabeth Holloway describes an overview of training in supervision. Her Systems Approach to Supervision (SAS) model is a comprehensive view of supervision within the context of organization and relationship. The SAS approach emphasizes training case conceptualization and strategies for supervisory intervention. Chapter 2 focuses on the generic tasks of supervision. Using his research, Michael Carroll systematically brings the reader through each of the seven generic tasks of supervision, outlining how trainee supervisors can be instructed and coached in each of them. In Chapter 3, Julie Hewson looks, in detail, at how supervisors can understand and be trained in 'contracting' in supervision, using not just theory, but her own gift for the visual. In Chapter 4 Susan Neufeldt posits supervision as a 'reflective' process and analyses what that means: she provides frameworks for helping supervisors to develop skills of reflection and to teach these skills to the supervisees. In Chapter 5, Willem Lammers takes a multi-professional approach, to examine team and group supervision within its ever-widening dimensions. Training for multi-cultural supervision is described by Hardin Coleman in Chapter 6. His focus illuminates the multi-cultural competencies needed in the profession. Maria Gilbert and Charlotte Sills, in Chapter 7, tackle how supervisors can be trained in the difficult supervisory task of evaluation, and in Chapter 8 Francesca Inskipp provides a model for educating supervisees in how to use supervision effectively. Shoshana Hellman describes, in the final chapter, the integration of a portfolio system for supervisors that is a self-instructional and peer collaboration process used in the training of supervisors in Israel.

As always, space confines us and not included are training supervisors in parallel process, training for ethical supervision and training in the supervisory relationship, to name a few, but we know there are other editors, other books and lots of experienced trainers who will fill the gaps in good time. Our editorship of this book has itself been a symbol for us. A Canadian in America and an Irishman in England, two international souls learning, laughing and listening across that vast expanse of water. The process has taught us both about how much enjoyment there is in learning and writing together. Our hope is that the future will see much more of this kind of collaboration widened by authors across countries, languages and cultures where supervision is being practised.

References

American Association for Counseling and Development (1988) *Standards for Counseling Supervisors*. Virginia: AACD Publication.

Association for Counselor Education and Supervision (1993) *Ethical Guidelines for Counseling Supervisors*. Alexandria, VA: ACES.

Bernard, J. (1981) Inservice training for clinical supervisors. *Professional Psychology,* 12: 740–8.

Bond, M. and Holland, S. (1998) *Skills of Clinical Supervision for Nurses*. Buckingham: Open University Press.

Bradley, L. (1989) *Counselor Supervision: Principles, Process, and Practice*. Muncie, IN: Accelerated Development Inc.

Bramley, W. (1996) *The Supervisory Couple in Broad-Spectrum Psychotherapy.* London: Free Association Books.

British Association for Counselling (1990) *Code of Ethics and Practice for the Supervision of Counsellors*. Rugby: BAC.

Carroll, M. (1995) *The Generic Tasks of Supervision*. Ph.D. Dissertation, University of Surrey.

Carroll, M. (1996) *Counselling Supervision: Theory, Skills and Practice*. London: Cassell.

Clarkson, P. and Gilbert, M. (1991) The Training of counsellor trainers and supervisors. In W. Dryden and B. Thorne (eds), *Training and Supervision for Counselling in Action*. London: Sage.

Hawkins, P. and Shohet, R. (1989) *Supervision in the Helping Professions*, Milton Keynes: Open University Press.

Holloway, E.L. (1995) *Clinical Supervision: A Systems Approach*. Thousand Oaks, CA: Sage.

Holloway, E.L. and Acker, M. (1989) *The EPICS (Engagement and Power in Clinical Supervision) Model*. University of Oregon (private publication)

Inskipp, F. and Proctor, B. (1993) *The Art, Craft and Tasks of Counselling Supervision. Part I: Making the Most of Supervision*. Twickenham: Cascade.

Inskipp, F. and Proctor, B. (1995) *The Art, Craft and Tasks of Counselling Supervision. Part 2: Becoming a Supervisor.* Twickenham: Cascade.

Loganbill, C., Hardy, E. and Delworth, U. (1982) Supervision: a conceptual model. *The Counselling Psychologist*, 10: 3–46.

Neufeldt, S., Iversen, J.N., and Juntunen, C.L. (1995) *Supervision Strategies for the First Practicum*. Alexandria, VA: American Counseling Association.

Page, S. and Wosket, V. (1994) *Supervising the Counsellor: A Cyclical Model*. London: Routledge.

Proctor, B. (1986) Supervision: a co-operative exercise in accountability. In M. Marken and M. Payne (eds), *Enabling and Ensuring: Supervision in Practice*. Leicester: National Youth Bureau.

Skovholt, T.M. and Rønnestad, M.H. (1992) *The Evolving Professional Self: Stages and Themes in Therapist and Counselor Development*. New York: Wiley.

Stoltenberg, C.D. and Delworth, U. (1987) *Supervising Counselors and Therapists*. San Francisco: Jossey-Bass.

Thompson, J. (1991) *Issues of Race and Culture in Counselling Supervision Training Courses*. M.Sc. Dissertation: The Polytechnic of East London.

1 A Framework for Supervision Training

Elizabeth Holloway

My work is held in a university that invites me to choose my question and then frees me to pursue it. The university knows full well that no definitive solution awaits me, but trusts that the pursuit will uncover new perspectives and relevant meanings for me and my fellow professionals. And so, what I have done over the last twenty years is practice, teach, study, and write about professional training. Early on as a graduate student it was my practice of supervision that fuelled my motivation to ask questions about this method of teaching. What was really going on in the conversation of supervision? What incidents in supervision were critical to a person learning to be a therapist? I spent the first ten years of my work recording, transcribing and analysing the talk of supervision. Empirical findings from these studies were interesting, informative, and dispelled some assumptions held about the supervision process. For example, supervision with a novice trainee is largely a teacher/student relationship in role, attitude and behaviour. These interactions are characterized by supervisors offering their opinions and suggestions and supervisees asking questions of clarification, or extending and agreeing with supervisors' ideas.

However interesting at the manifest level, these descriptions left out a large part of my experience in supervision. How was I thinking about supervision in the moment, as I designed training approaches or reacted to particularly intense interactions with supervisees? The empirical methods I was using were not uncovering the questions that emerged out of my experience. And so I sought a way to uncover the talk of supervision. What are the perceptions and attitudes that supervisors have about their role and actions? What do supervisees need at different junctures of their training? How do they name what they need? These among many other questions set me off talking with supervisors and supervisees to learn of their experience. Again I was interviewing, recording and transcribing, but in these cases I was looking for emergent understandings of the phenomena as remembered and articulated by the participants themselves.

This pursuit of understanding supervision has taken me to countries in Europe and Asia where I have met trainers and supervisors who have added immeasurably to my understanding of the practice of supervision. I remember in my early days in Britain when Terri Spy would look at me at the first tea break and say, 'Well, is it done?' I knew immediately what the 'it' was – a book on my model of supervision – a Systems Approach to Supervision (SAS) (Holloway, 1995). It wasn't until two years later I was able finally to exclaim in response, 'Yes, Terri, IT is done!' Yet, it is not at all done, for as I continue to be involved in different contexts of supervision practice the model has transformed itself (alphabetically!) to SAM-LP (Systems Approach to Mentoring in the Legal Profession), to SAM-A (Systems Approach to Mentoring in Academics), and to SAT-MT (Systems Approach to Training Multidisciplinary Teams). However, this is all in the making and Terri's question will prevail for a decade to come. For now, I present in this chapter the original framework for SAS.

Purpose of the SAS model

To me, supervision can be depicted as an instructional method that is hand held, parsimoniously constructed in the moment, accountable in the long term and remarkably intense as an interpersonal construction. One becomes, as a supervisor, a 'conversational artist'. The purpose of the Systems Approach to Supervision (Holloway, 1995) is to guide supervision teaching and practice by providing a framework based on empirical, conceptual and practice knowledge to guide supervision teaching and practice. Those factors that have consistently been identified as salient to the process and outcome of supervision (Bernard and Goodyear, 1992; Holloway and Neufeldt, 1995; Russell, Crimmings and Lent, 1984) have been used to build a dynamic model that can assist in systematic assessment of (a) the supervisee's learning needs, and (b) the supervisor's teaching interventions in idiosyncratically defined contexts. The model can be used as a frame of reference for an individual practitioner to think through a dilemma, for case consultation of supervision, or for training in supervision. It provides a strategy for systematically using a 'case method' approach that encompasses the presentation of client and supervisee histories, accompanied at times with examples of the supervision interaction, and followed with a conceptualization of the supervision situation and suggestions for interventions. It is an effort to understand supervision by offering a common language that is relevant to supervisors and educators across different theoretical points of view. The model is meant to raise questions about what each of us does as a supervisor rather than to tell a supervisor what to think and what to do.

The SAS framework provides four components of support for educators and practitioners to uncover their own thinking, attitudes, decision-making and behaviours: (a) a descriptive base, (b) guidelines stating common goals and objectives, (c) a way to discover meaning as it relates to participants and the profession, and (d) a systematic mode of inquiry to determine objectives and strategies for interaction during supervision. The confines of this chapter prevent the detailed discussion of the SAS structure, but none the less the heuristics of the model will be presented. The reader is referred to Holloway (1995) for a complete presentation of the theoretical and empirical underpinnings of the components of SAS.

Goals of the SAS model

The primary goal of supervision is the establishment of an on-going relationship in which the supervisor designs specific learning tasks and teaching strategies related to the supervisee's development as a professional. In addition, the supervisor empowers the supervisee to enter the profession by understanding the skills, attitudes and knowledge demanded of the professional and guiding the relationship strategically to facilitate the supervisee's achievement of a professional standard. The overall goals of the SAS model are:

1. The goal of supervision is to provide an opportunity for the supervisee to learn a broad spectrum of professional attitudes, knowledge and skills in an effective and supportive manner.

2. Successful supervision occurs within the context of a complex professional relationship that is on-going and mutually involving.
3. The supervisory relationship is the primary context for facilitating the involvement of the learner in reaching the goals of supervision. The essential nature of this interpersonal process bestows power to both members as they form the relationship.
4. For the supervisor, both the content and process of supervision become an integral part of the design of instructional approaches within the relationship.
5. As the supervisor teaches, the supervisee is further empowered by (a) acquiring the skills and knowledge of the professional work, and (b) gaining knowledge through experiencing and articulating interpersonal situations.

Dimensions of the Systems Approach

Seven dimensions have emerged from the empirical, conceptual and practice knowledge bases of supervision. These dimensions have been integrated conceptually into the SAS model as the seven factors depicted in Figure 1.1. The seven factors are represented as wings connected to the body of supervision, that is, the relationship. Task and function are represented in the foreground of the interaction with the more covert influences of supervisor, supervisee, client and institution in the background. The relationship is the core factor and contains the process of the supervision interaction. This is the foundation of SAS. It is understood that the components of the model are also part of a dynamic process in that they mutually influence one another and are highly interrelated. The graphic model is used to identify anchor points in this complex process and to encourage supervisors to discover and name the most salient factors in a particular piece of work as related to: (a) the nature of the task, (b) what function the supervisor was carrying out, (c) the character of the relationship, and (d) what contextual factors were relevant to the process.

The relationship of supervision

In the SAS model relationship is the container of dynamic process in which the supervisor and supervisee negotiate a personal way

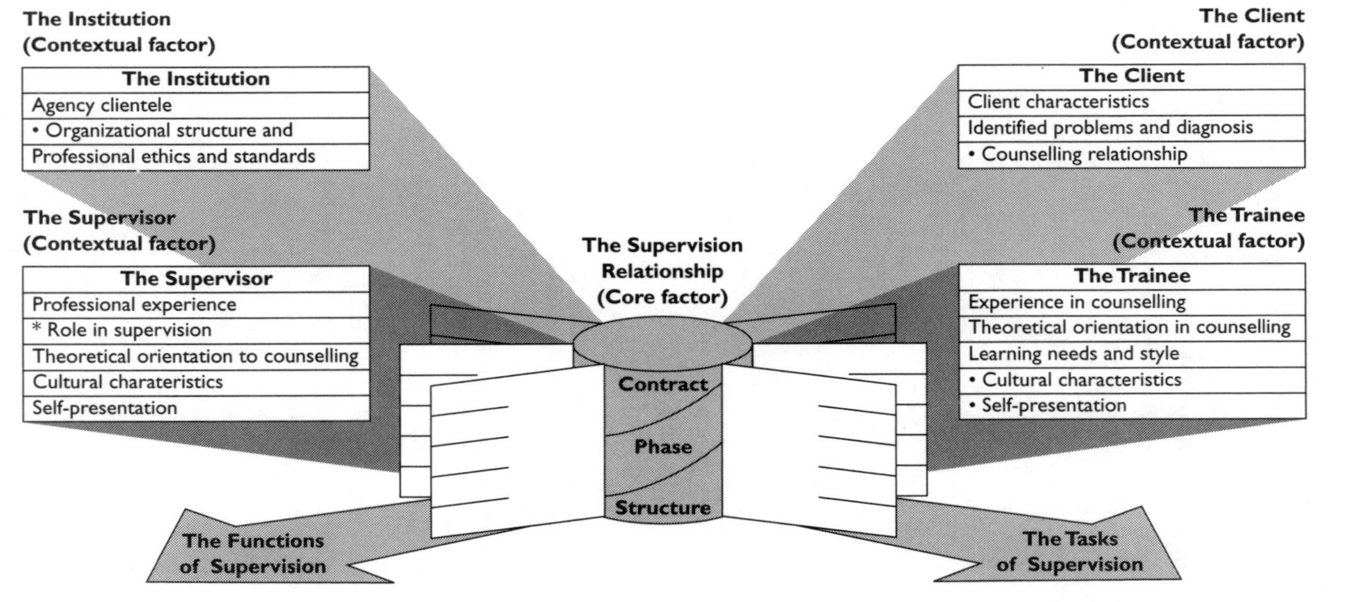

Figure 1.1 *The SAS model: tasks, functions, relationship and contextual factors (Holloway 1995; copyright by Sage Publications, Thousand Oaks, CA. Reprinted with permission of the author.)*

of utilizing a structure of power and involvement that accommodates the trainee's progression of learning. This structure becomes the basis for the process by which the supervisee will acquire knowledge and skills – the empowerment of the supervisee. Both the supervisor and supervisee are responsible for establishing a relational structure that is flexible enough to accommodate the trainee's particular professional needs in an intense, collaborative learning alliance. The supervisor, however, exercises the guiding function (that is, how the supervisor is different from the supervisee) of evaluation and support within the structure of this professional relationship. The structure and character of the relationship embody all other factors and in turn all factors are influenced by the relationship.

There has been considerable research on the relationship and process of supervision (Carroll, 1996; Holloway, 1992; Russell, Crimmings and Lent, 1984). From the empirical base and practice knowledge, I have identified three essential elements: (a) interpersonal structure of the relationship – the dimensions of power and involvement; (b) phase of the relationship – relational development specific to the participants; (c) supervisory contract – the establishment of a set of expectations for the tasks and functions of supervision (see Figure 1.1).

Interpersonal structure

Because of the centrality of relationship to the SAS model I have included a more extended description of the empirical literature that influences this dimension of the model. Note that research on relationships from a variety of contexts and disciplines is integrated into the conceptualization. Power and involvement are helpful constructs in understanding the nature of the supervisory relationship. Supervision is a formal relationship in which the supervisor's task includes imparting expert knowledge, making judgements of trainees' performance, and acting as a gatekeeper to the profession. Formal power, or power attributed to the position, rests with the supervisor, and in this regard the supervisory relationship is a hierarchical one. However, the exercise of power cannot be accomplished independently. The mutually influential process of relationship and the on-going interaction between individuals allow for a shared influence to emerge. Power may take very different forms depending on the personal and institutional resources available and the type of involvement of the individuals, a point of view not always given consideration (Hinde, 1979).

Three preferred methods have been used in supervision research to describe the power of the supervisor: French and Raven's sociological typology (1960); Strong, Hills and Nelson's (1988) circumplex model; and Penman's (1980) communication matrix. However, Leary's (1957) circumplex model, on which both the Strong et al. (1988) and Penman (1980) classification systems are based, provides a framework to place power in a relational system that includes an involvement or affiliation dimension which, in his view, every relationship has by definition. This theory of interpersonal relations undergirds the SAS interpersonal structure of the supervision relationship (power through involvement). Although the relationship takes on a unique character that can be defined by power and involvement, the participants bring their own history of interpersonal style. These interpersonal histories influence how the supervisor and supervisee ultimately present themselves in forming their new relationship.

Involvement might also be referred to as intimacy that includes 'attachments', the degree to which each person uses the other as a source of self-confirmation (Miller, 1976). This type of 'involved affiliation' influences the exercise and effect of power in the dyadic relationship and is crucial in creating more individualized versus more role-bound relationships. Both participants determine the distribution of power or the degree of attachment to one another (Morton, Alexander and Altman, 1976). The degree of relational influence potential will determine the degree of social bonding and thus the persuasiveness of the relationship. As the relationship develops, the participants will utilize more personally relevant interpersonal, psychological and differentiated information to make predictions of each others' behaviour and thus reduce interpersonal uncertainty. The basis of mutuality adjusts to these new levels of personal knowledge (Morton, Alexander and Altman, 1976).

Phases of the relationship

In the development of informal relationships two factors have consistently been observed. First, as a relationship evolves, the participants rely less on general cultural and social information and more on idiosyncratic information of the participant. Predictions regarding the other person's behaviours come from information that differentiates the person from other members of his or her corresponding social group. The other becomes unique in the eyes of the perceiver, and the relationship is said to have moved from a non-interpersonal to an interpersonal one (Miller, 1976). As the relationship evolves to an interpersonal one, there is a process of reduced uncertainty. After initial interactions, participants come to know one another better and are thus more accurate in their predictions about the other person's reactions to their messages. With decreased uncertainty, they are better able to use control strategies and communicative modes that will reduce the level of conflict in the relationship. Participants also become increasingly more vulnerable and more willing to risk self-disclosure, whereas in the initial stages genuine self-disclosure is seldom observed (Morton, Alexander and Altman, 1976). Extrapolating from the friendship studies, it could be suggested that the advanced supervisees, having a blueprint for the relationship of supervision from previous experience, were able to truncate the discomfort of uncertainty and resultant need for reassurance by relying on known general expectancies for supervisory roles. Thus, they could move more quickly to establish specific expectancies of an interpersonal (as opposed to non-interpersonal) relationship by self-disclosing aspects of self-relevancy to their counselling performance. On the other hand, the beginning level supervisee might still be discovering the role expectations of the supervisor and supervisee, because these general cultural, social and formal rules must be discovered before moving to an interpersonal relationship.

The development of an interpersonal relationship promotes a focus on shared idiosyncratic rules created just for that particular relationship. Nevertheless, supervision is a formal, professional relationship defined by certain relational rules and is more role-bound than friendship relations. Supervision initially provides a general expectancy base for certain interactive behaviours; however, as the relationship develops, it is individualized around the learning needs of the supervisee and the teaching approaches of the supervisor. These idiosyncratic reciprocal rules the participants will need to learn in the interactive process (Miller and Rogers, 1987).

In and of itself, phase does not determine the level of involvement in the relationship. Individual differences also play a part.

Altman and Taylor (1973) have named the process of providing more personal information 'social penetration', which is significantly affected by both the phase of relationship as well as by personal characteristics. Some individuals, because of their personal or cultural history, have a predisposition to reveal themselves, while others are more reluctant. There is evidence that still other factors may influence the course of supervision. For example, Tracey, Ellickson and Sherry's (1989) research demonstrated that both the individual presentational style of the supervisee (defined as 'reactance potential') and the urgency of the client's problem (whether a suicide threat or not) had a significant effect on the participants' need for a more structured and supportive approach. Research studies ultimately demonstrate the absolute need to consider all of the contextual factors that influence supervisory behaviours in devising any strategy in supervision.

SAS has described the relationship phases of supervision in a way that reflects the convergence of findings in friendship (Berger and Calabrese, 1975; Morton, Alexander and Altman, 1976) and supervision research (Mueller and Kell, 1972; Rabinowitz et al., 1986). Mueller and Kell's (1972) labelling system – beginning, mature and termination – has been used to describe phases of the supervisory relationship identified in the empirical literature (See Table 1.1; Holloway, 1992; Worthington, 1987).

Supervision contract

Each supervisor and supervisee will have idiosyncratic expectations of roles and function in supervision. Some will be the result of experience in engaging in supervision and others will be more directly related to the personal and cultural characteristics of both participants. As in any working relationship the clarity of these expectations directly affects the relationship and the establishment of specific learning goals. Because the supervisee is in a position of relatively less evaluative and expert power, the supervisor has a responsibility to ensure that the supervisee is clearly informed of the evaluative structure of the relationship, the expectancies and goals for supervision, the criteria for evaluation, and the limits of confidentiality in supervision.

Inskipp and Proctor (1989) and Proctor (1997) have identified the contract as critical to establishing a way of being together in the supervisory relationship. Not only do the participants nego-

Table 1.1 *Phases of the supervision relationship*

Developing phase
Clarifying relationship with supervisor
Establishing supervision contract
Supporting teaching interventions
Developing competencies
Developing treatment plans
Mature phase
Increasing individual nature of relationship, becoming less role bound
Increasing social bonding and influence potential
Developing skills of case conceptualization
Increasing self-confidence and self-efficacy in counselling
Confronting personal issues as they relate to professional performance
Terminating phase
Understanding connections between theory and practice in relation to particular clients
Decreasing need for direction from supervisor

Source: Holloway, 1995: 51.

tiate specific tasks, but they also define the parameters of the relationship. The negotiation of norms, rules and commitments at the beginning of any relationship can reduce uncertainty and move the involvement to a level of trust that will promote the degree of vulnerability needed for the task to be done. This clarification sets up both content and relational characteristics to be expected in the relationship and establishes a trajectory for types of interactions in which the supervisor and supervisee will engage. The supervisor, by initiating the contract, is dealing directly with the inherent uncertainty of the system. By acting openly and purposefully, the supervisor increases the probability that both participants will behave congruently with established expectations (Miller and Rogers, 1987). More importantly, the supervisee will receive an opportunity to participate in the construction of the relationship.

The supervisor must be alerted to the changing character of the relationship and thereafter initiate discussion on renewed goals and relational expectations. Not only will the trainee's learning needs change as experience increases or clients develop, but also his or her increasing skill and interpersonal confidence will influence issues of relational control. On-going negotiation of topics and processes is built on the initial contract for teaching and learning and the quality of relationship that the participants have built. The supervision session often begins with the supervisor asking the supervisee what he or she would like to discuss – a negotiation of the topic of conversation (Poulin, 1992). Although there may be shifts in direction throughout the course of the interview, these are often points of subtle negotiation between the participants.

Tasks of supervision

In the Systems Approach to Supervision the teaching tasks and supervisory function are used to describe the action of the supervision process. A task is defined as 'a definite piece of work assigned or expected of a person' (*Random House College Dictionary,* 1984). The tasks of supervision are defined by a body of professional knowledge that defines the counsellor role. It is from this larger pool of knowledge that the supervisor and student will choose those specific learning goals that match the individual needs of the supervisee. The numerous characteristics and skills identified in the literature can be grouped into five broad areas (Carroll, 1996; Holloway, 1992). Categories of teaching objectives include: counselling skills, case conceptualization, professional role, intra- and interpersonal awareness, and self-evaluation. Each of these categories is defined as follows:

Counselling skills

The task of developing counselling skills focuses on what action to take with the client, or on any of the specific skills that the supervisor identifies as both fundamental to counselling knowledge and specifically relevant to a particular supervisee. Counselling skills might include communication patterns, empathy, personalization, and techniques of counselling such as symptom prescription, desensitization, and reinforcement.

Case conceptualization

Case conceptualization involves the supervisor and supervisee understanding the client's psychosocial history and presenting problem. It requires the development of a conceptual framework that is applicable across many different types of clients, and that is simultaneously congruent with the therapist's ideas of human development and change.

Professional role

Professional role relates to how the supervisee will use appropriate external resources for the client; will apply principles of professional and ethical practice; will learn tasks of record-keeping, procedure, and appropriate inter-professional relationships; and will participate in the supervisory relationship.

Emotional awareness

Emotional awareness refers to the trainee's self-awareness of feelings, thoughts and actions that result from working with the client and with the supervisor. Both intra- and interpersonal awareness are relevant to counselling and supervision.

Self-evaluation

Self-evaluation is the willingness and skill to recognize one's own limits of competence, and effectiveness as it relates to client treatment and participation in supervision.

Functions of supervision

A function is 'the kind of action or activity proper to a person or thing; the purpose for which something is designed or exists; to perform a specialised action or activity' (*Random House College Dictionary*, 1984). Role labels have been useful in providing a common language for describing supervisor functions in educational and mental health supervision (Bernard and Goodyear, 1992; Carroll, 1996; Ellis and Dell, 1986; Ellis, Dell and Good, 1988; Hess, 1980). The five primary functions in which the supervisor engages while interacting with the supervisee are: monitoring/evaluating, instructing/advising, modelling, consulting, and supporting/sharing. Notice that here these roles have been transformed (from a noun to a verb) and simplified in order to emphasize their dynamic nature as well as to suggest a more cohesive approach to the role of supervisor. Each of these functions can be characterized both by behaviours typical of its respective social role, and by the form of relational power governing it.

Monitoring/evaluating

The monitoring and evaluative function is restricted to instances when the supervisor communicates judgements and evaluation of the trainee's behaviour as it relates to his or her professional role. In these instances, because the reward and coercive power of the supervisor is being exercised, the hierarchy of the relationship is accentuated and communication is largely controlled by the supervisor (that is, it is uni-directional). The supervisor's act of monitoring and evaluating performance is a function of supervision and is distinguished from the criteria for evaluation. In training situations, the evaluation may be a formal and standardized procedure, whereas supervision that takes place between peers or after training is often less explicit. In any case, the supervisor's opinion and judgement, implicit or explicit, is important.

Instructing/advising

The instructing/advising function consists of the supervisor providing information, opinions and suggestions based on professional knowledge and skill (Holloway and Poulin, 1994). Characterized as a 'teacher–student' communication it is largely controlled by the supervisor (that is, uni-directional) emphasizes the hierarchy of the relationship and is marked by considerable interpersonal distance.

Modelling

The supervisor acts as a model of professional behaviour and practice, both implicitly in the supervisory relationship, and explicitly by role-playing for the supervisee or client. As a mentor, a more implicit process, the supervisor becomes a role model of professional practice and conduct. Communication, here, is largely bi-directional: interpersonal distance is reduced because the exercise of referent power is a collaborative process.

Consulting/exploring

The supervisor facilitates the solving of of clinical and professional problems by seeking information and opinions from the supervisee. Again the use of expert and referent power is most relevant. Communication is bi-directional and interactive as the participants collaborate on fact-finding and problem-solving.

Supporting/sharing

The supervisor supports the supervisee through empathic attention, encouragement and constructive confrontation. Supervisors often support trainees at a deep interpersonal level by sharing their own perception of trainees' actions, emotions and attitudes. This direct communication may include confrontation, which can increase the affiliation of the participants if done constructively and appropriately. Communication is bi-directional and interactive, and the participants are highly engaged with little interpersonal distance.

Task + function = process

Supervisor tasks and functions are the combination of the supervisor and supervisee working together on a particular type of problem with a particular approach; in other words, what objectives and what teaching/learning strategies are adopted. This pragmatic, heuristic approach is characterized by the presence of task and function in the on-going interchange between supervisor and supervisee. The interrelatedness of identifying *what* is the teaching task with deciding *how* one will function to accomplish that task is known as the process of supervision. It is possible to identify the factors of task and function of on-going interaction and then use this information to chart the supervisor's use of skills. Hypothetically a supervisor may engage in any of the teaching objectives with any of the functions or strategies. Realistically, there are probably some task and function matches that are more likely to occur in supervision; for example, the use of a supporting function when working with interpersonal emotional awareness, or an advisory function when focusing on counselling skills. Using this method of matching task and function, supervisors can analyse the effectiveness of a prior session and plan the supervisory focus and strategies for subsequent sessions. The efficacy of matches between task and function in the interview can be examined because the analysis includes the trainee's immediate response to the supervisor's interventions as well as more long-term indices of supervisee learning, placing the immediate discourse within the context of the on-going teaching goals.

Teaching exercise for analysing process style

In a teaching setting, participants can actively use the matrix (Fig 1.2) to plot their development of skills. Have supervisors listen to an audio- or videotape of their supervision interaction. Have them use the matrix to identify functions or tasks, or use particular combinations. The completed matrix of 15–20 minutes of interaction with a particular supervisor's style of supervision will give a picture of the supervisee and the process. Specific knowledge about supervisory actions can encourage the supervisor to question or reflect upon past behaviour. Are the choices of task and function primarily a reflection of the supervisor's comfort with a particular style of presentation? Are there choices that are more frequent with a particular supervisee? Or at a particular phase of the supervisory relationship? Do the choices of task and function facilitate the empowerment of the supervisee? Questions can be generated from the simple identification of task and function and can encourage further exploration of factors influencing the supervisor's actions. Have supervisors consider the factors that have influenced their choice of learning objective and the approach to working with the supervisee. Although sometimes these factors are apparent, just as often they may exist only at a latent, rather than manifest, level of the interaction. The contextual factors of supervision are defined and uncovered in supervision interviews and, in some cases, in participants' comments on their supervisory behaviours. This exercise will introduce the concept of contextual factors and lead to the next part of the model.

Contextual factors of supervision

Contextual factors of supervision are conditions that are related empirically and practically to the supervisor's and supervisee's choice of task and function and the formation of the relationship. These factors are: the supervisor, the trainee, the client, and the institution or organization. The description of these factors completes the SAS model (see Figure 1.1). Whereas task and function are inferred from the process of communication, contextual factors are sometimes not obviously differentiated from the actual interactional process. Participants in an interaction are perceiving, intending, and understanding their own and the other person's messages 'inside their head' as they are engaged in the conversation. Factors that might influence information-processing and decision-making in supervision must be inferred by the observer. Although such inferential information is useful, it is different from information that might be gained from asking supervisors or trainees to reflect on their own or the other's actions (Holloway, 1995; Neufeldt, Karno and Nelson, 1996; Schön, 1983; Skovholt and Rønnestad, 1992).

Supervisor factors

The ideal supervisor has been described as a person who exhibits high levels of empathy, understanding, unconditional positive regard, flexibility, concern, attention, investment, curiosity and openness (Carifio and Hess, 1987). Although such personal qualities are valuable in any relationship, these descriptors focus almost entirely on the intra- and interpersonal characteristics of an individual. They implicitly suggest that supervisors are born and not made. All individuals bring to supervision their own interpersonal characteristics, knowledge, abilities and cultural values. Even so, supervisors express these characteristics uniquely as the foundation on which the supervisory role is built. Supervisors can enhance their own interpersonal style by the manner in which they use their repertoire of interpersonal skills and clinical knowledge to be deliberate, systematic and relevant in their professional role.

In SAS, five factors have been identified in the empirical or conceptual literature as relevant to the supervisor's performance. These are: professional experience in counselling and supervision; theoretical orientation to counselling; expectations concerning roles, for the supervisor and supervisee; cultural characteristics including race, ethnicity, and gender; and self-presentation. Brief

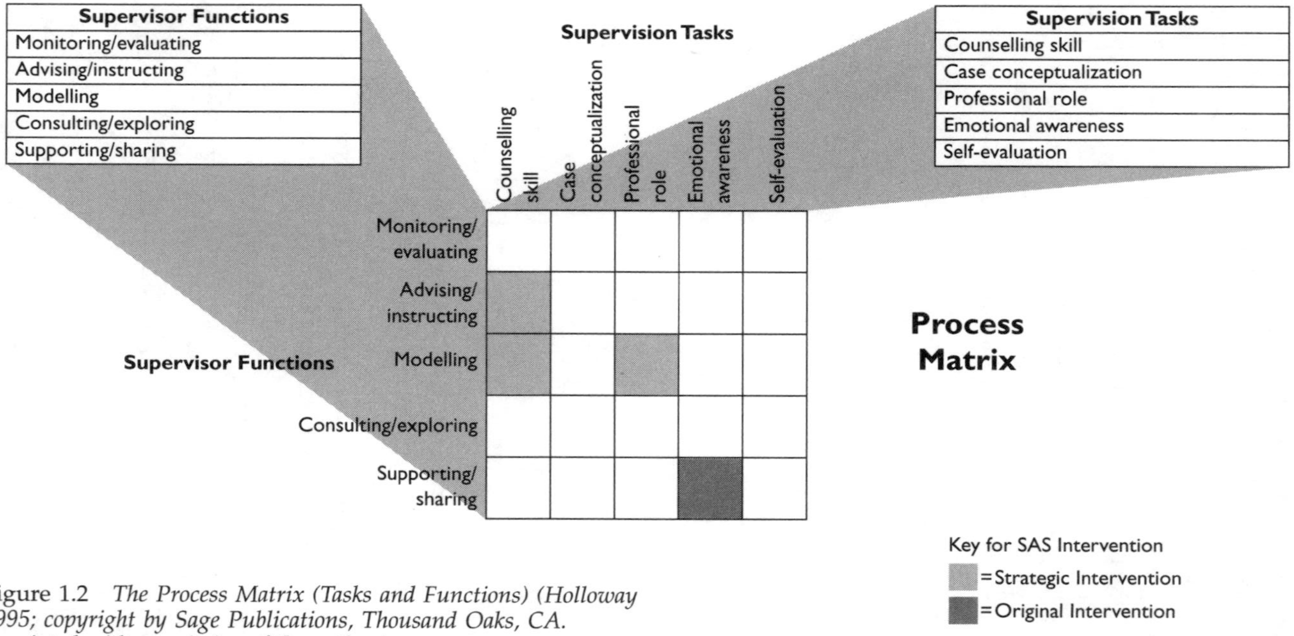

Supervisor Functions
Monitoring/evaluating
Advising/instructing
Modelling
Consulting/exploring
Supporting/sharing

Supervision Tasks
Counselling skill
Case conceptualization
Professional role
Emotional awareness
Self-evaluation

Supervision Tasks

Supervisor Functions

	Counselling skill	Case conceptualization	Professional role	Emotional awareness	Self-evaluation
Monitoring/evaluating					
Advising/instructing					
Modelling					
Consulting/exploring					
Supporting/sharing					

Process Matrix

Key for SAS Intervention
=Strategic Intervention
=Original Intervention

Figure 1.2 *The Process Matrix (Tasks and Functions) (Holloway 1995; copyright by Sage Publications, Thousand Oaks, CA. Reprinted with permission of the author.)*

definitions are included here to clarify their functional meaning in the SAS model.

Professional experience. It has been suggested in the supervision literature that the supervisor engages in a developmental process of change that unfolds as the supervisor gets involved in the unique demands of the supervisory role (see Walsh, 1994). Whether this is accurate remains to be determined. Empirically, at least, the amount of experience in counselling and supervision appears to be related to the types of judgements made by supervisors regarding self-disclosure, supervisee performance, and instructional approach to supervision.

Theoretical orientation. The supervisor has the task of teaching the supervisee the application of theoretical principles of counselling as they are relevant to the individuals and cases trainees will encounter. Thus, supervisors rely explicitly and implicitly on their own knowledge base to determine what to teach as well as how to teach it. Some theories of supervision generally maintain that the supervisor's method is intrinsically linked to the counselling approach. Cross-theoretical approaches have tried to create models unique to supervision that are not wholly dependent on theories of counselling. Nevertheless, supervisors' theoretical orientation to counselling or to particular aspects of human behaviour remains important when understanding their thinking and action.

Roles. Social role theories outline the behaviour considered to be a part of the supervisory relationship, specifically the role of the supervisor. The most frequently recognized roles are those of teacher, counsellor and consultant, but the roles of evaluator, lecturer and model of professional practice have also been used to describe supervisor behaviours and attitudes (Goodyear and Bradley, 1983; Hess, 1980).

Cultural characteristics. The supervisor brings to the relationship his or her way of viewing human behaviour, interpersonal relations and social institutions that is largely influenced by cultural socialization. Because cultural perspective is relevant to the conceptualization of both professionalism and mental health, the SAS model considers cultural values as salient to the supervisor's attitudes and actions. Cultural characteristics include gender, ethnicity, race, sexual orientation, religious beliefs and personal values that strongly influence an individual's social and moral judgements (Carroll and Holloway, 1999). In the SAS model, the relationship of supervision is understood from a perspective of power and involvement – inherent qualities in cross-cultural and cross-gender interactions that indicate the complex, sometimes subtle, but always critical aspects of supervisory work.

SELF-PRESENTATION. In SAS, the term self-presentation is used to refer to each participant's interpersonal presentation of self. This term originates in the social psychological literature concerned with impression formation. In the interpersonal psychotherapy literature, such behaviours are referred to as 'a person's style of relating', habitual ways of behaving that have been learned early in life and are maintained through adulthood (Teyber, 1988). It might be argued that in supervision self-presentational style is always a factor; however, it is under particular conditions that style becomes prominent and decidedly the primary factor in the course of communication.

TEACHING EXERCISE FOR SUPERVISOR REFLECTION. Ask supervisors to pair up and engage in a dialogue of reflection on their history and thinking about being a supervisor and being supervised. Have one person take the role of the interviewer and the other person of the interviewee. Have the interviewer guide the supervisor in talking about each of the five elements in the supervisor wing of the model. At the completion of the dialogue each participant should write a brief memo (a single page at most). The supervisor might reflect on what he/she learned about him/herself as a supervisor. The interviewer might reflect on what new things he/she learned about the interviewee, and/or supervision, and/or the experience of being the interviewer. Dyads can then switch roles and repeat the exercise. About thirty minutes per interview and memo-writing (total sixty minutes) should be allotted for this exercise.

Supervisee factors

Who is the ideal supervisee? The psychological health and personal character of the therapist has been considered to be of primary importance in the traditional training of the analyst. In-depth personal therapy has been regarded as a critical element in the training process (a) to enhance the therapist's ability as an unbiased clinical observer and to mitigate the effects of countertransference; (b) to demonstrate experientially the validity of therapy as a treatment; (c) to model first-hand the techniques of psychotherapy; and (d) to improve the psychological health of the therapist and ameliorate the stresses of practice (Wampler and Strupp, 1976). In the 1980s, as models of supervision began to attend to the actual process and strategy of supervision (Goodyear and Bradley, 1983; Hess, 1980; Loganbill, Hardy and Delworth, 1982; Stoltenberg, 1981), researchers became interested in characteristics of the supervisee that might influence the supervisory relationship (cf. Holloway, 1984; Russell, Crimmings and Lent, 1984; Worthington, 1987). The trainee's cultural experience, gender, cognitive and ego-development, professional identity, experience level in counselling, theoretical orientation to counselling, and self-presentation were identified in the empirical and conceptual literature as important factors in supervision. In SAS, these characteristics of the supervisee have been grouped into five supervisee factors: experience in counselling, theoretical orientation in counselling, learning style and needs, cultural characteristics, and self-presentation. A brief definition follows.

EXPERIENCE IN COUNSELLING. Experience level has been a frequently studied factor in supervision research. The trainee's familiarity with the professional role and tasks of counselling appears to be related to the supervisor's expectation of supervisee competence and the supervisee's needs. The experience of the learner has also been connected to the need for support and structure in supervision. Experience in counselling should not be confused with cognitive or ego-developmental factors that may influence the trainee's performance or the supervisor's choice of supervisory method. In SAS, developmental cognitive and ego characteristics of the supervisee are discussed under learning style and needs, and self-presentation, respectively.

THEORETICAL ORIENTATION. The theoretical orientation of the supervisee has not received much attention in the research literature (Holloway, 1992; 1995); however, most supervisors would concur that the views a supervisee holds about human behaviour and change will certainly be a part of supervision. Perhaps, because much research in supervision has been about supervisees early in their professional training, there is not a clear theoretical designation expected of these individuals. Instead, the focus is on the development of a personal model of counselling that matches generally expected principles of personality and counselling theory.

LEARNING STYLE/NEEDS. In the SAS model, learning style and needs refer generally to that identified group of developmental factors relevant to the trainee's approach to and perception of the supervisory experience (Holloway, 1995). Developmental characteristics such as conceptual level (Harvey, Hunt and Schroder, 1961) and ego-development (Loevinger, 1976) have been examined in light of the acquisition of counselling skills such as empathy and clinical hypothesis formation (for example, Borders, Fong and Neimeyer, 1986). Stoltenberg and Delworth (1987) prescribed matches between the developmental characteristic of conceptual level and the degree of structure in supervision. For example, the greater the tolerance for ambiguity and the more relativistic the thinking, the greater opportunity for the supervisor to offer a more unstructured approach to supervision. Unfortunately, there are few empirical findings to guide the supervisor in choosing those strategies that would reflect a structured versus an unstructured learning environment.

Poulin's (1992) dimensionalization of reflected interviews of expert supervisors found that the supervisor thought of supervisee characteristics in three categories: as a person, a counsellor, and a student. Within these categories the supervisor counselled trainees' learning needs within the context of the style in which they learned and their readiness to assimilate and make use of the knowledge (see Holloway, 1995).

CULTURAL CHARACTERISTICS. This area includes gender, ethnicity, race, sexual orientation, religious beliefs, and personal values that may be central to an individual's group identity, similarly to the cultural factors of the supervision. In SAS, cultural values are seen as salient to the trainee's attitudes and actions toward their clients and supervisors; that is, in any interpersonal situation. Research in this supervision area is relatively limited, although there has been significantly more research on the relation of cultural variables to counselling relationship and effectiveness (cf. Atkinson, Morten and Sue, 1989; Pedersen, 1985; Sue and Sue, 1990; Tyler,

Brome and Williams, 1991). The structure of power and involvement in the supervisory relationship may be particularly complex in a cross-cultural context because of the added complexity of power in society in general between oppressed and non-oppressed groups (Martinez and Holloway, 1997; Nelson and Holloway, 1999; Solomon, 1983). There has been limited research on the relation of gender and role (supervisor/supervisee) to process characteristics of power and involvement (Nelson and Holloway, 1990). Although similar studies examining ethnic or racial minorities in cross-cultural situations do not exist at this time, it is likely that the positional power of the supervisor or supervisee might be in contradiction to the usual social arrangements and thus conceivably be problematic.

SELF-PRESENTATION. Self-presentation is a social-psychological term that refers to the regulation of one's behaviours to create a particular impression on others (Jones and Pittman, 1982). A brief discussion of this construct appears under 'Supervisor factors: self-presentation' (this chapter, p. 23). The trainee's interpersonal and emotional characteristics in supervisory and counselling relationships have been included in the research of self-presentational behaviours (Ward, Friedlander et al., 1985). Constructs such as interpersonal patterns (Friedlander, Siegel and Brenock, 1989), reactance, potential defensiveness and counter defensiveness have been studied in relation to the process of supervision and relationship variables (Tracey, Ellickson and Sherry, 1989).

TEACHING EXERCISE FOR SUPERVISEE REFLECTION. Ask supervisors to pair up and for one to be in the role of supervisee while the other is the supervisor. You might also want to add an observer role to provide feedback on the interactional process. Have the supervisor engage the supervisee in a discussion of each of the five factors on the SAS supervisee wing. This exercise is practice for collecting information about the supervisee's experience and characteristics and using it to plan training interventions. Supervisors might think of using these topics for discussion in their first or second supervisory interview with a new supervisee. This interaction generally takes about thirty minutes with an additional fifteen minutes for feedback and discussion of the critical aspects of the interaction and the supervisee's training needs.

Client factors

The client is always present in the supervision. Indeed, the supervisor's *raison d'être* is to ensure that the supervisee can deliver effective service to the client. Yet, ironically, there is little research that examines client change or characteristics as an outcome or in relation to the supervision process (Holloway and Neufeldt, 1995). In SAS there are three client factors: client characteristics, client identified problem and diagnosis, and counselling relationship.

CLIENT CHARACTERISTICS. An important and frequently researched area has been on the variety of client attributes in relation to the process and outcome of psychotherapy. Characteristics and variables that have been studied include social class, personality traits, age, gender, intelligence, race and ethnicity. Some of these characteristics have some real practical value in determining the appropriateness of brief versus long-term therapy and pre-mature termination (Garfield, 1994). The relevance of these general client characteristics, rather than specific diagnostic attributes, has not been studied within the context of supervision and/or training. However, in practice, the supervisor frequently considers the client age, ethnicity, gender and race in determining the appropriateness of the match between counsellor and client as well as in problem-solving various difficulties that may emerge in the counselling relationship. The literature on matching client gender and/or ethnic minority status with therapists suggests that although there appears to be a preference for ethnically similar counsellors, this is not consistently evident in the empirical literature (Coleman, Wampold and Casali, 1994). It behoves the supervisor to recognize that variables such as social desirability, attitudes and values may play an important role in the potential effectiveness of the counsellor. Ineffectiveness may be attributed to the lack of similarity between client and therapist rather than discussing in depth other characteristics of the client and/or counsellor that may be inhibiting progress.

IDENTIFIED PROBLEM AND DIAGNOSIS. The identification of the client's problem is often the first topic for discussion in supervision. This might include a formal DSM IV assessment and diagnosis or a more problem-solving description of the client's presenting concern. New clients may be introduced to the trainee's caseload after careful screening by the agency and/or the supervisor. Supervisors in practice often screen clients for beginning level trainees to ensure that they will be assigned only cases appropriate to their level of competence. Supervisors also may choose cases for trainees based on the supervisor's areas of expertise. Occasionally, clients may be dealing with issues that are similar to a life circumstance that the supervisee has not yet resolved, and the supervisor then refers the client rather than risk the almost certain counter-transference that would emerge in the therapeutic relationship. Additionally, other characteristics of the client are relevant to the supervisor's and trainee's choice of topic of supervision and the manner in which they engage with one another. The supervisor is responsible for ensuring that the client will receive adequate treatment from the supervisee. In part, this assessment of the match between the supervisee's area and level of competence and the client's needs will depend on the severity of the client's problem. Axis IV of the DSM V is reserved for rating the severity of the psychosocial stressors in an individual's life. The degree of stress is then examined in light of the client's mental condition, or the nature of the problem and past adaptability to living, in order to determine the course of treatment. If a client is severely depressed or aggressive and is experiencing a very high number of stressors, then the supervisor and counsellor may need to do a specific assessment for suicide and/or homicide potential.

CHARACTERISTICS OF THE COUNSELLING RELATIONSHIP. The counselling relationship is an important basis from which to understand the impact of different treatment strategies as well as the effectiveness of the supervisee in creating a therapeutic relationship (Holloway and Neufeldt, 1995). The re-enactment of the relationship dynamics in the supervisory situation is a familiar phenomenon to supervisors and has been named the 'parallel process' (Doehrman, 1976; Ekstein and Wallerstein, 1958). Parallel process occurs when the central dynamic process of the counselling relationship is unconsciously acted out by the supervisee in the supervision relationship. The supervisee may be experiencing difficulty with the client and feels powerless to change the situation therapeutically, so he or she takes on interpersonal strategies similar to the client's form of resistance. If the supervisor does not recognize the dynamic as a part of the counselling situation and the trainee's feelings of powerlessness, then the supervisor may collude with this re-enactment by adopting a role similar to that of the trainee in the counselling relationship. The obvious result is an impasse in supervision. A supervisor who recognizes the parallel process can intervene directly with the supervisee, thus breaking the impasse in supervision while concurrently modelling effective interpersonal strategies for the supervisee. Thus, with effective supervisory intervention, the supervisee begins to understand, both experientially and conceptually, the meaning of the client's behaviour and is able to resume a therapeutic approach to the problem.

TEACHING EXERCISE FOR UNDERSTANDING THE CLIENT PROCESS. This exercise is designed to uncover parallel processes in supervision. The trainer can show a brief videotape of a counselling interaction. The trainer (or informed confederate) takes the role of the supervisee and a member of the group becomes the supervisor. The supervision interaction is done in front of the group and the supervisee creates a dilemma that encourages the development of a parallel process in supervision. The demonstration should take about twenty-five to thirty minutes, following which the group is able to use the SAS model to uncover the parallel process structure. (For an example of a parallel process training situation and the SAS analysis see Holloway, 1995: ch. 6).

Institutional factors

Supervision, whether a part of a training programme or continuing professional development, takes place in the context of institutional organizations, such as in-house departmental clinics, university counselling centres, hospitals, or community mental health or other service settings. The role of supervision in respect to the service demands of the organization is an important consideration in establishing goals and functions of supervision (Carroll and Holloway, 1999; Proctor, 1997). Yet the influence of organizational variables on supervision has rarely been investigated or discussed in the professional literature (Holloway and Roehlke, 1987). Institutional characteristics were first defined in SAS as an organizational clientele, the organizational structure and climate, and professional ethics and standards. However, the SAS model has been adapted to multi-disciplinary and organizational systems. In these environments the supervisor needs to attend to a more detailed knowledge of the organization's characteristics – for example, of such factors as mission, staffing practices, decision-making (formal and informal) and the history of the organization, among others unique to the supervisor's contract with the organization. These additional factors are described briefly here.

ORGANIZATIONAL CHARACTERISTICS. ***Mission***: The purpose and goals of the organization as they relate to both (a) internal organization and services, and (b) external relations with the community and other collateral organizations. ***Staffing***: personnel, full-time and part-time professional and support staff; recruitment and selection criteria and procedures; salary and promotion policies. ***Management structure***: management, lines of authority, lines of communication, supervisory relations, formal and informal decision-making processes, and formative and summative evaluation procedures. ***Climate and morale***: historical and current organizational culture, political agenda, attitudes and behaviours with regard to professional activities and co-workers. ***Ethics and standards***: mandated and/or expected standards for service within the organization, cost accountability, oversight regulation by external organizations, and individual ethics of the supervisors.

TEACHING EXERCISE TO UNDERSTAND THE INSTITUTION. Ask supervisors to form groups of three or four classmates. One volunteer is needed, to be interviewed by the group. The volunteer supervisor should be prepared to discuss various aspects of the organizational setting in which they work and to have a specific problem situation that is a result of the organization's structure in relation to supervision. The factors they might consider are on the institutional wing of Figure 1.1. Members of the group ask questions about the organizational setting to uncover the characteristics that might underlie the dilemma that the supervisor faces. This exercise usually takes about thirty minutes and is something like a detective game as members of the group try to figure out what the problem in the organization in relation to supervision might be.

Applying the SAS model to teaching supervision

I have described the seven components of the Systems Approach to Supervision (SAS) model used in analysing the supervision process. These have included the factors of supervision (task and function), the relationship of supervision, and the contextual factors (supervisor, supervisee, institution and client). I have suggested exercises to teach the differential nature of these dimensions while allowing for the specifics of their own context of practice and supervision. Although, for purposes of explication, these factors have been talked about in isolation, they are indeed interrelated, often occurring together in the same supervisory session. Potentially there is a multitude of relationships that are directly or indirectly part of any discussion of training in supervision. Each supervisor may have several trainees and in turn each supervisee may have several clients. Further, in the group consultation there is not only the relationship between each supervisor and the trainer, but also the relationships among the various supervisor members. Clearly not all of these relationships will be discussed explicitly in the group nor will the trainer know all of these relationships in detail. However, when supervisor members raise issues in the group, their perspective will be shaped by their observation and experience of these various relationships and contexts.

Any discussion of the teaching of supervision must involve a discussion of the practice of supervision and the practice of counselling. All three processes – teaching supervision, supervision practice and counselling practice – are necessarily linked by their concurrence and the supervisors' and supervisees' roles in the group consultation on supervision and the counselling relationship, respectively. Because the distinction among these three contexts of teaching and practising are easily confused, for the sake of clarity I have named them as follows. The *counselling relationship* refers to each or all of the counsellor trainee's counsellor-client dyads. The *supervisory relationship* refers to each or all of the supervisor's supervisor-trainee dyads. The *consultative group* refers to the group of supervisors who meet with a trainer to discuss and learn about their practice of supervision. By understanding the linkage among these three relational contexts, the tasks and processes of teaching supervision in a group setting might be further illuminated. The group consultation may deal with any of the roles or issues that emerge in these three interrelated contexts. Central to the purpose of the supervision consultation group are questions that relate to the supervisory performance of each relationship between the supervisor and individual members of the group. The supervisors face two central tasks: *What should I teach? How should I create a relationship that facilitates the supervisee learning the teaching objectives?* With these questions as a point of departure, the trainer can begin by providing a context for the supervisor's experience. Reference to the model may assist the supervisor in identifying the source or sources of the current dilemma, how these factors interrelate, and how the factors influence the three relational contexts. In the teaching of supervision, I encourage supervisors to consider the following questions while reflecting on their work.

1. What factors are influencing the participants' judgements in guiding the supervision process?
2. What characteristics of the contextual factors have they relied on in their decision-making?
3. What characteristics have they not considered but which, upon reflection, seem important in designing a teaching approach in supervision?
4. What kinds of roles do they tend to manifest in supervision, and are these the most beneficial for learning to take place?
5. What tasks of supervision do they focus on with particular trainees?

Supervision consultation case analysis

Through my years of teaching supervision I have collected tales of supervisors' struggles to become more effective in teaching the practice of counselling. Common themes have emerged across the years. I have chosen one common theme to illustrate the application of the SAS model in teaching supervision. The supervisor's original intervention and thinking is depicted in the 'The supervisor's dilemma'; in the strategic analysis, including salient factors and critical discoveries that emerged from the discussion; and, finally in the 'Process matrix of supervision' indicating the original task and function of the supervisor and the suggested target for intervention, is depicted in Figure 1.2. The purpose of the diagrams (Figures 1.1 and 1.2) is to emphasize the evolutionary change in focus throughout the process of the consultation and to demonstrate the way in which the SAS model may be used graphically in case analysis.

The supervisor's dilemma (see Figure 1.1)

Both supervisors came to me in disarray. Their trainees were not accepting supervision. They were unwilling to talk about their own feelings and thoughts about the counselling relationship and about the supervisory relationship. What was the cause of their supervisees' resistance? The supervisors were deeply concerned about the supervisees' futures as counsellors since they were unable to engage in the supervisory process. They were advanced in their clinical skills and experience and were dedicated professionals. They were supervising beginning level practicum students because of their commitment to training professionals and because of their enjoyment of the supervision process.

The clinical service setting

This was a small non-profit community agency that offered services to low-income people. All counselling sessions of trainees were audiotaped for supervision purposes.

The supervisees

The trainees were both mature individuals who had entered the counselling profession from other fields. They were eager to learn how to do counselling and were very involved in their placement setting. One supervisee was a European-American male who had been a teacher for five years. The other supervisee was a bicultural, European-American and American-Indian female and had worked extensively in community action organizations prior to returning to the university for counsellor training.

The supervisors' stories

Rebecca: 'My supervisee is having difficulty establishing boundaries with her client and it seems at times that the two of them are friends chatting on the street. I have explored with the supervisee the difference between friendships and therapy and felt that although she had an intellectual understanding of this, that she wasn't able to translate this into the practice of her role. The chatting, although somewhat diminished in the sessions, seems unpredictable and I don't think she can recognize the boundaries between the two roles. So that is when I decided to begin a process of emotional exploration with her. I've worked really hard at bringing her into her own awareness and felt satisfied with her willingness to self-disclose about her personal feelings in reference to this client. In fact, I followed this up with two more supervisory sessions in which we probed the meaning of friendships in her culture and the need to feel accepted as a person and professional. I really enjoyed the complexity and connection between the professional boundaries and their connection with the cultural background of the counsellor. I began to teach her about the importance of separation and the implications of dual relationships and ethics. She really became very tearful and then shut down. I didn't really understand what had happened and then in the last session before today she came in very angry with me for intruding into her personal world and for my lack of sensitivity to cultural background. She insisted that I stick to supervision and teach her the skills of the profession, not try to be her therapist. I was so shocked at the intensity of her reaction and even more shocked that she felt I was mixing up the boundaries.'

Georgine. I really know what you are going through. My supervisee seems completely incapable of exploring his own emotional response to his client. He's really trying to befriend his client and is actually giving her feedback on how he sees her as a woman. I think that he is trying to assure her that she is a nice person, someone that he would find attractive. I am so exasperated with him. He is unable or unwilling to get at what made it so necessary to reach across his professional boundaries like this. I have confronted him several times on this inappropriate behaviour with the client. Last time I observed his counselling session with this client I was totally undone. He seemed to be deliberately seductive with her. In the last supervision session, he told me in no uncertain terms to lay off him about exploring his feelings about the client and that what he really needed was to learn the skills of being a counsellor. If he wanted therapy, he'd pay a counsellor for it.

The consultation

Both supervisors sat across from me for their joint consultation hour. Rebecca is a very thoughtful, still type of person. Her quiet intelligence is probably the first view you have of her. There is a persistence and tenacity in the way she takes hold of an idea and runs underground with it. She has a keen set of antennae that pick up the nuances of behaviours and their meaning. She looked pretty discouraged today and running through it was something of a rage, at least what might be the glimpse of a rage for Rebecca. She started her tale at a higher pitch than usual and I was immediately alerted to the type of intensity she conveyed.

Georgine had a certain serenity about her. She has a great way of being quietly present, delivering searing confrontations with hardly a ripple in her composure and yet with a support and warmth that leaves a lingering feeling that you are cared about in spite of the fact that there are clearly things you need to change. They looked at me expectantly, knowing my predilection for complex interpersonal analysis. I could feel their suggestion that I begin an exploration of their feelings in their respective supervision relationships. I felt tugged by the seduction of their intensity and our history of untangling the webs of emotion and behaviour in relationship. I knew just as surely that it must be different this time. They needed to be taught rather directly the boundaries of their roles and the meaning of the contract and development of the supervisory relationship, just as surely as their students needed to understand the boundaries of their roles as counsellors. I needed to give to them what their students were asking – that is, to understand experientially the importance of skill acquisition in empowerment. As boring and interpersonally irrelevant as it may seem to them in this moment, I must remind them of the purpose of their supervision contract and the level of experience of their trainees. I offered them the possibility that their trainees did just not know how to show warmth and genuineness within the frame of a counselling relationship. This was indeed a parallel process with the counselling and supervisory relationship that needed to be stopped at the consultative level. We had to engage in a clear and careful analysis of their supervisory method. And so initially we began a process of examining the skills that the trainees lacked, and thought about supervisory approaches to teach these skills. We kept the focus on skills that might help facilitate the trainees in learning the role of counsellor. I could tell they were dubious and really wanted to divert our attention to their feelings about not being appreciated as supervisors after all their work and attention to these fledgling counsellors. I resisted and waited until we had dealt with the skills and teaching methods; and then we ventured into talk of relationship, culture and gender and how these factors were influencing their involvement with their trainees.

The SAS analysis (see Figure 1.2)

The supervisors had not misread the difficulty the counsellors were having in the development of the counselling relationships, but they had chosen a counselling function to focus almost exclusively on the trainees' emotional awareness to address this issue. The counsellors initially found themselves following this lead, but then felt that they were being seduced into a counselling relationship and being denied the skills that they needed to act differently. The supervisors needed to return to their understanding of the supervisory contract. Had they maintained the boundaries of the supervisory relationship? They needed to examine the phase of relationship and the level of experience of the supervisee. They were in fairly new relationships where deep self-disclosure might have been seen as premature. Their persistent focus on the trainees' self-disclosure was overly intense. Although initially an appropriate venture, it soon became too demanding and seemingly unrelated to the client the supervisee had to face each week. These were beginning-level counsellors and they needed to learn a level of skill that could help them implement their intellectual understanding of the counsellor role. They needed skills other than their friendship skills to create a facilitative and warm relationship. The supervisors' own preference for interpersonal awareness and counselling-type interventions in supervision – that is, their expectation of the role of the supervisor being too narrowly defined – prevented them from acknowledging the need to provide skill training to these supervisees. The importance of the gender and cultural differences between the supervisors and their supervisees also played a role in their lack of sensitivity to the supervisees' anger. The supervisors assumed that the trainees' use of relationship skills was based on some dysfunctional reason for needing to be friends with their clients. Although they were able to engage in a conversation with their supervisees about cultural mores and tradition in professional relationships, in action they were defying those norms in their persistence for self-disclosure and more intimate conversation. The supervisees felt that their behaviours with their clients were being interpreted in a way that maligned their intentions.

Eventually the supervisees were able to explain their intentions to their supervisors from a cultural and gender perspective. The supervisors were able to identify specifically those behaviours of the supervisees that were ineffective in the counselling context, and the supervisees were able to suggest ways they could be with the client that would ameliorate the situation but still feel genuine and culturally and gender congruent. Rebecca finally began a discussion of counselling approaches that were most effective with her trainee's own cultural groups and of the differences in relational structure and role that would be expected in cultures other than European-American. For both supervisors, understanding the meaning of their initial supervisory focus on personal awareness from a cultural and gender perspective was very important in finding a way to relate appropriately to their supervisees. The consultative process is situated in the Institutional Factors wing and the existing and potential parallel processes – between the supervisees' counselling relationships, the supervisory relationship, and the consultative relationship – are highlighted.

Concluding remarks

The SAS model invites practitioners and educators of supervision to reflection on what they do in supervision, to ask difficult questions about the meaning of their work, to uncover their own intuitive knowledge, and to use a common language to communicate this to others. The model attempts to integrate the research and practice knowledge of supervision and synthesize it in a way that is immediately practical and relevant to the understanding and teaching of supervision. I have tried to be explicit and concrete about a very complex instructional method without suggesting that there is a 'how to' or 'should do' of supervision.

References

Altman, I. and Taylor, D.A. (1973) *Social Penetration: The Development of Interpersonal Relationships*. New York: Holt, Rinehart & Winston.

Atkinson, D.R., Morten, G. and Sue, D.W. (1989) *Counseling American Minorities: A Cross-cultural Perspective* (3rd edn). Dubuque, IA: Brown.

Baumeister, R.F. (1982) A self-presentational view of social phenomena, *Psychological Bulletin*, 91: 3–26.

Berger, C.E. and Calabrese, A.M. (1975) Some explorations in initial interaction and beyond: toward a developmental theory of interpersonal communication, *Human Communication Research*, 1: 99–112.

Bernard, J.M. and Goodyear, R.K. (1992) *Fundamentals of Clinical Supervision*. Boston: Allyn & Bacon.

Borders, L.D., Fong, M.L. and Neimeyer, G.J. (1986) Counseling students' level of ego development and perceptions of clients, *Counselor Education and Supervision*, 26: 37–49.

Carifio, M.S. and Hess, A.K. (1987) Who is the ideal supervisor? *Professional Psychology: Research and Practice*, 18 (3): 244–50.

Carroll, M. (1996) *Workplace Counselling*. London: Sage.

Carroll, M. and Holloway, E.L. (eds) (1999) *Counselling Supervision in Context* London: Sage.

Coleman, H.L.K., Wampold, B.E. and Casali, S.L. (1994) Ethnic minorities' ratings of ethnically similar and European American counselors: a meta-analysis, *Journal of Counseling Psychology*, 42: 247–94.

Doehrman, M.J. (1976) Parallel processes in supervision and psychotherapy, *Bulletin of the Menninger Clinic*, 40 (1): 1–104.

Ekstein, R. and Wallerstein, R.S. (1958) *The Teaching and Learning of Psychotherapy*. New York: Basic Books.

Ellis, M.V. and Dell, D.M. (1986) Dimensionality of supervisor roles: Supervisors' perceptions of supervision. *Journal of Counseling Psychology*, 33, 282–91.

Ellis, M.V, Dell, D.M. and Good, G.E. (1988) Counselor trainees' perceptions of supervisor roles: Two studies testing the dimensionality of supervision. *Journal of Counseling Psychology*, 35, 315–24.

French, J.R.P., Jr. and Raven, B.H. (1960) The bases of social power. In D. Cartwright and A. Zander (eds), *Group Dynamics: Research and Theory* (2nd edn, pp. 607–23). New York: Peterson.

Friedlander, M.L., Siegel, S.M. and Brenock, K. (1989) Parallel processes in counseling and supervision: a case study. *Journal of Counseling Psychology*, 36: 149–57.

Garfield, S.L. (1994) Research on client variables in psychotherapy. In A.E. Bergin and S.L. Garfield (eds), *Handbook of Psychotherapy and Behavior Change* (4th edn, pp. 190–228). New York: Wiley.

Goodyear, R.K. and Bradley, F. (1983) Theories of counselor supervision: points of convergence and divergence. *The Counseling Psychologist*, 11: 59–68.

Harvey, O.J., Hunt, D.E. and Schroder, H.M. (1961) *Conceptual Systems and Personality Organization*. New York: Wiley.

Hess, A.K. (ed.) (1980) *Psychotherapy Supervision: Theory, Research and Practice*. New York: Wiley.

Hinde, R.A. (1979) *Towards Understanding Relationships*. New York: Academic Press.

Holloway, E.L. (1984) Outcome evaluation in supervision research. *The Counseling Psychologist*, 12, 4, 167–74.

Holloway, E.L. (1992) Supervision: a way of teaching and learning. In S.D. Brown and R.W. Lent (eds), *Handbook of Counseling Psychology* (pp. 177–214). New York: Wiley.

Holloway, E.L. (1995) *Clinical Supervision: A Systems Approach*. Thousand Oaks, CA: Sage.

Holloway, E.L., and Poulin, K. (1994) Discourse in supervision. In J. Siegfried (ed.) *Therapeutic and everyday discourse as behaviour change: Towards a micro-analysis in psychotherapy process research*. Norwood, NJ.: Ablex.

Holloway, E.L. and Neufeldt, S.A. (1995) Supervision: contributors to treatment efficacy. *Journal of Consulting and Clinical Psychology*, 63(2): 207–13.

Holloway, E.L. and Roehlke, H.J. (1987) Internship: the applied training of a counseling psychologist, *The Counseling Psychologist*, 2: 205–60.

Inskipp, F. and Proctor, B. (1989) *Skills for Supervising and Being Supervised*. Principles of Counselling audiotape series. St Leonards-on-Sea: Alexia Publications.

Jones, E.E. and Pittman, T.S. (1982) Toward a general theory of strategic self-presentation. In J. Suls (ed.), *Psychological Perspectives on the Self*. Hillsdale, NJ: Erlbaum.

Leary, T. (1957) *Interpersonal Diagnosis of Personality: A Theory and a Methodology for Personality Evaluation*. New York: Ronald Press.

Loevinger, J. (1976) *Ego Development: Conceptions and Theories*. San Francisco: Jossey-Bass.

Loganbill, C., Hardy, E. and Delworth, U. (1982) Supervision: a conceptual model. *The Counseling Psychologist*, 10 (1): 3–42.

Martinez, R. and Holloway, E.L. (1997) The supervision relationship in multicultural training. In D. Pope-Davis and H. Coleman (eds) *Multicultural Counseling Competencies: Assessment, Education, and Supervision*. Thousand Oaks, CA: Sage.

Miller, F.E. and Rogers, L.E. (1987) Relational dimensions of interpersonal dynamics. In M.E. Roloff and G.R. Miller (eds) *Interpersonal processes: New directions in communication research*. Beverly Hills: Sage.

Miller, G.R. (1976) *Explorations in Interpersonal Communication*. Newbury Park, CA: Sage.

Morton, T., Alexander, C. and Altman, I. (1976) Communication and relationship definition. In G. Miller (ed.), *Explorations in Interpersonal Communication* (pp. 105–25). Beverly Hills, CA: Sage.

Mueller, W.J. and Kell, B.L. (1972) *Coping with Conflict: Supervising Counselors and Psychotherapists*. Englewood Cliffs, NJ: Prentice-Hall.

Nelson, M.L. and Holloway, E.L. (1990) Relation of gender to power and involvement in supervision. *Journal of Counseling Psychology*, 37: 473–81.

Nelson, M.L. and Holloway, E.L. (1999). Gender and Supervision. In, M. Carroll and E. Holloway (eds) *Counselling Supervision in Context*. London: Sage.

Neufeldt, S.A., Karno, M.P. and Nelson, M.L. (1996) A qualitative study of experts' conceptualization of supervisee reflectivity. *Journal of Counseling Psychology*, 43, 3–9.

Pedersen, P. (ed.) (1985) *Handbook of Cross-cultural Counseling and Therapy*. Westport, CT: Greenwood.

Penman, R. (1980) *Communication Processes and Relationships*. London: Academic Press.

Poulin, K. (1992) *Towards a Grounded Pedagogy of Practice: A Dimensional Analysis of Counseling Supervision*. Dissertation Abstracts 9505214 UMI Dissertation Services, Bell & Howell Co., 3200 N. Zeb Rd. Ann Arbor, MI 48106 1–800–521–0600.

Proctor, B. (1997) Contracting in Supervision. In C. Sills (ed.), *Contracts in Counselling*. London: Sage.

Rabinowitz, F.E., Heppner, P.P. and Roehlke, H.J. (1986) Descriptive study of process and outcome variables of supervision over time. *Journal of Counseling Psychology*, 33, 292–300.

Random House College Dictionary (1984) New York: Random House.

Russell, R.K., Crimmings, A.M. and Lent, R.W. (1984) Counselor training and supervision: theory and research. In S. Brown and R. Lent (eds), *The Handbook of Counseling Psychology* (pp. 625–81). New York: Wiley.

Schön, D.A. (1983) *Educating the reflective practitioner*. San Francisco: Jossey-Bass.

Skovholt, T.M. and Rønnestad, M.H. (1992) *The evolving professional self: Stages and themes in therapist and counselor development*. Chichester: Wiley.

Solomon, B. (1983) Power: the troublesome factor in cross-cultural supervision. *Smith College Journal School for Social Work*, 10, 27–32.

Stoltenberg, C. (1981) Approaching supervision from a developmental perspective: The counselor complexity model. *Journal of Counseling Psychology*, 28, 59–65.

Stoltenberg, C.D. Delworth, U. (1987) *Supervising Counselors and Therapists*. San Francisco: Jossey-Bass.

Strong, S.R., Hills, H.I. and Nelson, B.N. (1988) *Interpersonal Communication Rating Scale (Revision)*. Unpublished manuscript, Department of Psychology, Virginia Commonwealth University, Richmond.

Sue, D.W. and Sue, D. (1990) *Counseling the Culturally Different: Theory and Practice* (2nd edn). New York: Wiley.

Teyber, E. (1988) *Interpersonal Process in Psychotherapy: A Guide for Clinical Training*. Chicago, IL: Dorsey Press.

Tracey, T.J., Ellickson, J.L. and Sherry, P. (1989) Reactance in relation to different supervisory environments and counselor development. *Journal of Counseling Psychology*, 36: 336–44.

Tyler, F.B., Brome, D.R. and Williams, J.E. (1991) *Ethnic Validity, Ecology, and Psychotherapy: A Psychosocial Competence Model*. New York: Plenum Press.

Walsh, J.F. (1994) One-way between subjects and design: simulated data and analysis using SAS. *Teaching of Psychology*, 21: 53–5.

Wampler, L.D. and Strupp, H.H. (1976) Personal therapy for students in clinical psychology: A matter of faith? *Professional Psychology*, 6, 195–201.

Ward, L.G., Friedlander, M.L., Schoen, L.G. and Klein, J.C. (1985) Strategic self-presentation in supervision. *Journal of Counseling Psychology*, 32: 111–18.

Worthington, E.L. (1987) Changes in supervision as counselors and supervisors gain experience: a review. *Professional Psychology: Research and Practice*, 18: 189–208.

2 Training in the tasks of supervision

Michael Carroll

Introduction

I have been involved with clinical supervision for almost twenty years now. My initial interest emerged during my first supervision experience when, during my training as a counselling psychologist, I arranged a placement (internship) in a youth counselling agency. I worked there for approximately 500 hours engaging in individual counselling with adolescents, training in parenting skills, doing group work with young people and becoming involved in a number of allied schemes around counselling and education. Overall, it was great experience. What was not so great was my experience of supervision. On my arrival and with my introduction to the service I was allocated a supervisor, an experienced trainer, counsellor and manager of the whole service. He was delighted to see me and greatly appreciated my work with the service, but not once did we meet for formal supervision. He was, as he put it, 'there if I needed him', giving the impression that supervision was for emergencies or instances of work I felt beyond my competencies. An occasional informal chat, as we drank coffee, met with the rest of the staff, or even when we played squash together was the sum-total of my supervision experience. I left, relishing my work in the agency but regretting not being supervised. Later I was to regret even more not having this experience to help me understand the tasks of supervision from both perspectives: those of the supervisor and those of the supervisee.

My next experience of supervision came about two years after qualifying and working as a counselling psychologist, and was a request to supervise. The request to become a supervisor propelled me into thinking through what it meant and how it could be set up. I found myself struggling with questions such as:

What was I supposed to do as a supervisor?
What were my responsibilities, ethical and legal?
What steps need I take to ensure the quality of the counselling work undertaken by my supervisee?
What were the tasks and roles in which we, supervisor and supervisee, were involved?

The issue of what were the tasks of supervision had again raised its head and I was, again, without clear answers.

Background Influences

Having forged some kind of working model of supervision to keep me going, I began to read up on supervision and eventually got some training in being a supervisor. During this training the question of supervision tasks emerged: what do supervisors and supervisees *do*? What tasks and roles do they engage in to meet the aims and purposes of supervision? I began to read the academic literature on supervision and I quickly discovered that supervision had quite a history, and a history that outlined a number of supervisory tasks.

These tasks crystallized around *six elements* that have influenced and continue to influence my work as a supervisor today and are the basis for my interest in and articulation of supervisory tasks. The first is the human and perennial need of people to have a forum of reflection. Reflexivity is the process by which learning emerges from experience and is integrated into new ways of engaging with life. Creating an environment to facilitate this reflection is no mean skill. My second influence is the concept of mentoring. Not quite a parent, not only a teacher, but a guide, an experienced adult, Mentor, friend of Odysseus, had the task of ensuring that the young man in his charge, Telemachus, son of Odysseus, grew up with the values and discipline needed. Mentor seemed to combine a number of complicated roles and tasks into a learning relationship with Telemachus. The third influence on my ideas of supervision is that of apprenticeship – the medieval notion of the young person apprenticing himself/herself to an experienced adult who taught them their trade. But not just the trade. A relationship was formed in which the young apprentice grew to adulthood, learning a trade, but also learning what it meant to be an adult. A fourth influence was connecting supervision to education. Supervision is, of itself, an educational process built around learning styles, and educational and training methodologies, and connects learning to teaching. A fifth influence on my understanding of supervision, and connected to supervision as an educational process, was an awareness of the developmental models of supervision. Realizing that the journey from novice to professional goes through various stages helps supervisors pitch their supervisory interventions according to the needs of the supervisee. And finally, the sixth influence was an awareness of the social role models of supervision which revolved around the roles and tasks in which supervisor and supervisee involve themselves. These six elements are the basis, in my view, for understanding and working with the tasks of supervision.

The tasks of supervision

My interest in the tasks of supervision led me to set up a research project to see if, and in what form, they existed and then to test them in reality. Were there generic tasks of supervision that crossed counselling orientation and were ingrained in all forms of supervision? I used four methods to help me identify these generic categories of supervisory tasks. The literature (both research and theoretical) was reviewed in depth to discover as many supervisory tasks as possible. In particular, the social role models of supervision were used. The second area considered was that of my own and others' experience of being supervisors. The third area for identifying tasks emerged from training supervisors. During a two-year training Diploma in Supervision I presented three classes of approximately twenty participants with a number of categories and asked them for further tasks of supervision. A fourth area was a small group in which I worked for a year as both a supervisee and a trainee supervisor. This group of four (the supervisor was a leading psychiatrist from the psychoanalytic tradition) reviewed their own client work and drew learning dimensions from it in respect of supervision. It was here that one element emerged as crucial, namely the administrative aspects of client work.

From the literature, from the experience of being supervised and being a supervisor, and from training others as supervisors, seven tasks emerged:

1. the relationship task
2. the teaching/learning task
3. the counselling task
4. the monitoring task (monitoring professional/ethical issues)
5. the evaluation task
6. the consultative task
7. the administrative task

I went on to set up three research projects on these seven tasks (Carroll, 1995). Besides researching the seven tasks I also tried to integrate them into training courses for supervisors, and to date have used this training with: treatment managers in the prison service; clinical psychologists; personnel/human resources officers; priests; counsellors, counselling psychologists and psychotherapists; youth and community workers; nurses; and managers in companies. These courses took place in a number of settings – hospitals, universities, counselling services and counselling centres and training programmes, companies and organizations both public and private. Using the tasks of supervision has enabled me to focus more clearly on training in supervision, covering areas where one individual meets another to help that person review his or her work.

The tasks of supervision

The practicality of being a supervisor means being skilled in the tasks of supervision: hence the importance of training aspiring supervisors in the generic tasks of supervision. This training takes place in two parts: the first presents the seven generic tasks of supervision and helps supervisors learn to understand and implement them with supervisees; in the second part they learn to work with and practise the skills of each task.

The first element in training in the tasks of supervision is to help participants understand what are the tasks of supervision and have a working knowledge of them. For this I go back to input on the tasks and look in some detail at the social role models.

Background

The 'tasks of supervision' have their roots in early understandings of supervision in which supervisor and supervisee adopt certain relationships towards one another. Bee and Mitchell (1984: 22) have defined the term 'role' as 'the content of a position or the behavioural implications of occupying that position'. From within a specific supervisory context, Holloway and Acker (1989: 3) have viewed roles as 'sets of behaviours that create certain expectancies of performance for the actor and the receiver in the encounter'. It is principally from these models that supervisory 'tasks' will be considered, tasks being seen as the crucial 'performance' or 'work' that is engendered by roles. The social role models attempt to tell us what supervisors and supervisees *do* within supervision, what tasks are performed and by whom.

Perhaps the central word used throughout is the term 'task'. A task has been defined as 'a piece of work imposed, exacted or undertaken as a duty or the like . . . a fixed or specified quantity of work imposed on or exacted from a person . . . the work appointed to one as a definite duty' (Onions, 1968: 2135). In the context of supervision the question that emerges is that of the specific work of supervisor and supervisee. What are the tasks (the specific work) of supervisors, and what are the tasks (the work appointed) assigned to supervisees?

Tasks are the behavioural side of roles. A role is person-centred (teacher/pupil); the task is action-centred (to teach/to learn). Even though a strong notional distinction is made between roles and tasks, in reality they combine.

A number of social role models of supervision that specifically address the roles of supervisors have been outlined (Bernard, 1979; Ekstein, 1964; Ekstein and Wallerstein, 1972; Hess, 1980; Holloway, 1984, 1995; Littrell, Lee-Borden, and Lorenz, 1979). Bernard's (1979) discrimination model is a pioneering study in roles; Ekstein (1964) and Ekstein and Wallerstein (1972) are the earliest to isolate supervisor roles; Hess's relationship model offers a different vantage point with its concentration on the supervisory relationship; Littrell, Lee-Borden, and Lorenz (1979) attempt to combine a developmental model with supervisor roles; and Holloway's work is the most recent and the most detailed role approach. In training potential supervisors I have found it helpful (and they seem to find it helpful too) to outline the essence of the history of tasks/roles in supervision and provide details of some models.

Bernard's Discrimination Model

Bernard (1979) divided supervisor roles into three categories:

- teacher: involving feedback, information, instruction;
- consultant: understanding the counselling process;
- counsellor: looking at the person of the therapist and his/her way of intervening.

Her training model for clinical supervision (1981) has described these three roles in terms of potential areas of focus, each of which demands consideration and attention if the role of a counselling supervisor is to be satisfactorily discharged: these are (a) process (where the focus is on the relationship between counsellors and clients and how trainees intervene in the counselling work), (b) conceptualization (which is concerned with understanding what is happening), and (c) personalization (which deals with the feelings and reactions of trainees). Each role can be combined with each area of focus (Bernard, 1979). In combining the roles and functions Bernard outlines a three-by-three matrix of focus points for supervisors. Bernard's work, designed and worked out as a training method for supervisors, is widely accepted in the supervisory literature as an important contribution to the various roles in which supervisors involve themselves.

Ekstein's Triangle and Ekstein and Wallerstein's Rhombus

Ekstein (1964) visualized the supervisor's tasks (he uses this word synonymously with roles) in terms of a triangle with the supervisor at the centre and lines going to each of the three corners. His aim was to ascertain if the supervisor's main task was one of therapist (looking after the patient and/or the therapist), didactic teacher (educating the therapist), or administrator (looking to the clinical setting in which clients are seen). Ekstein answered his own question by recognizing that while the supervisor will be pulled into each corner, his/her main objective is to remain 'equidistant' from all three, and at the same time fulfil each task when appropriate. He viewed 'equidistancing' as a function of supervision.

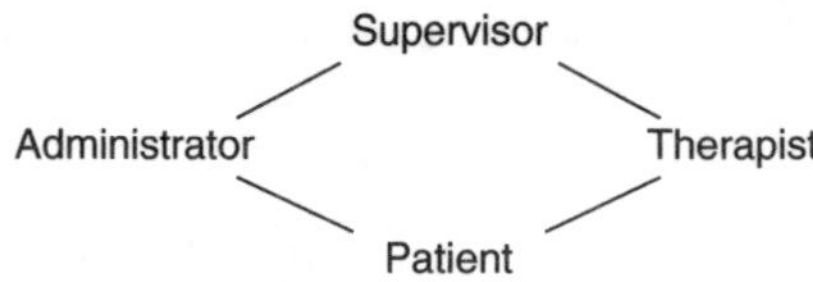

Figure 2.1 *The Clinical Rhombus*

What emerges strongly from this model are the clear tasks visualized by Ekstein, that supervisors take on different roles (tasks) at different times, sometimes as educators, sometimes as therapists, sometimes as administrators. He was insistent that the supervisory relationship was the context that held these tasks together.

The clinical rhombus devised by Ekstein and Wallerstein (1972) presents the same tasks from a slightly different perspective as outlined in Figure 2.1. Each of the other three roles can be viewed from the vantage point of the fourth; for example, the supervisor has a relationship with all three individuals (a teaching relationship with the therapist, the task of maintaining clinical standards with the patient, and a responsibility role with the administrator).

What Ekstein (1964) and Ekstein and Wallerstein (1972) have offered is a series of roles (tasks) in which the supervisor engages. What they have added to Bernard's model is the task of administration (sometimes the supervisor is also the administrator), and the notion of 'equidistancing'.

Hess's 'Relationship' Model

Hess (1980) viewed six forms of supervision in which he was concerned with the relationship parameters between supervisor and supervisee. Each role sets up a different task to be performed, with a different kind of relationship between supervisor and supervisee, and a different form of communication. Hess never viewed these as exclusive but envisaged superiors using a combination of roles when appropriate.

Role	**Task**
Lecturer	to inform
Teacher	to instruct (knowledge, skills, etc.)

Case conference facilitator	to clarify clinical understanding and make clinical decisions
Colleague-peer	to support and share meanings
Monitor	to protect client, trainee, agency, etc.
Therapist	to deal with the personal issues of the supervisee

Hess has brought the relationship task to the forefront and sees it as an underlying parameter in all forms of supervision. On the other hand he, unlike Ekstein, gives little attention to the administrative task.

Littrell, Lee-Borden and Lorenz

Littrell, Lee-Borden, and Lorenz (1979) have offered a model combining the tasks of supervision within a developmental framework. They connected four models of supervision with the tasks involved. Table 2.1 presents an overview of their model:

Table 2.1 *The tasks of supervision*

Supervisory model	Tasks involved
Counselling therapeutic	Helping the supervisee deal with personal and emotional reactions
Teaching	Instructing and facilitating conceptualization within supervision
Consulting	How best to intervene with clients
Self-supervision	Creating conditions where the supervisee monitors self on the three tasks above

Source: Littrell, Lee-Borden and Lorenz, 1979

Their suggestion is that rather than concentrate on one approach, which supervisors often do, the complete process of supervision combines these tasks within a developmental framework. Theirs is a four-stage developmental model presented in Table 2.2:

Table 2.2 *Developmental framework*

Stage 1	Stage 2	Stage 3	Stage 4
Relationship Goal-setting Contract	Counselling/therapeutic model Teaching model	Consulting model	Self-supervision

Source: Littrell, Lee-Borden and Lorenz, 1979

Movement through the stages of the model involves different tasks, decreased supervisor control and increased supervisee self-direction, increased professionalization, and the ability of the supervisor to help the supervisee progress through the various stages. Supervisory tasks change as supervision develops.

Littrell, Lee-Borden and Lorenz (1979) have introduced two elements into their task-directed model. First of all they emphasize the supervisory relationship as a key element in the learning process. Setting up and maintaining the relationship through goal-setting and contracting is a necessary prerequisite for the following stages. Second, they see self-supervision as an ideal towards which supervision should move, that is, the supervisee's ability to provide for self what the supervisor initially provides. What is new about their approach is the suggestion that supervisory tasks are 'developmental' – that different tasks predominate at different stages of the supervisory relationships.

Holloway's EPICS (Engagement and Power in Clinical Supervision) Model

Holloway (1984), Holloway and Acker (1989), and Holloway (1992, 1995) have contributed to the social role models of supervision with a number of approaches.

Holloway (1984) has pinpointed five supervisor roles and five corresponding supervisee roles as set out below (Table 2.3):

Table 2.3 *Holloway's roles of supervision*

Supervisor roles	Supervisee roles
Monitor: evaluating professional and ethical practice	Applying theory in an effective and appropriate way
Instructor: teaching	Conceptualizing practice
Consultant: conceptualizing client material	Understanding the client
Counsellor: facilitating personal growth	Being open to personal growth
Colleague: self-disclosure	Relating with supervisor and agency personnel

What is special about this model is its introduction of the 'monitoring' task as a method of 'gatekeeping' for professional/ethical issues. 'Professional behaviour' covers areas of professional practice such as 'being on time, maintaining confidentiality, the ability to effect an appropriate referral, and maintaining appropriate personal relationships with clients' (Lanning 1986: 193). Holloway, however, in the above model, also includes, like Hess, the relationship (is the supervisor a colleague?) as a task within supervision.

Holloway and Acker's (1989) model combined roles, tasks, teaching objectives and teaching strategies. Based on the supervisory relationship as involving the twin issues of power and engagement, their model connected teaching objectives (content areas that become students' learning) and teaching strategies (which are very similar to the roles outlined above and are concerned with the particular stance taken by the supervisor). It is possible, though still a bit premature, to see their EPICS model as a matrix of tasks/roles. The teaching strategies, or what they call 'roles within the supervisory position', are combined with teaching objectives (called the tasks in this study) and woven into what they call the 'EPICS matrix'. More on this can be found in Chapter 1 above. What Holloway has contributed to the debate on the tasks of supervision is a methodology for integrating five roles: monitoring, instructing, modelling, counselling and consulting. Moreover, around these tasks Holloway (1995) points out the centrality of the supervisory relationship as the context in which tasks are performed. For her, 'the structure and character of the relationship embodies all other factors of the supervision and in turn all other factors are influenced by the relationship. The process of supervision . . . is enacted within the relationship. Understanding the relationship is understanding the process' (1995: 51).

Conclusions

What conclusions can be drawn from the overview of these five social-role models of supervision in respect of generic supervision tasks? That tasks exist is in no doubt: supervisor and supervisee are present 'to do' something, to involve themselves in specific behaviours. The five models review present tasks from different angles. Some are universally agreed (such as teaching), and other tasks are particular to individual authors. An analysis of the literature on teaching, counselling and consulting since Bernard's model shows these to be definitive tasks. Holloway (1992) and Lanning (1986) add the evaluating task (assessing the work) as a key role within supervision, and this has been widely accepted as fundamental by practitioners and by recent literature (Bernard and Goodyear, 1992; Borders and Leddick, 1987). The supervisory relationship has always been viewed as essential to supervision and in recent writings seen more as a 'task', that is, something to be done (Efstation, Patton and Kardash, 1990; Hawkins and Shohet, 1989; Holloway, 1995). It is presumed to be a container for the many supervisory roles that make up supervision. Monitoring the administrative aspects of supervision is very high in the social work supervision literature (Kadushin, 1985), but has been mentioned only somewhat in the counselling supervision literature. However, in recent publications it is slowly being recognized as an important, and indeed often neglected area (Bernard and Goodyear, 1992: Holloway, 1992). Thus, administration seems like an important supervisory task. The role of ethical/professional issues within counselling has been recognized for some time in the profession (ACES, 1993; Bradley, 1989), but there has been a lack of clarity around its place within supervision. None the less, this role is common to most practitioners.

The generic tasks/roles outlined here may not be acceptable to all models of supervision; for example, some supervisory arrangements refuse to 'evaluate' the supervisee on the basis that it affects the supervisory relationship adversely. Furthermore there may well be different models of supervision that stress different roles/tasks: some are more teaching-based (e.g. rational-emotive supervision), others more counselling-based (person-centred supervision), others more relationship-based (psychodynamically oriented supervision). Designating generic tasks does not mean that all are found within all counselling-oriented supervision models.

Despite the fact that the literature is quite extensive on the tasks involved in supervision, there is little explanation for the conditions or criteria for choosing particular roles by supervisors (Kurpius and Baker, 1977). Agreement on the importance of a task or a role in no way indicates that the individuals or groups who agree actually carry out the task/role in similar ways; for example, few would disagree with the 'teaching' task of supervision but there is wide variation in the way the teaching task is implemented by different supervisors. Some refuse to give 'information' to the supervisee and believe information-giving should take place on the training course. Furthermore, it may well be that the tasks designated by supervisors and supervisees as the ones in which they engage may differ from what actually happens.

Although there is reasonable agreement across supervisory models and, indeed, across professions (psychiatry, social work, counselling psychology, teacher training) about the main supervisory tasks, there is little to help supervisors to understand the conditions for performing certain behaviours. Developmental models of supervision locate these in the stages through which supervisees move. Other variables influencing the choice of task may be the orientation of the supervisor, the limited choice of task by the supervisor because of his/her limited skills, allegiance to a particular counselling orientation, the needs of the supervisee, and the relationship between the participants.

Tasks are the behavioural side of functions and roles. The role is person-centred; the task is action-centred; the function is a combination of both roles and tasks. If the function is education, then the roles of the participants are teacher/pupil, and the task teaching/learning.

Training in the seven tasks of supervision

Training in each task will be presented as having five areas:

- understanding each task: information and readings
- discussion points: key questions to facilitate sharing
- learning the skills underlying each task (experiential work)
- practising the skills in actual supervision sessions
- summarizing learning

Table 2.4 summarizes this training:

Table 2.4 *Training outline in seven tasks of supervision*

	Teaching method				
	Understanding	Discussion	Skills	Practice	Review
Task					
Relationship					
Teaching					
Counselling					
Consulting					
Monitoring					
Evaluating					
Administrative					

In the training course it is important not to be rigid about the chronology of the five approaches above: participants can start with discussion or experiential work: information and readings may come last. Good trainers vary their approach to maintain creativity and learning.

Setting up a learning supervisory relationship

If one of the tasks, both an initial and on-going one, is to establish the kind of relationship between supervisor and supervisee/s that facilitates the learning of the supervisee, it is imperative to try to determine what kind of relationship this is and how to set it up and maintain it as a learning relationship over time. Supervisors have described the supervisory relationship in many ways (Carroll, 1996), in general seeing it as between the teaching relationship and the counselling relationship, but not either. So training in this task means struggling with the concept as well as working with the practicalities of setting it up.

Input

Looking at the supervision relationship.
Research on the supervisor relationship.
Characteristics of the supervisory relationship.
Some open areas: the supervisory relationship and gender, and Cross-cultural issues, changes over time.
Readings on the supervisory relationship (Carroll, 1996).

Discussion points

What is the nature of the supervisory relationship?
How does it compare and contrast with the counselling relationship?
What kind of relationship is most effective for supervision and what are its characteristics?
What roles and tasks are engaged in by supervisors and supervisees as part of the supervisory relationship?
What elements need to be negotiated within the supervisory relationship?
How might the supervisory relationship change over the course of supervision, especially as it moves into a more collegial relationship?

How might supervisor/supervisee go about contracting in supervision?

Experiential learning

Feedback on how I relate: strengths and weaknesses in areas of relationship I contract to work on, for example challenging, working with emotions, dealing with transference.

Taking the five relationships outlined by Clarkson (1995) and applying them within supervision.

Coming from one of the TA ego-states outlined by Eric Berne (1961) and negotiating with the supervisor/supervisee around expectations from supervision.

Learning how to set up learning objectives for myself and how to help supervisees do the same.

Practising the task

Negotiate the learning relationship as the initial step in setting up a supervisory relationship. The aim is to work through an initial supervision contract.

Work with a supervisory relationship that is not going well, for example where the supervisor is demanding, etc.

Negotiate a supervisory relationship with a skilled and qualified counsellor (consultative supervision).

The teaching task of supervision

Trainees would consider what teaching means in the context of supervision and how best to instruct, coach, model, and set up appropriate learning experiences for supervisees. They would experiment with various teaching methodologies ranging from direct information-giving to setting up experiential learning to further the skill and knowledge of supervisees.

Input

Different forms of teaching: instructing, modelling, demonstrating, coaching, lecturing, role-play, experiential learning.

Formal and informal teaching.

Learning styles.
Models of learning.
Reading: Bond and Holland (1998: ch. 4).

Discussion points

List the various teaching methods and evaluate yourself against each of them.
How can you pitch your teaching to the learning stage of supervisees?
What teaching methods seem best suited to different stages of supervisee development?

Experiential learning

Fill in a Learning Styles Inventory and look at the characteristics of your own learning style.
Have another member of the group fill in the Learning Styles Inventory and work with them about what kinds of teaching/learning experiences would help them learn most effectively.
Arrange how to use Interpersonal Process Recall (Kagan, 1980) with one of the other members of the group.
During a supervision training session, in an appropriate manner, bring in your own experience as a method of teaching others.

Practising the task

Give a lecture for five minutes on a subject of your choice to the group and get feedback on your clarity, delivery, presence, etc.
Work with one other member of the group who shares a 'learning style' with you. How might you adapt your supervision to their learning style?
Within the supervision session see if you can think of an appropriate experiential learning exercise to help the supervisee gain insights into work with the client they are presenting.

The counselling task of supervision

Although supervision is not counselling or therapy with supervisees, and supervisees are very adamant that they do not want it to be so, supervisees need a forum where they can deal with their personal feelings and reactions to work with clients. Supervision uses the work with clients and the reactions engendered by supervisees as a springboard for learning about themselves, their clients and about appropriate interventions.

Input

The 'counselling task of supervision'.
How can there be a counselling task without supervision becoming therapy?
Stances on how to use counselling in supervision.
Read Burns and Holloway's article (1990), 'Therapy in supervision: an unresolved issue'.

Discussion points

What would you do if it was clear to you that a supervisee needed some personal counselling to deal with some issues arising in their work with clients?
When is it appropriate to suggest that supervisees engage in their personal therapy?
When would supervisors leave aside some time to deal with personal issues in the life of supervisees?
How might they negotiate the boundaries between the two roles?

Experiential learning

Listen to a supervision tape and monitor the use of the counselling task.
As a supervisee, use a supervisory session to look at the client you like most/least and see if you can trace the reason why this is so.
What are your personal reactions to your supervisee/supervisor?

Practising the task

Have a supervisee bring to supervision a client who raises major personal issues for him/her. Watch how you deal with this from a supervision/counselling perspective.

In a practice supervision group have the supervisor try to turn supervision into a counselling session. Monitor what happens to yourself as supervisee.
In the practice supervision group have one of the supervisees try to turn supervision into a counselling session.

The consulting task of supervision

The consulting task of supervision is the most used task (Carroll, 1995). Consultation is about problem-solving and reviewing all aspects of the counselling work, for example what is happening to the client; what interventions are most appropriate; how counsellors can be more effective; how the therapeutic relationship is helping clients; and whether there are parallel processes between what is happening in counselling and what is taking place within the supervisory relationship.

Input

What is meant by the consulting task of supervision?
Use Hawkins and Shohet's (1989) process model as a consulting model.
Parallel process as part of the consulting task.
Unconscious element in supervision.
Read Hawkins and Shohet (1989: ch. 6).

Discussion points

How can supervisors help supervisees assess clients in particular contexts?
Give some examples of parallel process and look at how best to deal with it within supervision.

Experiential learning

Use Brandenburg Orchestra exercise as outlined in Hawkins and Shohet (1989: 97).
Set up a counselling session followed by a supervision one and watch for parallel issues.

Practising the task

In the supervision group focus on what is happening between supervisor and supervisee and see if it is related to work with clients.
Review as many possible interventions with a particular client as you can think of.
Help a supervisee work on assessing a client for brief therapy.

The evaluation task of supervision

The evaluation task within supervision comprises both formal and informal elements, the first consisting of the on-going feedback mechanisms built into supervision – feedback from supervisor to supervisee, self-feedback by both supervisor and supervisee, and feedback from supervisee to supervisor. The second is about summative evaluation – those occasions when formal assessment and even report-writing takes place. There is some evidence that evaluation is the most difficult task for supervisors (Carroll, 1995) because it involves the assessment elements that can affect the future of supervisees.

Input

What is evaluation?
Methods of evaluation within supervision?
Formats for evaluating supervisees, supervisors and supervision
Formal and informal evaluation
Feedback
Writing formal reports on supervisees.
Read: Bernard and Goodyear (1992: ch. 8) and chapter 7 below (Gilbert and Sills), on evaluation.

Discussion points

What are the components of effective feedback?
What criteria should be used to evaluate supervisees?
How to evaluate in a way that can facilitate learning in supervisees?
What might go wrong in evaluation?

Experiential learning

Give feedback to one of the group members and listen to what observers tell you about your manner of delivering it.

Tell one of the members of the group that you think he/she should not continue their counselling training. Get feedback from the group on how this was done.

Practising the task

Give clear feedback to the supervisee on how you see him/her work. Let the group evaluate how this was done.

Work with a supervisee to see how, together, you might write a formal evaluation report for their training course.

Create a supervisory role-play where you and the supervisee disagree about your evaluation report.

Monitoring the professional/ethical dimensions of client work

This 'gatekeeping role' of supervision ensures that supervisees are working ethically and professionally with clients and are continuing to sensitize themselves to the implications of their actions. Supervisors have responsibilities to clients (BAC, 1995) and, with their supervisees, work so that clients can obtain the best service possible.

Input

Look at codes of ethics for supervisors (read BAC *Code of Ethics and Practice for Supervisors*, 1995 and Carroll, 1996: ch. 8).

How can we monitor what supervisees do?

Discussion points

Whose job is it to ensure that supervisees know about ethical codes and ethical practice? What is the role of the supervisor here?

What would you do if you felt that a supervisee was not working ethically?

Experiential learning

Use given examples of unethical behaviour to review professional stances.

Bring examples of lack of professionalism by supervisees and look at how you might deal with it.

Work in small groups to come up with a process for ethical decision-making in supervision.

Practising the task

Have a supervisee bring an instance (real or role-played) of unethical behaviour with a client to supervision.

Role-play with a supervisee an instance in which you give feedback on an agreed unprofessional action by the supervisee. Get feedback on your way of giving feedback.

Prepare a five-minute input for your supervisees on the ethics of 'touch' in counselling. Get feedback on how well you did this.

Reviewing the administrative aspects of client work

The administrative task of supervision has an eye to the context in which counselling takes place and in which supervisors, supervisees and clients live and work (Carroll and Holloway, 1999). Supervisors help supervisees become aware of the impact of surroundings and systems on their work and on their clients.

Input

The organizational aspects of supervision.

Looking at how organizations impact on supervision and counselling.

Setting up supervisory contracts with an organization.

Tasks of supervisors where counselling takes place in an organization.

Reading: Carroll and Holloway (1999), Carroll (1996: ch. 6).

Discussion points

What are the critical points for you working as a counsellor/supervisor in an organizational setting?

How can you position yourself *vis-à-vis* the organization (as supervisor/counsellor) in order to be most effective?

Experiential learning

Set up a counselling programme within an organization (medical, industrial, educational) with a supervision system as part of it.

Set up a role-play of an organizational setting in which members of the organization (shareholder, union representative, manager, head of personnel, an employee) give feedback on how they view the counselling and supervisory arrangements.

Practising the task

Review, in supervision, a client issue that has organizational implications.

Set up a supervisory session in which the counsellor is being pressurized to be more involved in the organization in ways which could conflict with the counselling role.

Look, with a supervisee, at how you might help him/her keep records of their work and present a report to the organization.

Conclusions

Research has pointed out that supervisors often adhere to a few of these roles/tasks rather than develop a portfolio or range of options that cover all seven (Carroll, 1995). I am arguing here for the ability to utilize any of the seven tasks when appropriate for the learning of supervisees. Flexibility in supervisors creates more learning opportunities for supervisees. Training in the seven generic tasks of supervision allows supervisors to choose which task is most appropriate for this supervisee, with this learning style, at this stage in their development, working with these clients, in this context. Overall training in the seven tasks helps aspiring and experienced supervisors review which tasks they do well and which they tend to ignore or do poorly. By knowing this they can then concentrate and contract to build their skills in areas in which they are weak. This not only helps them as supervisors, but models for supervisees and others that learning is truly lifelong.

References

Association for Counselor Education and Supervision (1993) *Ethical Guidelines for Counseling Supervisors*. Alexandria, VA: ACES.

BAC (British Association for Counselling) (1988, 1995) *Code of Ethics and Practice for Supervisors*. Rugby: British Association for Counselling.

BAC (British Association for Counselling) (1992) *Code of Ethics and Practice for Counsellors*. Rugby: British Association for Counselling.

Bee, H.L. and Mitchell, S.K. (1984) *The Developing Person* (2nd edn). San Francisco: Harper & Row.

Bernard, J. (1979) Supervision training: a discrimination model. *Counselor Education and Supervision*, 19: 60–8.

Bernard, J. (1981) Inservice training for clinical supervisors, *Professional Development*, 12: 740–8.

Bernard, J.M. and Goodyear, R.K. (1992) *Fundamentals of Clinical Supervision*. Boston: Allyn & Bacon.

Berne, E. (1961) *Transactional Analysis in Psychotherapy*. Guernsey: Souvenir Press.

Bond, M. and Holland, S. (1998) *Skills of Clinical Supervision for Nurses*. Buckingham: Open University Press.

Borders, D. and Leddick, G. (1987) *The Handbook of Counseling Supervision*. Alexandria, VA: ACES.

Bradley, L. (ed.) (1989) *Counselor Supervision: Approaches, Preparation, Practice*. Muncie, IN: Accelerated Development Inc.

Burns, C.I. & Holloway, E.L. (1990) Therapy in Supervision: An Unresolved Issue. *Clinical Supervisor*, 7, 4, 47–60.

Carroll, M. (1995) *The Generic Tasks of Supervision*. Unpublished Ph.D. Dissertation: University of Surrey.

Carroll, M. (1996) *Counselling Supervision: Theory, Skills and Practice*. London: Cassell.

Carroll, M. and Holloway, E. (eds) (1999) *Counselling Supervision in Context*. London: Sage.

Clarkson, P. (1995) *The Therapeutic Relationship*. London: Whurr.

Efstation, J.F., Patton, M.J. and Kardash, C.M. (1990) Measuring the working alliance in counselor supervision. *Journal of Counseling Psychology*, 37 (3): 322–9.

Ekstein, R. (1964) Supervision of psychotherapy: Is it teaching? Is it administration? Or is it therapy? *Psychotherapy: Theory, Research and Practice*, 1: 137–8.

Ekstein, R. and Wallerstein, R.S. (1972) *The Teaching and Learning of Psychotherapy*, New York: International.

Gilbert, M. and Sills, C. (1999) Training for Supervision evaluation. In E. Holloway and M. Carroll (eds), *Training Counselling Supervisors*. London: Sage.

Hawkins, P. and Shohet, R. (1989) *Supervision in the Helping Professicns*. Milton Keynes: Open University Press.

Hess, A.K. (1980) Training models and the nature of psychotherapy supervision. In A.K. Hess (ed.), *Psychotherapy Supervision: Theory, Research and Practice*. New York: Wiley.

Hess, A.K. (1987) Psychotherapy supervision: stages, Buber, and a theory of relationships. *Professional Psychology*, 18 (3): 251–9.

Holloway, E. (1984) Outcome evaluation in supervision research. *Journal of Counseling Psychology*, 12 (4): 167–74.

Holloway, E. (1992) Supervision: a way of teaching and learning. In S. Brown and R. Lent (eds), *The Handbook of Counseling Psychology* (2nd edn). New York: Wiley.

Holloway, E. (1995) *Clinical Supervision: A Systems Approach.* Thousand Oaks, CA: Sage.

Holloway, E. and Acker, M. (1989) *The EPICS (Engagement and Power in Clinical Supervision) Model.* (University of Oregon; private publication).

Inskipp, F. and Proctor, B. (1993) *The Art, Craft and Tasks of Counselling Supervision. Part 1: Making the Most of Supervision.* Twickenham: Cascade.

Inskipp, F. and Proctor, B. (1995) *The Art, Craft and Tasks of Counselling Supervision. Part 2: Becoming a Supervisor.* Twickenham: Cascade.

Kadushin, A. (1985) *Supervision in Social Work* (2nd edn) New York: Columbia University Press.

Kagan, N. (1980) 'Influencing Human Interaction – 18 years with IPR'. In A.K. Hess (ed.) *Psychotherapy Supervision: Theory, Research, and Practice.* New York: Wiley.

Kurpius, D.J. and Baker, R.D. (1977) The supervision process: analysis and synthesis. In D.J. Kurpius, R.D. Baker and I.D. Thomas (eds), *Supervision of Applied Training: A Comparative Review.* Westport, CT: Greenwood.

Lanning, W. (1986) Development of the supervisory rating form. *Counselor Education and Supervision,* 25: 191–6.

Littrell, J.M., Lee-Borden, N.A. and Lorenz, J.R.A. (1979) Developmental framework for counseling supervision. *Counselor Education and Supervision,* 19: 129–36.

Onions, C.T. (ed.) (1968) *The Shorter Oxford English Dictionary.* Oxford: Oxford Clarendon Press.

3 Training Supervisors to Contract in Supervision

Julie Hewson

Introduction

The supervisory questions that have intrigued me from the outset are: Why has some supervision, in which I have been supervisee, been so ineffective, destructive and arresting of confidence and development? Why has some supervision been beautifully pleasant but banal? Why have other experiences of supervision been incredibly useful, invigorating, helpful and growth promoting? I need to know what has made the difference. And so, I begin this chapter with a series of questions:

- What are the ingredients of good supervision as opposed to bad?
- Can I begin to describe supervision in terms of good and bad?
- What were the key factors that helped make sense of the varying experiences of supervision for me?
- Is it possible to design a supervision training to take account of these matters?
- Where does contracting fit into the whole schema of supervision training and can supervisors be taught how to supervise?

I wonder if the last of these questions, about contracting and the elements in contracting in supervision, is a key question overall.

Background

My varied background, educational and experientially, says something about why contracting is of such importance to me. My first degree was in Sociology and Psychology, I had specialized in history and literature at school, and was a painter and potter professionally for a time. That is already quite a bagful to keep together and keep integrated. Perhaps it was because I had studied the Renaissance period where it was not unusual for educated people to be fascinated by many things and competent in many (Elizabeth I, Leonardo da Vinci, and Sir Philip Sidney, for example) that I too saw myself as straddling professions and integrating skills from numerous professional backgrounds. In my book this could be a richness, not a problem. Later I taught in school, in community education, colleges, university and a college of management studies. I trained in psychotherapy, in social work and ran management training for local government agencies, the NHS and industry. I have supervised trainees, practitioners in counselling, psychotherapy, social work and management. I currently manage, with a team of staff, a training centre that I founded with my husband over twenty years ago and which currently offers four Master's degrees with a fifth, on supervision, in progress.

To add spice and variety to my supervision questions it makes sense to tell you that I am qualified as a training and supervising Transactional Analyst and a BAC accredited supervisor and assessor of supervisors. I work as a management consultant and trainer to the NHS, with teams in specialist areas such as cancer and leukaemia in children (CLIC), general managers of large directorates with a multiplicity of staff and resource problems, accident and emergency units and special care baby unit staff. I have taught supervisory skills, methodology and concepts to nurses, doctors, osteopaths, social workers, teachers, managers, psychotherapists, counsellors and, more recently, lawyers.

Is it any wonder, with such a background, that contracting, in whatever relationship I have with individuals or groups, becomes an essential ingredient of my work. Contracting and supervision issues cover a wide span of applicability, and with my background as a teacher, clinician, businesswoman, management consultant, author and ordinary everyday person, I see the need for contracting most days – not just a need but a necessity if I am to be clear about my roles and responsibilities, if my clients, varied as they are, are not to build up unrealistic and unreal expectations and if our relationship is going to be well-negotiated and well-structured while still being spontaneous and creative.

Contracting: overt and covert

Contracting is an agreement between two parties, of lawful object, of mutual benefit undertaken with full agreement on both sides. This is the *overt process*. Alongside this are all kinds of *covert contracts* and these, if not brought into conscious awareness from time to time, affect both psychotherapy process, counselling, management and supervision. However, the contractual method which derives from the process of contracting, has as its assumption that everyone is personally responsible for the goals they are trying to achieve, and makes overt what each is willing to do to achieve this end. The supervisor decides whether he or she is willing to work with the supervisee to achieve their chosen goal, which may well be on-going professional development, case-load management, diagnostic accuracy or consultancy, and to undertake to use the best of their professional skills in this venture.

Part of the role of the contracting process is to minimize the risk of humiliation which is the transactional reinforcing relationship to the original existential experience of shame. The importance of teaching contracting needs to be set against a backdrop of understanding the pervasive nature of shame in many adult learners as well as in experienced practitioners.

Contracting raises a number of questions and issues that need to be addressed. *It affects the relationship* and poses many questions that we sometimes have to wrestle with, for example:

- *What is the contracted nature of the relationship?* What are the parameters? Is there a dual role or responsibility? Does that help or hinder?

- *Is what the supervisee asks for, the contract, or does the supervisor, in the process of negotiating, discover what underlies the original request?*

- *Does the supervisee know what it is they really want, as they struggle to make sense of a difficulty or find a way through?* Does the supervisory process include the process of the supervisor sometimes knowing 'best' and giving information, theory or strategy. Has this been agreed as part of the relationship?

- *What is the contract when the supervisee is stuck in parallel process with the supervisor as they have been with their client?*

What do we as supervisors agree to when dealing with counter-transference issues in supervision? Do we have a contract to do a piece of boundaried therapy, or does this fly in the face of the overall contract of supervision and breach the professional boundary? Is the contract one of merely identifying the supervisee's personal issue? What happens if the supervisee is seeing the client in the next twenty-four hours and not seeing their therapist for two weeks?

- *What is the contract on matters of ethics and professional practice?* What are the agreements on confidentiality and responsibility?

Each of these points will be addressed during this chapter as a basis for on-going discussion.

Contract-making

This section of the chapter, and the central tenet of the chapter, will focus on ten points that go to make up the contract within supervision, and which are listed below.

1. Both parties become actively involved in developing the nature of the supervision process.
2. A contract provides a mental set or overall perception of what end goal is being aimed at.
3. The supervisor and supervisee should know that they have completed the Gestalt of their work together.
4. Contracting creates a mutuality and a guard against an abuse of power.
5. Contracts are designed to minimize covert agendas.
6. Three or multi-handed contracts as part of supervision.
7. Contracting for content.
8. Contracting in supervision when supervision relies on meta-models rather than a specific counselling or professional approach.
9. How do I teach contracting in supervision?
10. How can we teach the process of contracting in supervision?

We will look at each of these in turn:

Both parties become actively involved in developing the nature of the supervision process

The nature of the supervisory relationship, and contract, will change as the supervisee moves from novice to apprentice to journeyman to master craftsman. The needs of each stage are different and need to be re-negotiated in order to provide the right mixture of support and challenge. The supervisory contract, like all healthy relationships, needs to be re-negotiated at each stage of its development.

For novices and apprentices there is often a degree of trepidation associated with the term supervision, and linked to being found wanting, or caught out. Their needs are different, with much more emphasis placed on support rather than challenge, except in areas of danger to the client.

I have developed a menu of supervision to enable supervisees and those training as supervisors to be helped to understand the range of possibilities within the supervisory relationship. The menu of supervision provides a kind of smorgasbord and helps to create the climate of *à la carte* rather than a set menu.

Below are items on the supervisory menu which can be added to or deleted from depending on the context and parameters of the supervisory relationship. It allows both parties to negotiate according to need.

MENU OF SUPERVISION

Appetizer – awakens the jaded palate

Knowing what is available
Experiencing care
Hearing from others
Permission to ask for help
Desire to increase learning and professional direction

Starter – sets the scene for a good meal

Personal time
Support
Self-awareness
Confidence-building
Appropriate challenge
A safe place to explore difficult professional issues
Books, articles, resourcing

Sorbet – palate cleanser

Ventilation
A place for the supervisee to say 'I don't know'
Permission to ask for what is needed
The start of contracting

Main course – choosing the most nourishing or sustaining item

(Continuation of contracting process)
Assessment/diagnosis of problem or case
Skills-building
Teaching theory
Ethical issues and dilemmas
Counter-transference issues
Case-load review
Treatment planning: what strategies/interventions needed?
Uncovering areas that may have been discounted
Monitoring
Mentoring
Coaching
Addressing self- and client-presentation
Pin-pointing therapy issues to be addressed in the therapeutic relationship
Professional development issues
Validation of intuition and hunches and finding the words and evidence to support them
Understanding parallel process
Discussion of sessional contract for the client in the context of the overall contract
Alternative perspectives on the case or problem for the supervisee
Team-building and workplace issues
Constructing or reworking a philosophy

Dessert – to include cheese board: a sweet or salty complement to the meal

Celebrating good work
Providing inspiration
A forum for discussing existential themes, for example, why am I doing this work?
Constructive criticism and pointers for future development
Enjoyment

Integration of learning with other models
A meta-perspective

Wine list or other drinks: different kinds for each course

Types of communication
Responsivity (Garcia, 1991)
Six-Category Intervention Analysis (Heron, 1990)
Functional ego-states (Berne, 1961)
Five kinds of relationship (Clarkson and Gilbert, 1991)

Coffee – the best ground types, not instant

Review of session
Review of relationship
Creative moves forward
Consolidation
Increase in the professional developmental direction
Clarification of care to the client

(With acknowledgement to Frances Derbyshire and Gill Smith)

A contract provides a mental set or overall perception of what end goal is being aimed at

An example of this occurred with my then excellent supervisor.

I often 'knew' what was the matter, intuitively, physically and emotionally. I was finely tuned to the process of projective identification and parallel process. I could identify a lack of skills, knowledge or theory, but at the start I couldn't always find the precise words to express what it was I *knew*. I tended to need to paint verbal pictures, fine in their way but somewhat time-consuming and diffuse. Thus on the menu as described above I took permission to ask for help from the appetizer section, from the starter took regular personal time and appropriate challenge as my confidence grew. I asked for and was provided with books, articles and resourcing and from the main course I worked with a number of them. However, the overriding contract running like a theme throughout was ***validation of intuition and hunches and finding the words and evidence to support them***. The dessert has been how this experience of supervision has led me to develop my own supervisory philosophy, skills and enthusiasm.

The supervisor and supervisee should know that they have completed the Gestalt of their work together

Supervisors and supervisees, knowing what the completion of their work together 'looks like', can use this as a monitoring device so that at the end of the session the supervisee has a way of checking whether what they came for has been addressed. For example: if for some reason, because of the re-negotiating of the contract, this original aim has been changed, both parties are agreed as to why, and are able to gauge the efficacy of such an alteration in terms of the original request. Perhaps the supervisee brings a client's case believing that what they want help with are some 'how to's', that is, interventions that will expedite the healing process. However, during the course of the negotiation of the contract it becomes clear that the key issue is not one of knowledge about interventions but rather one of counter-transference. If this is agreed to be the focus of the supervision, it is necessary to check at the end whether the supervisee, having resolved the personal factors clouding his or her vision, can now access appropriate intervention resources to move the client forward in the direction of contracted change.

Contracting creates a mutuality and a guard against an abuse of power

In the negotiation of the supervisory relationship it is essential that both parties, or three parties if an organization is involved, clearly negotiate so that mutuality is assured and the abuse of power minimized. For this reason it is often contra-indicated for a line manager to supervise clinically a member of staff. It is unlikely that a person would feel able to bring a difficult case to their supervisor if by doing so their supervisor's line-manager role might be activated in a way that could lead to conflict rather than help. This happened, when a nurse felt too ashamed to tell her supervising line manager that she did not know a certain procedure, and so caused an accident. Changes in our regional Social Services have separated the roles of line manager and supervisor very effectively, but unfortunately in the NHS this situation of dual roles happens more frequently.

There are different levels of responsibility involved in the supervisory relationship depending on whether the supervisee is a trainee or a qualified practitioner. These aspects of the relationship need to be clarified, as a trainer should exercise authority if, for example, a trainee is working with clients beyond his or her level of competence. This would also be an ethical matter for a supervisor of a qualified practitioner, though the nature of the authority relationship is different.

Contracts are designed to minimize covert agendas

Contracts are, or should be, negotiated from the here-and-now integrated part of our being. However, we know that transference and other factors of an unconscious nature can sabotage even the most clearly open communication, when they are not addressed. Thus, as mentioned in Hawkins and Shohet (1989), the occasional surfacing of unconscious agendas or relationship issues keeps the process clean.

An example of the emergence of an unconscious agenda might be a situation in which a person starts as a novice, moves into a stage of being an apprentice and is glad for the careful developmental help needed to build some confidence and a degree of competence. During the transition from apprentice to journeyman, the supervisee might hit a developmental transference issue associated with adolescent rebellion and begin to behave in ways inappropriate to the collegial and responsible relationship with the supervisor. Where the transference issues are non-resolvable, a change of supervisor is indicated.

Three or multi-handed contracts as part of supervision

When working for an agency, either as an employee or as a paid consultant, the supervisor is engaged in a contract with more than one person. In this situation, clarity of contracting with each part of the system is essential. If the bond between one part of the triangle is perceived as closer than that of another, there is the danger of unconscious but tricky rivalries, collusions and conflicts. These are what in Transactional Analysis would be described as psychological games, played out of awareness as a form of repetition compulsion. The way to stay out of these is to be potent, responsive and aware of one's own as well as another's vulnerability.

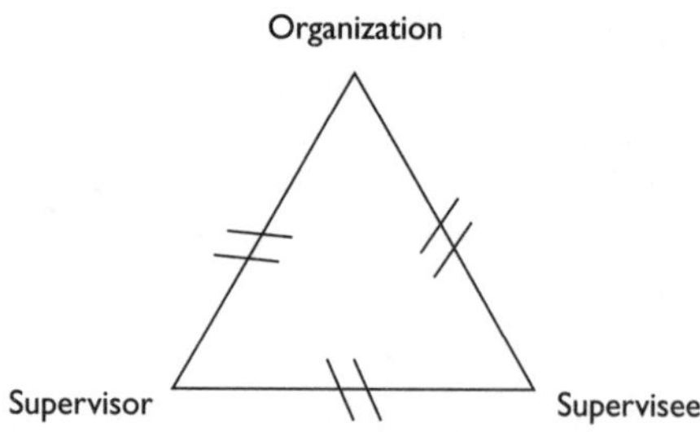

Figure 3.1

The equilateral triangle (Figure 3.1) is the ideal configuration, for in this there is equidistance between each party, showing a balance between the contract from agency to supervisor, from supervisor to supervisee and supervisee to agency. This leads to clear boundaries and equality of expectations, albeit different in nature, for example a supervisor for a staff counsellor in an agency where the contract with the agency is one of confidentiality and boundaries understands and agrees this contract. The contract with the supervisee is for clinical/counselling case supervision and the supervisee has a clear agreement from the agency to take external supervision far removed from the organization, so that staff confidentiality can be maintained.

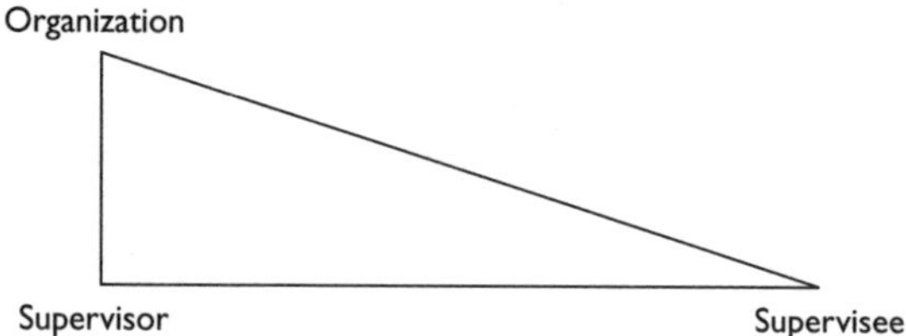

Figure 3.2

The triangle in Figure 3.2 demonstrates an imbalance in relationships and can lead to collusion between the agency and the supervisor. This might occur when someone is brought in to deal with 'a marginal performer'. Figure 3.3 might occur when there is a great deal of pressure on an organization and illustrates what

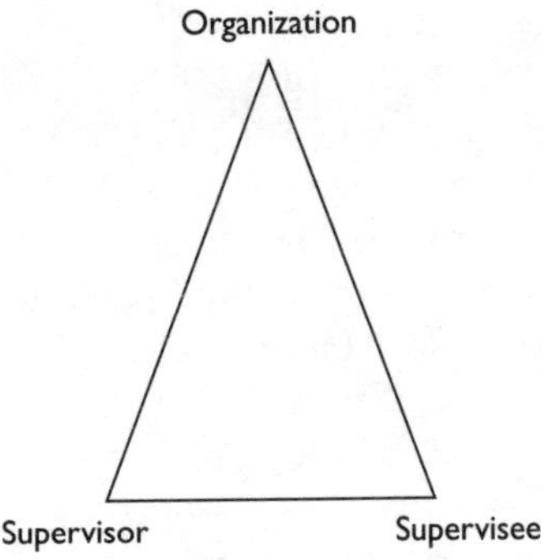

Figure 3.3

happens when supervisor and supervisee collude against the organization – which may not be functioning well and may require some intervention.

Another factor is the problem some supervisors have of a dual role or responsibility, which often occurs in social work. Recently, reorganization in some parts of the UK has separated practice and case supervision from managerial supervision so that one person can no longer hold both roles. This enables the process of contracting to be clearer, simpler and easier to manage, although the context of both areas can be complex.

Contracting for content

In supervision, as in therapy and counselling, what we think we are coming for is not always what we need. A very experienced counsellor, for example, came asking for interventions to deal with a client who had had a severe traumatic experience. As the session progressed it became clear that the supervisee had herself been traumatized by the unfolding story, and the key issue was not one of client interventions but of counter-transference and shock on the part of the counsellor. The focus of the supervision was respectfully to honour this shock and help to dissolve the *mesmeric quality of the trance*. (The client herself had been so traumatized by an event she had witnessed that she had gone into a shock-induced trance and in telling her story had traumatically entranced the counsellor.) Once this had been addressed, the supervisee/counsellor found herself able to reclaim her own resources and remind herself of a range of creative interventions that could help her client. One useful model developed by Clarkson helps to unravel the focus of supervision and facilitate the contracting process. This model is 'a tool for identifying categories or bands of key issues in supervision' (Clarkson, 1992: 273).

With the emphasis on contract and relationship, the bands highlight potential areas of focus for the supervisory process. The supervisee may have contracted for help in how to assess the client, situation or problem. This may be based on their belief that they do not know how to *think* about the situation. In the process of contracting, it may become clear that the supervisee does know how to diagnose, assess and form a hypothesis about what is clinically problematical. Thus, to take this as a contract would lead the supervisor along the wrong route. Here the menu of supervision can give the supervisor and supervisee time to reflect on what the real area of concern is. For example, a counselling student came to me many years ago with a very highly developed skill in interpersonal awareness and an acute sense of her own body's reactions to her clients' stories. She had been trained in Rogerian methods and had also encountered Gendlin's Focusing Techniques, which she had found immensely helpful. I enjoyed exploring with her what she already knew descriptively, intuitively and physically about the cases she brought to supervision. She often asked for help in interventions and yet I noticed that what she actually did was frequently spot on, but she didn't know why. We therefore re-contracted to develop conceptual frames to help her understand both the significance of the assessment and the efficacy of her interventions.

Contracting in supervision when supervision relies on meta-models rather than on a specific counselling or professional approach

As a supervisor and trainer of supervisors I am interested in models that transcend any one school of psychotherapy or counselling, and which take account of intrapsychic, interpersonal, systemic, task- and function-based approaches. Contracting needs to take place against a backdrop of these and other models and each of the following interventions will develop some thoughts against some of the main approaches from which I draw.

When supervision is solely 'counselling or profession-specific', a variety of assumptions may be made about what constitutes supervision which may cut out a range of valid areas for consideration. For example, if supervision comes purely from a psychodynamic approach, there is a danger that environmental and systemic issues, context and ecology might be overlooked.

Figures 3.4 explains how this works:

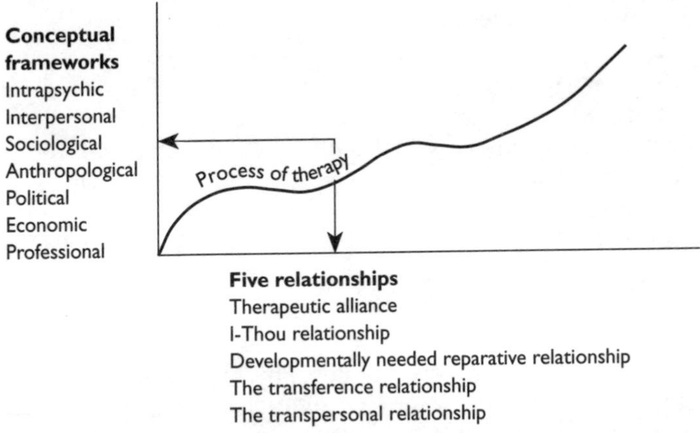

Figure 3.4 *Matrix of conceptual frameworks and therapeutic relationships*

For example, a supervisee brings a client with whom the relationship appears in some difficulty because the counsellor is exclusive in her approach to the counselling relationship (for example, using only the working alliance and missing the transference). It may be freeing for the counsellor to appreciate another framework in respect of the relationship, the transferential relationship, and at least understand it, if not work with it. In supervision we start with a basic contract or working agreement. This will vary depending on the experience/needs and context of the supervisor/supervisee.

In the process of contracting, the supervisor will be assessing both at the beginning and throughout the session the supervisory functions needed to fulfil both the primary and secondary contract. As is often the case what is originally asked for may be not what is actually needed, and that requires re-negotiation during the course of the session.

How do I teach contracting in supervision?

As I become more aware of the subtleties involved in contracting, I teach it by encouraging supervisees to:

- think with their senses as well as their intellect;
- be aware of the covert agendas and invitations to play games;
- notice what they are picking up through the use of their intuition;
- pay attention to the social, political, organizational and professional contexts in which they work (and from which their clients come);
- pick up subtle shifts in expectations for which they have not contracted;
- keep track of the prevailing relationship so as not to collude with any uncontracted transference needs;
- be clear about their own philosophy, values and beliefs and check that these are congruent with what is being requested by supervisees (contracting is a two-way process and supervisors have choices too).

I use the following sequence and encourage people to pay attention to the following:

1. Listen to, look at and get a sense of the opening transaction (which ego-states are being used by the supervisee?).
2. Log it (mentally or jot it down).
3. Listen to what is actually asked for.
4. Check on all seven levels as to resonance with request (Clarkson and Lapworth, 1992).
5. Note feedback from body, intuition, thinking and feeling.
6. Dialogue with supervisee in relationship I-Thou – sharing the process and negotiating further, perhaps using the menu of supervision.
7. Give supervisee time to do a personal check so as not to over-adapt.
8. Go ahead with the following criteria in mind in order to double-check at the end:

Have we identified the key issue (Clarkson, 1992: 275)?
What is the nature of the relationships involved?
Have we reduced any potential for harm (Clarkson, 1992: 257)?
Have the supervisee (and supervisor) learned something new as a result of this supervision contract?
What is the contract both with the client and for the supervision, and are there any parallels either in content or process?
Have I (as supervisor) modelled a good I-Thou relationship?
Is the asked-for contract masking something else? If so what?

How can we teach the process of contracting in supervision?

- Use eyes, ears, body-sensation.
- Notice overall response to supervisee and client (supervisor's counter-transference).
- What names jump out at you, words and phrases?
- What should be happening?
- What has led to this situation
  (a) for the client
  (b) for supervisee to bring it to supervision?
- What is your hunch/hypothesis or metaphor for what is arising between client and supervisor, or yourself and supervisee? What light does this shed on the current dilemma?
- What is the transpersonal level in operation at this time – issues of compassion, recognition, humanity or other?

Conclusion

Contracting in supervision may well be the most important task engaged in by supervisor and supervisee. Think of the opposite, of not having a negotiated contract. An unsatisfactory outcome may occur for either one or both participants: having no 'benchmark' against which to judge the success or failure of their supervisory endeavour leaves both open to lack of clarity and lack of focus. Collusion is a major danger when there is no contract – collusion with unconscious issues, covert agendas, avoiding difficult cases and not learning in an effective manner. Clear contracting, on the other hand, creates a negotiated and mutually respectful supervisory relationship where tasks, functions and responsibilities are understood by both parties and where the professional development of the supervisee is paramount and the care and protection of clients is assured. Covert agendas can be dealt with openly and outcomes can be gauged against the original agreements made. The importance of contracting in supervision means it should rate high on the training needs of supervisors.

Appendix

Exercises in Training Supervisors in Contracting in Supervision

Exercise One

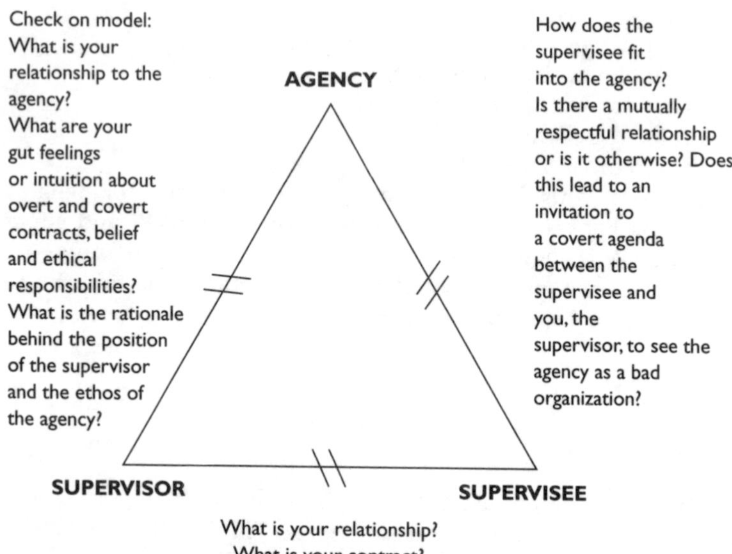

Check on model:
What is your relationship to the agency?
What are your gut feelings or intuition about overt and covert contracts, belief and ethical responsibilities?
What is the rationale behind the position of the supervisor and the ethos of the agency?
AGENCY
How does the supervisee fit into the agency?
Is there a mutually respectful relationship or is it otherwise? Does this lead to an invitation to a covert agenda between the supervisee and you, the supervisor, to see the agency as a bad organization?
SUPERVISOR
SUPERVISEE
What is your relationship?
What is your contract?
At what level is the supervisee?
What does she/he need?
How can we identify needs in context and meet them effectively?

Figure 3.5 *There is more than one contract in supervision. Look to them all*

Exercise Two

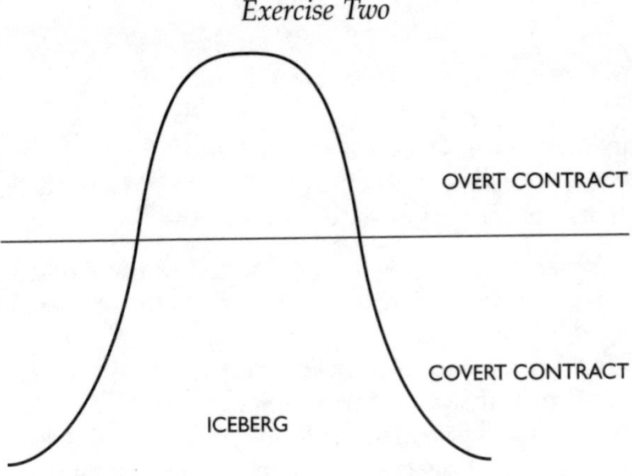

How do you find out what is below the water-line?

Ideas: Image it.
Name it.
Discuss any transference/counter-transference.
Supervisor takes supervision on supervision for his/her learning needs.

Figure 3.6 Uncovering overt and covert contracts

Exercise Three

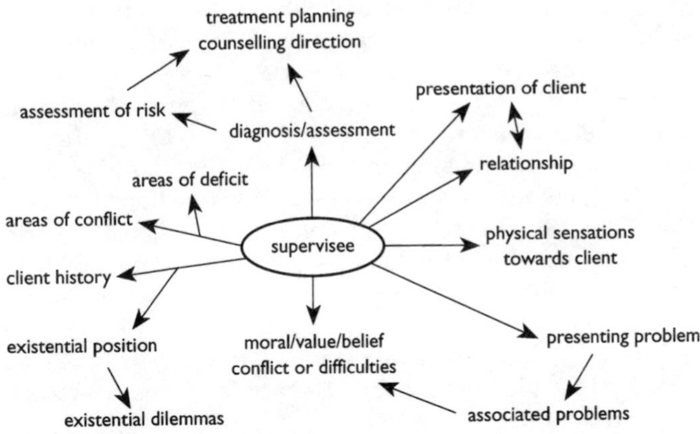

Figure 3.7 Spidergram to teach and encourage supervisees to know what they know

Exercise Four

A method of assessing a contract for clarifying an ethical or professional practice boundary.

Thompson (1990) outlines six areas of focus to assess the existence or otherwise of an ethical dilemma. When teaching this I ask students and supervisees to consider the following:

1. ***Beneficence***: was your intervention done from a place of good-will, good heart and respect for the client, or was it coming from a place of over-nurturing which might indicate a counter-transference response or the inappropriate encouragement of an unhealthy dependency relationship? This would require a supervisee or student to consider their assessment of a developmental need on the part of their client.
2. ***Non-maleficence***: above all do no harm. Apart from the possibility of actual dislike of the client, in which case it would be unethical to continue working with the client and a referral would be indicated, this usually refers to neglect or lack of competence on the part of the practitioner. As I am sanguine enough to believe few people go into the profession in order to inflict harm on their clients, it is important for the supervisor to check on competence, the professional support and knowledge of supervisee.
3. ***Justice***: has there been equality of reward, both ways, and is there a clear working contract in which both parties benefit and one is not working at the expense of the other?
4. ***Fidelity***: this refers to a mutual exchange of promises, both implicit and explicit and these need to be brought to the surface in supervision, to be clear that the supervisee is on track. (Refer to Exercise Three.)
5. ***Autonomy***: 'maximising the client's ability to choose freely and competently on how to conduct his or her life' (Thompson, 1990: 13). This requires careful monitoring of the original contract and the interventions you use in relation to that contract. Heron's Six-Category Intervention Analysis is very useful here (1990).
6. ***Self-interest***: that is taking care of oneself by means of a healthy lifestyle, supervision, therapy and good referral and support systems.

Exercise Five

Contracting is a behavioural activity which is part of an attitude. An attitude is traditionally comprised of three components – cognition, affect and behaviour. In writing about cure, Erskine (1980) includes a fourth dimension, physiology.

When teaching or learning, what is happening is the potential for a change in attitude. Some of these attitudes will be more easily accessible, others much deeper seated. So when teaching contracting it is important to emphasize:

Cognition

For the supervisee
What is it I know about this client?
What do I call things?
Where does what I observe fit into the theories I have learned?
What is it I know about my knowledge base?
What is it I know about my stage of development?
What is it I want to know more about?
Does my supervisor know more than I do? Can she see where my gaps are, even if I can't?
Will I, on the basis of this checklist, feel willing to make a contract with her about increasing my knowledge in a way that furthers my personal and professional development and gives greater protection to my clients? If the answer is no, what does this tell me about the nature of my relationship to my supervisor?
Can it be changed?
Do I know how to think about my client and the problems he presents?
Do I know how to proceed from there?

For the supervisor
At what developmental stage is the supervisee?
What is his/her knowledge base?
Has he/she developed a coherent philosophy?
Is he/she familiar with more than one model of the person or situation?
Are our two approaches complementary?
Have I got good supervision of my supervision?

Affect

For the supervisee
How do I feel about this client in the here and now?
Do these feelings influence what I want to contract for?

How do I feel about this client not being sure whether it is about the here and now?
Will this confusion affect what I contract for?
What are my beliefs, values and cultural norms? Are they being challenged by this client or situation?
Am I being faced by an ethical dilemma?
Am I touched by this client in a way that transcends the individual meeting?
What are the images or metaphors that inform my emotional response to what I bring to supervision?
What is my feeling towards my supervisor?
Do any of these affect the way I contract?

For the supervisor
How does the supervisee impact on me?
Am I affected by the case he/she has brought (supervisor's counter-transference)?
Is this information useful?
Are any emotional responses I have affecting the process of contracting?
Am I clear about long-term, short-term and any covert contracts between myself and the supervisee, the supervisee and his client?
Do I look forward to seeing this supervisee?

Behaviour

For the supervisee
Have I the skills to make appropriate interventions?
Do I know what to do?
Do I understand when an approach is contra-indicated?
Can I ask my supervisor to teach me some creative interventions?
Should I have taken this client/situation on?

For the supervisor
Do I have a range of creative interventions I can share with the supervisee?
Am I modelling the kind of relationship that is needed here?
Am I having appropriate levels of supervision as I expect my supervisees to have?

Physiology

For the supervisee
What is my physical sensation to the case I am presenting?
Can I work with this sensation in my supervision?

Will it inform how I contract to work in this session?
Do I need to find a supervisor who will listen to the wisdom of my physiological feedback as well as to my verbal articulation?
Can they help me integrate the two?

For the supervisor
What is my physical reaction to the supervisee's presentation?
What is my physical and emotional response to the plight of the client (if any)?
What physical sensations and bodily cues do I as the supervisor pick up from the body language of the supervisee?
What are the factors in this domain that the counsellor or supervisee picks up from the situation he/she has brought to supervision?

Exercise Six Using a transcript

Transcript of a supervisee/trainee contracting for feedback. This supervisee has been using the seven-level model (Clarkson and Lapworth, 1992) as a checklist and wants to know how well he has contracted in his work with his client, Paul.
S=Supervisor (Supervising Supervisor)
J=Supervisee (Supervisor)

S: You have just asked that the contract that we have is that you can reflect on your practice in this particular instance, using the seven-level model we have just discussed. Is that right?

J: Yes, and what would be useful for me are some how to's, there are lots of possibilities. I think how to . . . . What exactly do I want? That is an interesting question. I think a start would be how to contract clearly.

S: Isn't that interesting because I don't think you had a problem with contracting with Paul. So let's stop and reflect on why would you be asking that. I think it's because you didn't finish the sentence. And, as I reflect, I notice you expanding your request for three things. You're right, there is a level at which you did not contract clearly. May I say more about that as I think on my feet?

J: Yes do.

S: What I wrote down at the beginning, when I was tracking your supervision with Paul, when you worked earlier, was that the first part of the contract was very clear and the second part, as an observer, for me wasn't clear. I don't think you firmed up what he actually wanted. You both said 'Oh that's fine', so that could be mine or it could be yours and if I had taped it I could have heard if I had missed it. With you now, you and I in the present, I notice you saying you would like to reflect using the seven-level model to see what you have focused on. So that is very clear and then you said I want some how to's and it was left 'how to's for what'?

J: Yes, yes.

S: So.

J: There is a slight feeling of helplessness at that level because in a sense I don't feel I've fulfilled the contract with Paul. At maybe the level of sensation and, 'Aha' at level 4. And there was a fairly complicated and unfinished ending which even if I had had longer time I don't think we would have resolved.

S: OK, I think you are right there is something about the completion of the Gestalt.

J: That's right. [*We start tracking the supervisory process.*]

S: I think you are aware, intuitively aware, at level 2 then you go on to name it.

J: Yes.

S: And in the process of being aware and naming it [the key issue], you become aware as you reflect now, that you might have missed something. Let's use your intuition to discover what it was you might have missed.

J: Yes, let's do that.

S: OK, so what's the piece that would have brought about complete resolution. Shall we look for that?

J: Yes.

S: So if you would like to come closer to the board, we can track back over the supervision that you have just delivered, using this model and then we will do what we did yesterday, which is to ask our observer to give feedback on what he experienced, once his experience of supervision with you has had time to settle, is that acceptable to both of you?

J: Yes, that would be helpful.

S: OK, how shall we do this? Do you want to talk about what you think you did? Do you want me to talk about what I saw you do? What's the most useful approach to you?

J: I would like to talk about what I think I did.

S: That sounds good.

J: I would like you by all means to affirm or challenge or check anything that you think you experienced as different and help me become more conversant with this model.

S: Go ahead, I will do that.

J: I was interested to see which level in the model I would automatically make contact with. I suppose what I was noticing was, as P was talking, that I was feeling a little bit clumsy with myself. It's interesting because if I was in this situation again, I think I would have changed my physical position and got more comfortable. It was a bit restrictive; it was an interesting observation. (*He had a glass of water and was trying to balance it.*) It's interesting I notice that at one point he asked me if his contract was OK and I thought is that what he is thinking, *'Am I doing it right?'* and I wondered how to give that to him as I moved from a sensation to awareness and I also became aware that his eyebrows were lifted up and I went into an archaic child Ego State . . .

Commentary of supervisor on the above

He, the supervisor, then went on to track all seven levels and realized he had focused on helping the supervisee name the problem – and had left an incomplete Gestalt about what to do next.

There are many ways of processing what was helping in this overall piece of supervision. There was a parallel process of physical clumsiness in the supervisor in response to listening to the supervisee talking about a client with learning difficulties who bumps into things a great deal. There was the fact that both supervisor and supervisee wanted to 'get it right', which can lead to a tendency to over-include (the second transaction leads to an expansion of these possibilities). The supervisee had two roles in relation to a client, being both manager of the residential home, and in overall charge of the client's well-being. Sometimes the role felt clumsy.

The invitation could have been to be over-inclusive with the supervisee but we were tracking a way of thinking to clarify what he had covered, what still needed attention. This helped with structure and focus. The first contract was to track the process using the seven-level model that had just been learned. This is what it did, and the additional issue of subcontracts was addressed in the early part of the supervision and provided a subtext for the short piece transcribed.

Further exercises useful in teaching contracting in supervision

Exercise (a) In a role-play or a transcript of supervision count the number of times the supervisor contracted with the supervisee. (I sometimes refer to this as contracting on the hoof. It is a series of transactions which leads to some agreement between the two parties about what is to be focused upon.) The purpose of this is to show that contracting does not have to be a mechanistic and artificial process but a constant dialogue.

Exercise (b) Tape a session with a supervisee and transcribe a section. Look for clear evidence of contracting in your tape. Do the same with the tape (if you have one) of the supervisee's work with his or her client. So often when supervisees feel they have lost their way it can be because the contract with the client is unclear, or has become diluted over time.

Exercise (c) If the notion of contracting is anathema to you because of your philosophical stance or particular counselling approach, how would you describe to an intelligent lay person what you think you are doing together with this client? How does that fit your philosophy? Is that what the client needs or is there any danger of imposing an approach on a client which may simply reinforce old patterns? For example, if a person has experienced him or herself as always having to work things out on their own, is the withholding of some of Heron's authoritative interventions helpful? How would you justify this?

References

Berne, E. (1961, reprinted 1993) *Transactional Analysis in Psychotherapy*, Guernsey: Souvenir Press.

Carroll, M. (1996) *Counselling Supervision: Theory, Skills and Practice*. London: Cassell.

Clarkson, P. (1992) *Transactional Analysis Psychotherapy: An Integrated Approach*. London: Routledge.

Clarkson, P. and Gilbert, M. (1991) The Training of counsellor trainers and supervisors. In W. Dryden and B. Thorne (eds), *Training and Supervision for Counselling in Action*. London: Sage.

Clarkson, P. and Lapworth, P. (1992) Systemic integrative psychotherapy. In W. Dryden (ed.) *Integrative and Eclectic Psychotherapy: A Handbook*. Buckingham: Open University Press.

Erskine, R. (1980) Script cure: behavioural, intrapsychic and physiological. *Transactional Analysis Journal*. 10(2) 102–6.

Garcia, P. (1991) Responsivity. *Transactional Analysis Journal*. 21(4): 212–17.

Hawkins, P. and Shohet, R. (1989) *Supervision in the Helping Professions*. Milton Keynes: Open University Press, Chapter 6.

Hay, J. (1992) *Transactional Analysis for Trainers*. Maidenhead: McGraw-Hill.

Heron, J. (1990) *Helping the Client: A Creative Practical Guide*. London: Sage.

Hewson, J. and Turner, C. (1992) *Transactional Analysis in Management*. Bristol: The Staff College, Bristol.

Holloway, E. (1995) *Clinical Supervision: A Systems Approach*. Thousand Oaks, CA: Sage.

Page, S. and Wosket, V. (1994) *Supervising the Counsellor: A Cyclical Model*. London: Routledge.

Sills, C. (ed.) (1997) *Contracts in Counselling*. London: Sage.

Thompson, A. (1990) *Guide to Ethical Practice in Psychotherapy*. New York: Wiley.

4 Training in reflective processes in supervision

Susan Allstetter Neufeldt

Throughout my professional life I have been torn between two keen professional interests, teaching and the practice of psychotherapy. Educated at Stanford University, where I received a B.A. and M.A., I became a public school teacher for five years, before returning to the University of California for my Ph.D. in counselling psychology. Three years of teaching undergraduates in psychology was followed by twelve years of private practice primarily within an interpersonal process model. Principal mentors for me were Jules Zimmer, Ed.D., and James H. Wells, M.D.

In 1990 I was invited to the University of California, Santa Barbara, as clinic director and supervisor of beginning students in a basic practicum and advanced students in a supervision practicum. At last my interests in teaching and counselling were united into the discipline of supervision! While I have continued to see a few clients myself, I have focused my energy on the training and supervision of therapists and supervisors. As I study the professional literature on supervision and training, I integrate my experience as teacher, therapist, and now supervisor, as I continually develop and revise my approach to supervision.

Reflective[1] processes as a key to therapist development

Training and supervision of therapists are endeavours to help novices become experts (Lichtenberg, 1997; Rønnestad and Skovholt, 1998). Expert therapists display a high level of intellectual ability and a rich conceptual structure in the cognitive domain (Jennings and Skovholt, in press; Skovholt et al., 1997). They differ from novices particularly in their ability to manage difficult cases

(Binder and Strupp, 1993; Skovholt et al., 1997) or problems that are poorly formulated by clients (Lichtenberg, 1997). Skovholt et al. (1997) observed that novices can perform effectively with clients who have positive relationship histories and relatively straightforward developmental problems; it takes experts, on the other hand, to work with clients who have poor relationship histories and characterological problems. Experts must also define the problem to be addressed from a vast array of clinical data. Schön (1983) stated that 'When we set the problem, we select what we will treat as the "things" of the situation, we set the boundaries of our attention to it, and we impose upon it a coherence which allows us to say what is wrong and in what directions the situation needs to be changed' (p. 49). Novice therapists of many theoretical persuasions display difficulty in setting the problem (Binder and Strupp, 1997; Shaw, 1984).

One critical goal of training and supervision is building skills, the basis for the intellectual ability described by Jennings and Skovholt (in press). Sternberg (1990) might have referred to therapy skills as the 'intelligence' of psychotherapy. 'The intelligent person welcomes automatization. He or she is intelligent largely by virtue of the numbers of automated routines available for information processing' (Sternberg, 1990: 153). The second goal in training is to help the trainee develop strategies for continued development, strategies that lead to clinical wisdom (Neufeldt, 1999). Sternberg has described the wise person as someone who 'resists automatization of thought but seeks to understand it in others' (1990: 153), a concept akin to our ideas of clinical wisdom.

The development of both counselling skills and strategies for continued growth are necessary for the development of novice therapists into expert therapists. In this chapter, I will focus my discussion on that second aspect, the trainee's development of strategies for continued growth towards clinical wisdom. The literature on therapist and counsellor development is instructive.

Therapist development

Considerable work has focused on therapist development (see, for example, Bernard and Goodyear, 1992, 1998; Holloway, 1987; Skovholt & Rønnestad, 1995; Stoltenberg and Delworth, 1987; Stoltenberg and McNeill, 1997). Only Skovholt and Rønnestad

(1995) systematically examined the development of counsellors and therapists beyond the years of training as graduate students or interns. They interviewed 100 practitioners who ranged from untrained counsellors to therapists with forty years' experience in practice, in a carefully constructed qualitative study.

While illuminating the stages of development, Skovholt and Rønnestad (1995) also isolated a critical factor in facilitating professional development. That factor, which distinguished therapists who continued to develop from therapists who stagnated and 'burned out', they called continuous professional reflection. Schön (1983, 1987) likewise has described the importance of reflection-in-action and reflection-on-action as skills required for expert practice.

Nature of reflectivity

Schön's concept of reflection and Skovholt and Rønnestad's continuous professional reflection appeared similar. Neufeldt, Karno and Nelson (1996) elected to explore that similarity. They conducted a qualitative study to determine whether these authors' conceptualizations were isomorphic and what elements were included in the concept of reflectivity. They interviewed Schön, Skovholt and Rønnestad, along with two scholars, Willis Copeland and Elizabeth Holloway, who had utilized the concept of reflectivity in teaching and supervision respectively. All five agreed on the common processes included in the concept of reflectivity.

The experts identified the causal event, which is where reflectivity (and development) begin, as a problem in counselling 'ripe for reflectivity' (Neufeldt et al., 1996: 6), signified by the trainee's feelings of uncertainty. A problem is really a dilemma for the supervisee; they are surprised by the turn of events in the counselling session and feel confused and 'stuck' (ibid.). Trainees can reflect on dilemmas if they have the personality characteristics; cognitive capacities for complexity, invention and imagination; and a situation in a safe institutional and supervisory environment that encourages these qualities.

Reflective processes can occur when these conditions are met. Reflectivity was described along a number of dimensions. First is the locus of attention. When reflective, therapists focus on their own actions, emotions and thoughts in the counselling session. In addition, they attend to the interaction between the client and therapist. The second dimension, which several experts considered the most important, was a 'stance' of reflectivity. Four elements characterize that stance: the intention to examine one's actions in order to act further, active and critical inquiry about one's own covert and overt activity in session, continued openness to a variety of alternatives for interpreting what is being conveyed, and the willingness to become vulnerable and try out new ideas both in supervision and in session. Third, reflective persons use two important sources for understanding what they see. Theory is one source which enables them to explore the phenomena they wish to understand, a kind of lens through which to view their experiences. A second, and significant element of novice-to-expert development, is the use of 'past personal and professional experiences, particularly previous surprising, puzzling clinical experiences and the interpretations one has made of them' (ibid.: 7).

Reflectivity is apparently a meta-skill that enables two critical therapist activities. Reflection-in-action (Schön, 1983) enables therapists to make the in-session decisions to utilize a specific strategy tailored to a particular client at a particular time, and continuous professional reflection (Skovholt and Rønnestad, 1995) facilitates the development of the professional counsellor as he or she moves from one level of professional competence and clinical wisdom to the next. It is therefore necessary to teach this skill to beginners, who will need it to advance. Likewise, more advanced therapists will need reflectivity both for continued development and for moment-to-moment decision-making within sessions. Our task is to develop that meta-skill as we supervise therapists at all developmental levels.

Use of reflective interventions in supervision

A number of strategies for reflective supervision have been described fully in a manual for supervision (Neufeldt, 1999). Much of the training and supervision of beginning students involves basic skill-building, with modelling and practice. However, even at this early stage, I look to encourage the habit of reflection and cogitation where it is appropriate. It is challenging to do this and even more challenging to teach it to beginning supervisors. As Carl

Rogers once said to Rod Goodyear (Goodyear, 1982), on a videotape where he conducted and then described his feelings about supervision, 'I just want to say, "Move over; let me take over."' It is difficult for any of us not to answer supervisees' questions immediately nor to give 'brilliant' advice; we were therapists first, and we often want to provide a therapeutic solution. This difficulty is greater for the beginning supervisor (Skovholt and Rønnestad, 1995) who feels the pressure to generate answers and perform credibly by being helpful. However, when our goal is the development of a reflective therapist, we can attend to that goal instead of showing the supervisee, in that moment, how the 'best' therapy might look (and how clever we were to figure it out). A number of active strategies encourage reflectivity on the part of the supervisee (Neufeldt, 1999). In this chapter I will illustrate their use in a particular supervision session.

The therapist, in this instance, was a doctoral student in her second year of academic and clinical training, with exactly one year of counselling practicum experience behind her. We had worked together the previous year, when I regularly supervised her student supervisor's work with her and occasionally directly supervised her client work myself. We had developed a relationship where she seemed comfortable and occasionally asked questions that involved some level of risk, so I believed our supervision could occur in what she might experience as a safe environment. On this occasion, I asked her whether she had a dilemma in any of her cases that I could help her with. In that way I made certain that the critical causal event was in place, and I explained that I would be using this discussion for illustration. She agreed to these conditions and then proceeded to tell me about her case and her questions. I responded by exploring how she had felt about what she did in the session and any other thoughts or feelings she experienced in her meeting with the client. From there I explored the other dimensions described above as elements of reflectivity. Because she was a second-year student, I was able to ask more questions and still get responses than I might have done had I directly questioned a beginner; beginners typically respond to questions with silence (Holloway and Wolleat, 1981).

In this supervision session, I addressed some but not all aspects of the reflective process. My primary goal, however, was to enlist the supervisee's collaboration in our mutual effort to understand the events of the counselling session. I hoped to engage her curiosity to the degree that it could override any anxiety she might feel in discussing the case with me.

N: I've seen this woman for three sessions and last time she told me some things that I didn't know what to make of.

S: Umm-hmm.

N: Yeah, she said that after she's been in a relationship for a while, like right now, when she is involved in the physical part of the relationship, it feels just like all the other relationships she's been in, like the physicality of it, almost as if she couldn't differentiate between her experience with her present lover and her experience with a different person. And I thought that was kind of odd, and I didn't know if it was sort of psychotic.

S: So when you were in there, you were trying to figure out what was going on, what this meant.
[Here, I was asking her to focus on what she was thinking.]

N: Yeah. So I just kept asking her about it. And she said that it's happened before. And I said, like, maybe he reminds her of someone else. And she said he reminds her of everyone, that it all feels the same after a while. Then I said, 'Well, maybe the relationship's getting kind of old.' And she didn't pick up on that. So I didn't know. She came in because of problems in relationships and said she often gets kind of numb after a while. So I asked if maybe this was the beginning of that process, and she said it probably was.

S: Umm-hmm. And so how were you feeling while all this was going on.
[I shifted from the counsellor's thoughts in session to her feelings.]

N: Well, I was really curious, but at the same time it was kind of eerie.

S: So you were kind of uncomfortable?

N: Well, yeah, it just felt eerie. I mean, I had never heard of anything like this before and I just wanted to know if it was normal.

S: And you were a little bit worried.

N: Yeah. I mean, I wondered if this was some sort of psychotic process. You know, she came in with a previous diagnosis of manic depression and they get psychotic sometimes, don't they?

S: Sometimes. But what would it mean to you if she were psychotic?

[I moved from her thoughts and feelings to the meaning she made of the experience.]

N: Well, I don't know. I mean, my regular supervisor said I should just be calm and stable with her.

[She described what had been suggested for her to do in future sessions. So I shifted back to what she intended and experienced in the session under discussion.]

S: But really, you still don't know what it all means. And so you were really trying to understand it while you were in there.

N: Yeah.

S: And you're still wondering about it.

N: Yeah.

[Now I shifted from her thoughts, feelings and actions, to her experience of the relationship and interaction between them.]

S: So let's explore it a little further. What was your interaction like?

N: I think it was pretty good, I mean, I don't think she realized I was uncomfortable or anything.

S: Good. And what was the nature, the feel, of the interaction between you?

[I realized she hadn't really understood my question, so I tried again, by asking for a deeper response to the interaction between them.]

N: Oh, well it wasn't very different from the way it usually is. She doesn't show much emotion. But I think we have a pretty good relationship, I mean, as good as we could. I think this is probably how she is in any relationship. And I think she could feel that I was really interested in understanding her.

S: How did you get that impression?

N: Well, she just kept talking and answering my questions and trying to explain what I wanted to know.

S: Okay . . . Do you feel as engaged, connected to her as you usually do with clients?

N: Well, it's more connected than I feel with adolescents, but it's a lot less than with my other client, who is very social and just has a particular relationship problem he's trying to figure out.

S: So this sounds like a client who may not have had a good relationship history and is kind of hard to form a relationship with.

N: Yeah, but I think she's a good client to work with; she talks very easily and she comes in for all her appointments.

S: But you're saying there isn't much 'flavour' to the relationship with her. And you think that's pretty characteristic of her.

N: Yeah.

S: Okay. And do you have any opinions about what you did in the session?

N: Well, at the time, I just asked her the questions I could think of, but now that I've had more of a chance to consider it, I wish I'd asked her more about whether it happens in other relationships, going numb or feeling disconnected, I mean.

S: Sure. And can you think of anything else you might want to try?
[I encouraged her not to settle for the first idea, to remain open and consider additional alternatives.]

N: Well, I'd want to know if it was connected to something in her past. So I'd ask about that.

S: Ah, so you are interested in the similarity of the relationship between the two of you and her other relationships. And you want to know about things in her past. Is that something you think you might pursue in session with her?
[I rather quickly shifted here to checking out whether she planned to risk trying out her ideas in a future session.]

N: Yes.

S: So it sounds as if you have a plan that you're willing to try.

N: Yeah.
[And then I checked her sources of understanding in terms of both theory and experience.]

S: As you seek to understand her, what kind of theory are you using? What's the lens through which you view these events?

N: What? O yeah. Well, it's a combination, I think, of interpersonal and psychodynamic.

S: Yeah. That seems to fit what you've been saying you wanted to know about. And besides those theories and your experience with this client, what else do you use to understand her? I know you haven't had a lot of counselling experience, but what past experiences might have helped you here?

N: Well, I think I'm not really judgemental in relationships, that I can ask about experiences that are not like my own and not have too strong a reaction. I mean, like once I was talking with this homeless guy in San Francisco, and his life was nothing like mine, but I was just curious about it. And that's kind of how I am with her; I just ask questions.

S: Okay . . . You know, this was a pretty short session, and I'm wondering how this discussion was for you?
[Finally, I asked her to reflect on our interaction in supervision.]

N: Well, it was pretty helpful. We went a little deeper into it. I mean, I hadn't really thought much about my own feelings. And then when you said I seemed to have a plan, that felt good.

The challenge for me always occurs when I'm trying to encourage reflectivity rather than build skills. With many years of practice in therapy and supervision, I still occasionally find it difficult to back off and encourage therapists to consider their own thoughts, feelings and behaviours. In this way, I try to build in a pattern of thinking about difficulties with clients, a reflective process, that will continue to help the supervisees long after they leave me. I also train supervisors to do this, and I am struck by how the novice supervisors' efforts to encourage reflectivity in their supervisees facilitate their own reflective attitudes and processes.

Exercises for practice

The practices described above encourage the supervisee to use reflective processes while discussing a counselling dilemma during supervision. I enjoy the process of drawing out therapists and encouraging them to consider their work from different angles, to approach it with curiosity. The goal, however, is to enable therapists to do this exploration on their own. To that end, I developed the following exercises for supervisees to do on their own.

Self-reflection on a dilemma

Supervisees are directed to respond to the following questions in writing immediately after the next therapy session in which they face a puzzle, a dilemma. It will take the therapist quite a while to carry out this endeavour, but it can help to establish a habit of thinking through a clinical problem.

1. Describe the therapy events which precipitated your puzzlement.
2. State your question about these events as clearly as you can.
3. What were you thinking during this portion of the session?
4. What were you feeling? How do you understand those feelings now?
5. Consider your own actions during this portion of the session. What did you intend?
6. Now look at the interaction between you and the client. What were the results of your interventions?
7. What was the feel, the emotional flavour, of the interaction between you? Was it similar to or different from your usual experience with this client?
8. To what degree do you understand this interaction as similar to the client's interactions in other relationships? How does that inform your experience of the interaction in session?
9. What theories do you use to understand what is going on in session?
10. What past professional or personal experiences affect your understanding?
11. How else might you interpret the events and interaction in the session?
12. How might you test out the various alternatives in your next counselling session? (Be sure to look for what confirms and what disconfirms your interpretations.)
13. How will the clients' responses inform what you do next?

Exercise for listening to audio or videotape of session

Up to this point, I have described ways of encouraging therapists to reflect back on their actions in session, what Schön (1983) called reflections-on-action. It is, however, important to train therapists to reflect in action, to examine what is happening while the session is going on. While we cannot interrupt the session with questions about the therapist's experience in the moment, we can closely approximate it by asking therapists, as soon thereafter as possible, to recall what they were experiencing during the session. Schön called this 'reflections-on-reflections-in-action' (personal communication, 1994). Arrange for a supervision session directly after the taped session to make the experience more immediate. Ask the supervisee to play a tape of the most puzzling interaction in the session. After *each* therapist intervention (aside from minimal verbal responses designed to keep the client going), ask the therapist to describe her or his experiences during that time. In particular, ask about the therapist's in-session feelings and thoughts, as well as the intentions behind the behaviour. Encourage the therapist to explore the results of the intervention and consider what that meant to the therapist during the session itself.

Make every effort to keep the therapists' attention focused on their experiences *during* the session. In this way you encourage them to pay attention to their own thoughts, feelings and behaviours, and to client reactions while they actually conduct therapy. Only after discussing those, do you allow them to shift in supervision to the ways they now experience what they saw and how they intend to move forward in the next session.

Effectiveness of the reflective approach to supervision

To date, there is no research that supports the effectiveness of this series of interventions on therapists' regular use of reflective processes during or after their sessions. As Binder has noted, however, 'Because empirical data are lacking, any discussion about problems with the supervisory process is speculative and must be based upon personal experience and relevant clinical literature. Nevertheless, such problems are sufficiently critical to the therapy training endeavour to warrant even speculative discussion' (1993: 305). In my personal experience with supervisees, I have observed these results: (a) Those who naturally reflect will do it whether I ask them to or not. It is a habit of thinking, which is akin to 'psychological mindedness.' (b) Those who have not yet learned to reflect can do so, albeit awkwardly at first, if I pose the specific kinds of questions I have described above. (c) While sometimes supervisees will reflect aloud in supervision, in many cases I would have no idea of what they were experiencing unless I asked explicitly. (d) I can sometimes facilitate their learning reflective skills by modelling my own reflective processes.

These interventions work well in one-on-one supervision and I have also found them easy to use over the telephone. In addition, when I use them in supervision groups of two or more, I find that the other supervisees also reflect. Group members sometimes interject their thoughts or feelings during the discussion of the case.

It is important to remember that teaching and practising reflective processes is only one aspect of supervision. As indicated earlier in this chapter, there is a definite place for the specific teaching and modelling of new or ineffectively applied skills. Certainly, we begin their training with skills training, and we continue to offer new possibilities as they advance. As well, there is evidence that supervisees prefer structured supervisory interventions during a crisis (Tracey, Ellickson and Sherry, 1989), and it is likely that they cannot readily reflect in those crisis moments when their anxiety is high.

The continuous use of reflection, however, appears to lead to significant development in therapists and prevent stagnation and deterioration (Skovholt and Rønnestad, 1995). Training can create a habit of reflective practice that may lead to addressing clinical problems 'in the swampy lowland where "messes" are incapable of technical solution' (Schön, 1983: 42). It may also assist in the development of the ability to form successful alliances with difficult clients, as well as with those who bond to the therapist and others rather easily, for that appears to be the critical element in successful psychotherapy (Strupp, 1996).

Notes

[1]Throughout this chapter, the terms *reflection*, *reflecting*, and *reflectivity* refer to an internal process of attention and thought rather than to a counsellor's verbal response to a client.

Suggested Reading

The works which follow are listed by author and title; the complete references can be found in the next section.

Recommendations for improving psychotherapy training based on experiences with manual-guided training and research (Binder and Strupp, 1993)

Supervision Strategies for the First Practicum (Neufeldt, 1999)

Supervision of beginning and advanced graduate students of counselling and psychotherapy (Rønnestad and Skovholt, 1993)
Educating the Reflective Practitioner (Schön, 1987)
The Evolving Professional Self (Skovholt and Rønnestad, 1999)

References

Bernard, J.M. and Goodyear, R.K. (1992) (2nd edn, 1998) *Fundamentals of Clinical Supervision*. Boston: Allyn & Bacon.

Binder, J.L. (1993) Is it time to improve psychotherapy training? *Clinical Psychology Review*, 13: 301–18.

Binder, J.L. and Strupp, H.H. (1993) Recommendations for improving psychotherapy training based on experiences with manual-guided training and research: an introduction. *Psychotherapy*, 30: 592–600.

Binder, J.L. and Strupp, H.H. (1997) Supervision of psychodynamic psychotherapies. In C.E. Watkins, Jr. (ed.), *Handbook of Psychotherapy Supervision* (pp. 44–59). New York: Wiley.

Goodyear, R.K. (1982) *Psychotherapy Supervision by Major Theorists* (Videotape series). Manhattan, KS: Kansas State University.

Holloway, E.L. (1987) Developmental models of supervision: is it development? *Professional Psychology: Research and Practice*, 24: 1094–1119.

Holloway, E.L. and Wolleat, P.L. (1981) Style differences of beginning supervisors: an interactional analysis. *Journal of Counseling Psychology*, 28: 373–6.

Jennings, L. and Skovholt, T.M. (in press) Characteristics of Master Therapists. *Journal of Counseling Psychology.*

Lichtenberg, J.W. (1997) Expertise in counseling psychology: a concept in search of support. *Educational Psychology Review*, 9: 221–38.

Neufeldt, S.A. (1999) *Supervision Strategies for the First Practicum* (2nd edn). Alexandria, VA: American Counseling Association.

Neufeldt, S.A., Karno, M.P. and Nelson, M.L. (1996) A qualitative study of experts' conceptualization of supervisee reflectivity. *Journal of Counseling Psychology*, 43: 3–9.

Rønnestad, M.H. and Skovholt, T.M. (1993) Supervision of beginning and advanced graduate students of counseling and psychotherapy. *Journal of Counseling and Development*, 71: 396–405.

Rønnestad, M.H. and Skovholt, T.M. (1998) Berufliche entwicklung und supervision von psychotherapeuten [The professional development and supervision of psychotherapists] *Psychotherapeut*, 42: 299–306.

Schön, D.A. (1983) *The Reflective Practitioner*. New York: Basic Books.

Schön, D.A. (1987) *Educating the Reflective Practitioner*. San Francisco: Jossey-Bass.

Shaw, B.F. (1984) Specification of the training and evaluation of cognitive therapists for outcome studies. In J.B.W. Williams and R.L. Spitfire (eds), *Psychotherapy Research: Where Are We and Where Should We Go?* New York: Guilford.

Skovholt, T.M. and Rønnestad, M.H. (1995) *The Evolving Professional Self: Stages and Themes in Therapist and Counselor Development*. Chichester: Wiley.

Skovholt, T.M., Rønnestad, M.H. and Jennings, L. (1997) Searching for expertise in counseling, psychotherapy, and professional psychology. *Educational Psychology Review*, 9: 361–9.

Sternberg, R.J. (1990) Wisdom and its relations to intelligence and creativity. In R.J. Sternberg (ed.), *Wisdom: Its Nature, Origins, and Development* (pp. 142–59). Cambridge: Cambridge University Press.

Stoltenberg, C.D. and Delworth, U. (1987) *Supervising Counselors and Therapists*. San Francisco: Jossey-Bass.

Stoltenberg, C.D. and McNeill, B.W. (1997) Clinical supervision from a developmental perspective: research and practice. In C.E. Watkins, Jr. (ed.), *Handbook of Psychotherapy Supervision*. New York: Wiley.

Strupp, H.H. (1996) Some salient lessons from research and practice. *Psychotherapy*, 33: 135–8.

Tracey, T.J., Ellickson, J.L. and Sherry, P. (1989) Reactance in relation to different supervisory environments and counselor development. *Journal of Counseling Psychology*, 36: 336–44.

5 Training in group and team supervision

Willem Lammers

Introduction

Originally trained in social psychology, I have been working with groups, teams and small organizations for approximately twenty years, in the roles of psychotherapist, supervisor and organizational consultant. For the past ten years I have been training professionals in psychotherapy, counselling and supervision, using my own background in transactional analysis Neurolinguistic programming (NLP) and different forms of group psychotherapies and trainings. The context of my work is the Institute for the Application of the Social Sciences which I founded with a colleague in 1987 in Switzerland and which specializes in training programmes for supervision, coaching, team development, and different forms of counselling, for example transactional analysis and trauma counselling. Our institute also offers services in these fields alongside the training we provide.

One of the areas in which I work and train substantially is that of supervising teams and groups. For effective work in this area supervisors need specific competence in the complex processes which are part and parcel of groups and organizations. These processes can stimulate or inhibit the learning of the individual supervisee and the group as a whole. In this chapter, I will describe my understanding of group and team supervision within the context of the Systems Approach to Supervision (SAS model, Holloway, 1995). I will then draw out the consequences of this thinking for the training of group and team supervisors.

Tasks, roles and context

The tasks and roles of a supervisor working with groups or teams vary with the context. Types of groups and teams are very different. A few recent examples from my own practice illustrate this variety. I work with:

- professional counsellors and psychotherapists who need support in their daily work with clients;
- professionals from different disciplines in a drug ward of a psychiatric hospital;
- professionals preparing for the exams of the International Transactional Analysis Association;
- nurses from the management of a rehabilitation hospital who have conflicts among themselves and with the medical staff;
- staff responsible for a training programme of social workers in the first year of the curriculum;
- staff members of a broadcasting corporation preparing a meeting in which they have to develop a strategic plan with a larger team;
- a team of a 'birth house' who want to discuss the level and strength of co-operation among themselves;
- a team from an insurance company who want to learn to manage conflicts;
- a team of schoolteachers who want to discuss their communication problems with the school board.

The size of these groups varies from three to twelve, the meeting arrangements vary from just one occasion to intensive co-operation on a day-to-day, hour-to-hour base. The activity may be labelled group supervision, team supervision, team development, coaching, crisis intervention, conflict management or process facilitating. The labels or titles given to the work differ across countries, corporate culture and context. In German-speaking countries the word 'coaching' is used for the counselling of business managers, while in Britain the word 'mentoring' covers the same area. In a few Swiss hospitals, the word '*Praxisberatung*' (practice counselling) is used for team supervision. At first this may seem irrelevant, but its importance was realized when the hospital management reserved a budget for '*Praxisberatung*' but not for 'team supervision'. One trainee I know was reluctant to call herself a team supervisor until she realized she was doing team supervision under the title of 'organizational development'. In a corporate context (and this is where care in the use of terminology needs to be exercised), 'supervision' is a controlling function and we have found it is more acceptable to talk about 'coaching', 'team development' or 'workplace counselling'.

In this chapter I will describe differences between group and team supervision and then describe the characteristics of each. In general, to become a team or group supervisor, training and competence in individual supervision is a basic condition. From this starting point, competence has to be built at different systemic levels for those who wish to proceed to being a team or group supervisor. The skills involved are around working with (a) the individual in the group setting; (b) the group as a complex system in itself; and (c) the group as part of a system in which it is embedded. These three aspects pertain to group supervision as well as to team supervision. Table 5.1 is an overview of the characteristics of both group and team settings.

Characteristics of group supervision

I will review the features of group supervision from a systemic perspective as well as from the three aspects mentioned above.

From a systemic stance we can see group supervision as a forum in which trainees or professionals meet regularly with an experienced professional to discuss professional issues. The goals include all five supervisory tasks of Holloway's SAS model: counselling skills, case conceptualization, professional role, emotional awareness and self-evaluation. The group members may come from the same profession or have different professional backgrounds. Participants in the group usually do not meet outside sessions. At the beginning of each session, a list of topics is agreed and the group decides, with the supervisor, how these topics will be prioritized. Work on a specific topic usually takes between twenty minutes and an hour. Depending on the goal and on the style of the supervisor, an individual may be supervised by the group with the supervisor in the role of a facilitator of the group process, or the supervisor will work with the individual in front of the group. In the latter case, group members offer their observations later in the session. As a support system, group supervision is still usually restricted to professionals from non-profit organizations. In commercial organizations, the need for a professional's reflection on self, the team, and the organization is not yet widely recognized. It is quite the opposite sometimes, and for some professionals in a business context it may still be difficult to admit that self-reflection and self-evaluation is not a weakness.

The individual in the group

The role of the individual in the group is especially relevant in group supervision, where group members come from different

Table 5.1 *Group and team characteristics*

Categories	Group supervision		Team supervision		
Subcategories	Training group	Support group	Corporate	Non-profit	Management
Contract partners	trainees, professional association or institution	trained professionals	management, team	management, team	management
Goal	learning counselling, psychotherapy, supervision	professional support	crisis intervention, problem-solving, group process	problem-solving, group process, case supervision	problem-solving, conflict management
Membership	professionals in training	trained professionals	team members	team members	management team
Leadership name and status	Training supervisor	group supervisor	team coach, organizational consultant	team supervisor	team coach
Group size	5–8	5–8	3–20	3–12	3–5
Duration of contract	until end of training with different supervisors	one year, may be prolonged			
Frequency/duration	1–2 times a month/3 hrs	monthly/3 hrs	according to needs, usually not regularly	monthly/2–3 hrs	according to needs, usually not regularly
Main focus	cases of clients, professional role/identity	cases	team problems/co-operation	cases/team problems/co-operation	co-operation/strategic thinking
Termination	with end of training	end of contract	after stabilization of co-operation	after 2–3 years	when problems are (not) solved

work settings with the primary task of developing and maintaining professional competence. There is usually no other connection between members than this shared interest. Most of the time concentration is on issues around problems with clients, colleagues or the management of the institution in which the supervisee works. Depending on the exact goal of the group, members may come from the same or different professions. This kind of supervision may be very similar to individual supervision, with clear roles negotiated by the supervisor and the supervisee. This kind of group has additional advantages similar to those outlined by Yalom (1970) when he describes the advantages of group over individual psychotherapy. Many experienced supervisors prefer this type of group work to engaging in individual work because of the extra options available to them. At a theoretical level, group supervisors must be familiar with:

- the elementary structure and process of working groups (Bion, 1961);
- stages in the development of working groups (Tuckman, 1965; Lacoursiere, 1980);
- the extension of parallel processes into a supervision group (Stoltenberg and Delworth, 1987).

The role of the group supervisor is a combination of the individual supervisor and a group process facilitator.

The group as a complex system in itself

Every supervision group creates a culture of its own which determines, to a large degree, the working relationships between the members and the environment. Intimacy, trust, creativity and productivity of the members of the group individually and the group as a whole are key elements in the effective working of the group. Supervisors play an important role in building the culture in how they conduct the first sessions. Supervisees may be encouraged or inhibited in expressing their thoughts and feelings and the group may develop either towards a network or towards a hierarchical basic structure. The risk of group supervision is that it is implicitly paternalistic and authoritarian and can create a sense of dependency in the members. It is important to invite contributions from all members of the group as a way of helping them become more autonomous and create a culture of participation.

The group as a part of a hierarchical system

Group supervision can take place as part of professional training and as a supportive measure for those finishing their professional training. In the former case, the rules of the training institution, a professional association or the law will apply to the supervision group. When there is no explicit training task in the supervision, usually the ethics and professional practice rules of the association the supervisor and the group members belong to will apply. Group supervisors in training must become aware of the larger structures they are working in and which may limit their range of interventions and tasks, for example where confidentiality or dual relationships are concerned. Group supervisors must also realize that they have a containing or embedding function towards supervisees and clients. This means that the old rule '*primum non nocere*' (literally translated as 'firstly, no harm') still applies: the first task of the supervisor is to reduce danger for the clients of the supervisees and the supervisees themselves, in this order.

Contract partners

In group supervision, each individual participant has a separate contract with the supervisor, usually for a fixed number of sessions. The trainees of psychotherapy or counselling contract with the professional organization, institute or association which supports the training. It is recommended that the supervisees also contract with each other around issues such as confidentiality and participation.

Goals

The goals of group supervision are the same as what Holloway (1995) describes in her book as supervision tasks. These goals will shift with experience and with the phase of group development: beginning counsellors tend to focus more on their identity in the profession and on technical and diagnostic issues, while experienced professionals put the main emphasis on the therapeutic relationship and counter-transference.

Membership

The membership of a training supervision group is part of a larger training programme. This larger training will include elements on theoretical and technical training as well as personal experience in the taught method and sometimes also practice in a psychiatric hospital or another context where the taught method is used. A support supervision group consists of professionals who have finished their training and use the group to exchange their experiences with clients. In the last few years, our institute has started to offer supervision to groups consisting of members from mixed professional backgrounds, such as teachers, business trainers, and organizational consultants.

Labels and titles

In group supervision the leader of the group is called a group supervisor. The supervisor is usually a professional with a number of years' experience in the field. However, groups of experienced professionals may work without a designated leader. Such groups may also be called *intervision* groups, or peer groups.

Format

The group size may vary from four to eight, with an optimum of about six members. The group usually meets once a month, and the presence of all members is expected and highly valued. A session duration of three hours allows members to treat a number of issues in depth. The duration of the contract must recognize the fact that mutual trust is a necessary condition for the exploration of working relationships and counter-transference issues. It is therefore desirable that a group does not change more than once or twice a year.

Main focus

The main focus in group supervision where the focus is on psychotherapy and counselling is on working with clients. In groups of mixed professional background, the contact with other types of client systems, such as pupils in schools, patients in hospitals or employees for managers, may be important. Issues regarding the supervisee's professional role within an organizational and professional context may also be on the supervisory agenda.

Termination

Usually supervision groups exist over a long time, with individuals joining or leaving the group at fixed moments in the year. Members leave a training supervision group after finishing their professional training. A support group may stay together for years, with changes taking place only when members feel they have learned what they can from the group and consider it is time to move on.

Characteristics of team supervision

Having reviewed the features of group supervision, I will now present the characteristics of team supervision, which differs somewhat from group supervision. Again, I will look at these features through their systemic aspects and then through the same three lenses: the individual member, the group system and the group as part of a larger system.

A team is a group of people with a common task within the structure of an organization. The word team may have many different meanings depending on the context: there is quite a difference between seven nurses in a psychiatric ward responsible for the care of a group of patients on a day-to-day basis and a group of psychotherapists who have in common that they share their consulting rooms. There are also differences in the way teams are managed. A manager may be a *primus inter pares* who works closely with the team, or he or she may be a physically and psychologically distant person at the other end of a telephone line. Team supervision may take place with or without the presence of the manager or team leader. In general, the closer a manager stands to the team the more important is his or her presence.

Contract partners

In general, in team supervision there will be a three-cornered contract, in which the supervisor has contracts both with the team and with the management of the institution. The team has contracts with the management and with the supervisor. When supervisors work within an institution, it is important that they are able to support the goals of the institution, while at the same time having sufficient distance from power in the organization to be able to recognize problems regarding organizational structure and culture. In contract negotiations before the start of the supervision process, there must be clarity about the exact role of the supervisor regarding the teams and the level of the organization at which work takes place. In addition, the content of reports to the management and the issue of who will have access to these reports must be defined. The different aspects of contracts become clear in the three-cornered contract diagram (English, 1975) as outlined in Figure 5.1.

Goal

In general, team supervision will help the team in the fulfilment of their goals within and outside the organization. In working with clients, many tasks of group supervision are also present in team supervision. Additional issues are:

- the position of individuals within the team;
- the co-operation and communication of the team members;
- the relationship of the team with the management and with other structures in the organization.

Cultural aspects and leadership styles play an important role in team supervision.

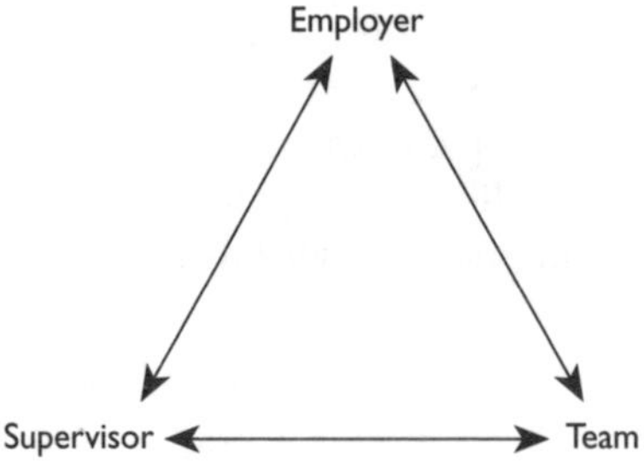

Figure 5.1 *The three-cornered contract*

Membership

Membership in team supervision may differ according to context, organizational culture and team goals. If supervision focuses on expanding the competence of the team members in coping with clients, like a team in a drug ward, they may well end up with individual supervision in the context of the team supervision. In such a context the presence of the head of the ward might be counter-productive as members may become aware of personal emotions or have to confront personal issues which may be difficult to do with the leader of the team present. Participants may consider that this could affect their career or how they are perceived within the team as a strong member or a weak one. When, however, team supervision is focused on resolving conflicts in the team, the presence of the leader may be mandatory. A discussion about the team philosophy, the tasks and the roles to fulfil the tasks may be very ineffective when the leader is not present.

Labels

Supervision in a team may be team supervision as such where focus is on the team, it could be coaching and team development, and/or workplace counselling. The name of the activity is less relevant than the fact that the supervisor gains acceptance for the work done. However, the choice of a name that has a familiar and positive connotation is of utmost importance, especially in a corporate context where asking for help may equate with admitting one's incompetence. It may be, in some instances, essential to find the label which supports the process at the level of the organization. The name supervisor may sound too controlling. Therefore consultant, counsellor or coach may be a better and more acceptable title.

Format

Formats in team supervision may differ greatly. In non-profit organizations that treat or educate clients, supervision may be a regular monthly activity for a few hours. In working with corporate or management teams, any format might be possible: small groups, large groups, days or hours, long-term contracts or single sessions. This is the same for the membership. Sometimes groups want to work with three hierarchical levels at the same time, which may point to serious difficulties regarding the structure and the management of the organization. Formats must be adapted to the task and the availability of resources. Usually there is a gap between what the supervisor considers necessary and what is available, especially in corporate settings.

Main focus

The main focus in team supervision has to be formulated in the contract. There are three different possible foci:

CASE SUPERVISION In case supervision, team members present cases from the population they are working with. For a team of psychiatric nurses, this could be a patient who does not want to leave his bed; or, for a team of school psychologists, a pupil who does not make contact with others in the class. The task of the supervisor is to develop theories and methods for the immediate work with the client system.

TEAM CO-OPERATION When the supervisor has a contract to improve team co-operation, there is a wide array of options. A primary issue is co-operation regarding clients for whom different team members may have tasks. This may be the same task, as in a psychiatric ward where all nurses may have the same roles at different times, or different ones, like psychotherapists and nurses in a treatment centre for borderline adolescents. Team supervision may thus focus on managing boundaries between roles. Another issue is communication between team members and the group dynamics in the team. Emotional problems between team members often have their roots in unclear contracts regarding roles and tasks. In such a case, conflict management means managing roles, boundaries and group dynamics in the team. A third issue is the relationship of the team and the outer world, and how this outer world is represented by the management. For many professionals on the floor, it is very difficult to cope with the realistic limits the management has to move within. In supervision of teams who work with groups of clients, special attention is needed for parallel processes between the client group and the team. A team working with borderline adolescents may be subject to all kinds of splitting dynamics as they are seen in the client group. On the other hand, organizational issues can support splitting mechanisms.

TEAM STRATEGY When the focus of the supervision is on team strategy, the team has to define the primary task. This must be done because different team members may have different views. I worked for a long time in a pulmonary rehabilitation hospital in which the primary task was seen differently by medical and socially trained personnel. The medical staff thought that the primary task was to return people to a healthy physical condition. They therefore wanted to design a rigid physical fitness programme. Other staff members, social workers and psychotherapists, thought a rigid programme would make patients very dependent on an external structure. As soon as the structure was gone, there would be no internal drive to maintain the fitness of patients. These are strategic problems which cannot be solved on a day-to-day basis; the team must take the time to find a clear definition of the primary task, in which different aspects of health are represented. Only then can a structure with corresponding roles be designed around this task. The job of the supervisor is often to bridge the gap between different disciplines.

Termination

Because team supervision is often task-oriented, it is usually terminated when the task is fulfilled, or when it becomes clear that the task cannot be fulfilled and other goals are formulated. Often there are no long-term contracts, but contracts are made from stage to stage. From the beginning, team supervision is much more complex than group supervision. Participants are not only there for their personal learning goals, but also to solve interpersonal problems and to help the team as a whole fulfil the primary task. In a training programme, therefore, the teaching of team supervision comes after the trainee supervisor has learned to manage the basic dynamics of a supervision group as described above. The above-mentioned aspects – the individual in the group, group dynamics and embedded and embedding hierarchies – are infinitely more complex and each deserving of a book in its own right. The most important difference between team and group supervision is the fact that the team as a whole has a primary task to work on which is different from the task of the supervision group. This primary task has four key aspects, which have to be taken care of and which can lead to different roles for different team members. These aspects are illustrated in Figure 5.2 (Hilb, 1998).

In team supervision, team members bring their external roles into the relational context of the supervision process. This process must not only enhance the learning of the participants, as in group supervision, but also has to support the fulfilling of the primary task. This has ethical consequences: if the supervisor cannot support the primary task of the system to which team members belong, a supervision contract should not be made. There is a difference between the primary task itself and the way the people in the organization work on it. If they work on an ethical goal in unethical ways, supervision might well help to work on the goal in a different way. Therefore supervisors must learn to take ethical considerations about the primary task into consideration. An example of an ethical consideration is confidentiality. In team supervision it is usually not possible to keep information within the boundaries of the sessions in the way this might be expected in group supervision. In group supervision, confidentiality contracts can be made and breaches of the contract can be confronted. In team supervision, negotiations must take place about whether and how information might go beyond the session. The key concept in these negotiations must be respect. If

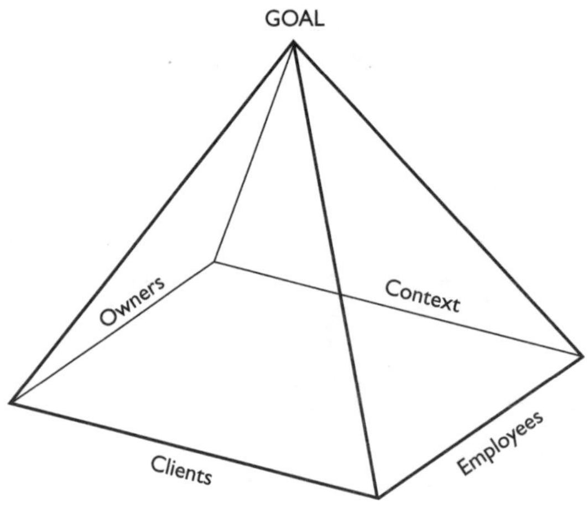

Figure 5.2 *Four key roles*

information is badly managed, people might easily lose face if they show their vulnerability within the context of supervision.

We will now look at the three levels of focus for team supervision which were also used for group supervision.

The individual in the supervision system

When working with individuals in team supervision, the supervisor has to take into account that the supervisee will meet his colleagues from supervision in other situations between sessions. This means that individual participants have to be protected in ways that enable them to take their roles in the team and in the system after supervision is over. The supervisor has to offer protection in a way that corresponds with the level of trust and intimacy in a group. The more trust exists, the more the supervisor can concentrate on vulnerable aspects of the individual. If this is not the case, the emphasis will lie upon the clarification of roles and tasks within the context of the organization.

The dynamics of the supervision system itself

The interaction between team members is an explicit part of the supervision contract. Conflict, competition and co-operation are connected to the fulfilment of the primary task of the group. In the system dynamics, the supervisor can focus upon the interactions between individuals and on the dynamics of the team as a larger system, in which individual positions represent aspects of the system as a whole. These interactions may be connected to roles, especially to the roles of management. In the team, there are formal and informal roles. In figure 5.3 M stands for management and the circles represent individual team members.

Team dynamics may have an immediate influence on the position of the supervisor. If a team has a strong, hierarchical, critical leader, the supervisor will be invited to be supportive, to avoid confrontation with the reality of the management as it is. If the management takes a *laissez-faire* stance, the team might turn to the supervisor for clarity about their tasks and roles. The system might thus be stabilized, but the chances are that the learning will be minimal.

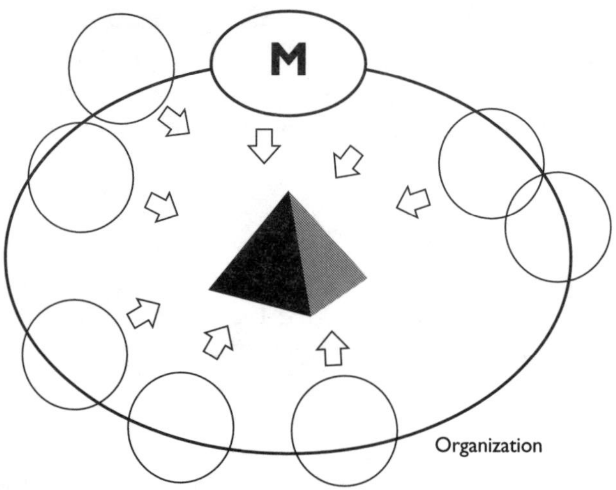

Figure 5.3 *Formal and informal roles in teams*
This diagram was developed after an unpublished model by V. Auer-Hunzinger.

A supervisor must learn to hear the invitation for a specific form of the supervisory relationship as a diagnostic tool for the function of the team as a system or within a larger system.

The supervision system as a hierarchical system

Usually, a team is part of a larger organization and at the same time builds a larger organization for another system. A team of psychiatric nurses is the ruling context for a group of inmates and at the same time is part of a larger system with other teams and even hospitals. The team usually takes one part of the primary task of the larger structure, treating drug addicts, for example, while another team is treating schizophrenics. Conflicts within the team may mirror conflicts at another level of the hierarchy. In multi-disciplinary teams, in particular, many of the dynamics of the supervision systems depend on how differences of opinion between representatives of different disciplines are managed at a higher level of the institutional hierarchy. Examples are the relationships between medical staff and nurses in hospitals, between teachers and caretakers in children's homes, or between marketing and production staff in industry.

A supervisor must be aware of these differences and of the

fractal nature of co-operation and conflict in organizations. This means that if any departure from the work on the primary task in an organization is found in an individual, in a team or in the management, similar phenomena may be observed at any other place in the organization. Schwartz (1990) gave an excellent example in his description of the *Challenger* catastrophe, but it can observed in any organization at any time. The fractal nature becomes clear in Figure 5.4.

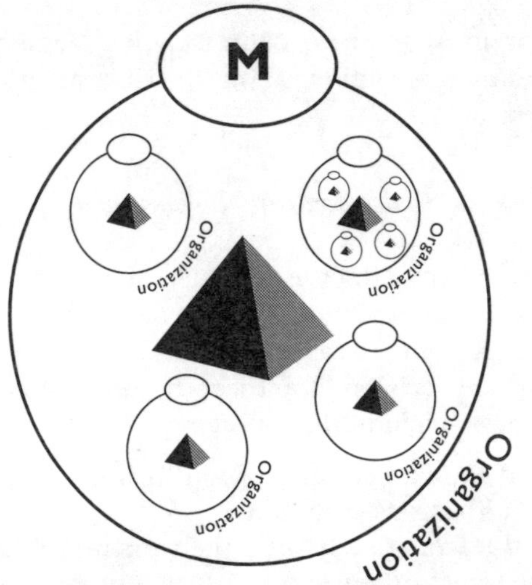

Figure 5.4 *Fractal nature of teams in organizations*

Team supervisors must learn to develop a high level of awareness at these three levels of attention. Training has to offer opportunities for learning about organizations. Supervisors have to become familiar with the above dynamics. It means that they have to learn a number of elementary concepts which allow them understanding of the system dynamics while at the same time being in it, even being part of it.

Skills and methods

Group and team supervisors need the skills and methods demanded by individual supervision. However, they must also be able to use the resources of the group in the supervision process by means of:

- facilitating group processes;
- containing the group process in different developmental stages (Clarkson, 1992);
- timing confrontation and support for group members;
- role-playing techniques;
- feedback and evaluation methods;
- visualization techniques for the group process;
- interpretation of unconscious group processes about leadership and intimacy.

A supervisor must learn to contract with members and representatives from organizations about the content and context of the supervisory task.

Conceptualizing organizations

A group and team supervisor must be able to use a broad spectrum of theoretical models for group and organizational dynamics, apart from the case conceptualization models necessary in individual supervision. Topics, to be understood and worked with in this area, include the following:

- power and intimacy in groups and teams
- anxiety and basic assumptions
- individual learning styles and their interaction in groups
- the influence of organizational structure and culture on team process
- the role of the management in team supervision
- formal and informal roles in the group
- personal vs. team and organizational issues
- the changing economic environment in group and team supervision
- boundaries between supervision on one side and organizational development

Role competence

Supervisors who work with groups and teams require awareness of the compatibility or incompatibility of the different roles they employ. Some of these roles are:

- organizational development consultant
- skills trainer
- team supervisor

- group supervisor
- individual supervisor
- counsellor
- psychotherapist

The professional role of the supervisor is also connected to ethics. In the SAS model, ethical issues may show up in the supervisor tasks of professional role and self-evaluation, with emotional awareness as a subtle instrument for the perception of ethical dilemmas. Ethical issues connected with the professional role may be covered by the ethical code of the professional association to which the supervisor belongs.

Emotional awareness

With regard to emotional awareness, group supervision is much more complex than is the individual supervision process. Other group members might become involved in transference/counter-transference issues. Supervisors develop a kind of radar for what is going on for different individuals in the group and how these emotional experiences represent aspects of the situation of the supervisee, of the situation of the other group members and of the supervision group as a whole.

To evaluate what is happening in a group or a team, a group supervisor has three kinds of instruments at hand: the information given by the supervisee and the group, the information derived from non-verbal communication, and his or her own counter-transference. Counter-transference may be defined, as does Kernberg (1998), as the total emotional reaction of the supervisor to the supervisees in the supervisory situation. The emotional awareness of the supervisor in individual supervision is based on the dyadic relationship and mostly connected to the parallel process between a client and the supervisee. Emotional awareness in group supervision is much more complex and mirrors the complex situation of the supervisee. Emotional awareness is not only important in respect of individual supervisees but the supervisor has to learn to be aware of the mood of the whole group.

Self-evaluation

A good supervisor has the skills and the capacities to learn and to teach at the same time: supervision is a learning process for the supervisor as well as for the supervisee. A supervisor mirrors this duality to the supervisee. Bion concluded that supervision cannot be made. The same might be true for supervisors. Self-evaluation is necessary to find out one's own boundaries regarding skills, understanding and the ability to work with certain categories of professionals and groups.

Ethical rules only make sense when supervisors have gone through a process in which they find personal ways of coping with issues of ethics. According to ethics rules dual relationships in supervision and psychotherapy must be avoided. However, there might be extremely specific situations in which a psychotherapist decides that a combination of both roles is useful, and even indicated. Ethics appear in the choice of professional roles and in the way supervisors perceive their supervisees and themselves. Ethical issues of group and team supervisors are similar to those of counsellors and psychotherapists. However, the looser professional boundaries between supervisees and supervisors and the complexity of the task, especially in the context of an organization, build in more risk of transgressing boundaries.

Supervision training

Supervising a group or a team is an extremely complex professional role. Supervisors have to find a way through a number of paradoxes which are also present in individual supervision. The trainee supervisor must develop a basic attitude from which he or she is able to question what is happening and at the same time offer enough protection to encourage the supervisees to ask themselves what is going on. He/she must learn to recognize when group dynamics has to be taught or explained and when it has to be experienced. The supervisor must contain the group process in a way that is not paternalistic, but at the same time may not – physically or emotionally – leave the group in a state of disarray in the face of difficult professional problems. He/she must focus on the goal of the session without neglecting the group process which eventually mirrors key issues of the supervisee or the team. This role can only be learned in a group, where the experiences of the complexity of the group and organizational processes are reflected upon within the same context. Containing dynamic processes is only possible when such processes are part of the learning process in the training group. Professionals working with groups and teams must be able to diagnose, intervene and evaluate at different levels and be able to diagnose and act at three levels, namely (a) the intervention level; (b) the session level; and (c) the long-term process level.

(a) The micro-level: the intervention

At the micro-level the supervisor must listen carefully to what is said and how it is said and react to it in a way which stimulates the learning of the supervisee and the group. Interventions must be made which empower the supervisee professionally.

(b) The meso-level: the session

At the session level a good supervisor can identify the key issues within or behind a supervisee's or a team's presented problem. A session contract must be made and judged to see if this contract has been fulfilled. Possible harm for the supervisee and for the client is thereby minimized. The professional learning process never stops. At the end of the session supervisors help the supervisees or the group identify the next steps in the learning process. For supervisees learning about the professional role in the group process supervisors are the most important role models. They must be able to describe why they work with the group as they do and thus allow the group to reflect on professional behaviour. The supervisor does this within the context of an equal relationship in which the difference in professional experience does not lead to a paternalistic attitude (Clarkson, 1992).

(c) The macro-level: long-term process

The long-term process level describes the development of the group or the team as professionals within the context of the institution or the practice in which they work and within the boundaries of the overall contract. The contract can be directed towards the support of the team and thus be continuous in character. Goals have to be set and the supervision evaluated from time to time, regarding results and process. Where a supervisor is asked to intervene and solve a problem in a specific situation, a structure must be developed and evaluated to achieve this. This mostly applies to working within institutions and has the character of conflict management or crisis intervention. The long-term process is intricately intertwined with organizational structure and culture. The supervisor has a difficult stance: he/she must be at sufficient distance to discriminate organizational and group dynamics and at the same time close enough to be taken seriously by the team or the group.

Stages of group and team supervision training

A group supervisor needs, firstly, techniques to help the group understand the supervision process, and needs to be able to use skills and knowledge as a counsellor and individual supervisor to help supervisees solve problems on the level of diagnosis and technique. The supervisor learns to facilitate the group process and to use the resources of the group members in a structured way. He/she needs this structure to reassure the group and himself. Attention is restricted to the current session. Supervision and training at this stage are directed toward structuring and facilitating the group process. In training workshops, a beginning group supervisor usually makes a number of mistakes. In our model, trainees get an opportunity to play the supervisor role in a group of six to eight peers, for a time span of half an hour. Usually the supervisor starts to offer supervision on an individual basis, as learned in the first year of the training. He/she loses touch with the group and discovers after twenty minutes that the resources of the group were not used at all. In that time, group members get bored, resign and withdraw or become somewhat rebellious. The supervisor has to learn to involve the group in the clarification, contracting and intervention stages. Once able to do this, the supervisor can relax and utilize group resources in the supervision process. In the later stages he/she starts to use knowledge of complex systems with teams and larger organizations, thinking in informal and formal roles and recognizing the primary task of organizational systems. The supervisor is able to recognize repeated patterns in the behaviour of the group and group members, and is able to recognize parallel processes and similarities between team members, and can diagnose more complex patterns in group behaviour, such as scapegoating team members and how group behaviours are used to reduce anxiety. Supervision at this stage is directed toward the recognition of complex patterns and the function of these patterns with regard to anxiety reduction and system stabilization. Teaching will be in the field of complex dynamic systems. An experienced supervisor is able to discriminate group and organizational process with the help of his/her own counter-transference process. Supervision is now directed toward keeping the supervisor in contact with his/her own skills and intuition and the utilization of counter-transference experiences and behaviour within the context of the supervision process.

A training programme

In illustrating the consequences of the above for supervision training, I will refer to the diploma course at the Institute for the Application of the Social Sciences (IAS). The institute offers a three-year programme in supervision, team development and coaching, covering sixty-three days of classroom learning and sixty hours of supervised supervision. In the first year, the techniques and theory of individual supervision are taught and trained. The second year focuses on group and team supervision, and the third year teaches the basics of organizational consulting as considered relevant for supervisors.

The programme consists of six parts:

- seminars on theory and applications
- skill-training seminars
- yearly one-week intensive seminars
- supervised supervision
- intervision groups
- supervision given by the trainee

The IAS offers working conferences in which a number of training groups together build a large transitory organization in which different tasks have to be fulfilled by different groups in a number of different learning events. Large group meetings make it possible to explore the dynamics of the system as a whole.

The skills training consists of ten one-day workshops, in which specific techniques for group and team supervision are taught in groups of twelve to fourteen participants. In these sessions, group processes are taught at the level of single interventions and at the level of sessions. Video recording is used to analyse the process at a micro-level. Topics regarding group and team supervision are:

- acquisition and contracting

- verbal intervention techniques
- non-verbal methods
- training group supervision
- role-play
- visualizing group processes
- training team supervision
- ethics and professional practice

Conclusion

Training in group and team supervision is a complex task, which is built upon basic skills in individual supervision, but requires additional skills in the field of group dynamics, management and organizational consultancy. It is recommended that such training programmes be staffed with experts from different fields, because every trainee must develop his or her own voice from a broad variety of models. It is also strongly recommended that trainees collect their own experience as a member of different types of working groups, to be able to find a still point in themselves when around them everything is in uproar. More than in individual supervision, trainees must become aware of issues of group, political and organizational culture, because these issues play important roles in the dynamics of groups and organizations.

References

Bion, W.F. (1961) *Experiences in Groups*. New York: Basic Books.

Clarkson, P. (1992) *Transactional Analysis Psychotherapy. An Integrated Approach*. London: Routledge.

Dryden, W. and Thorne, B. (eds) (1991) *Training and Supervision for Counselling in Action*. London: Sage.

English, F. (1975) The three-cornered contract. *Transactional Analysis Journal*, 5: 383–4.

Hawkins, P. and Shohet, R. (1989) *Supervision in the Helping Professions. An Individual, Group and Systems Approach*. Milton Keynes: Open University Press.

Hilb, Martin (1998) *Integriertes Personalmanagement*. Berlin: Luchterhand.

Holloway, E. (1995) *Clinical Supervision: A Systems Approach*. Thousand Oaks, CA: Sage.

Kernberg, O.F. (1998) *Narcissistic Personality Disorder*. Philadelphia, PA: Harcourt Brace Jovanovich.

Lacoursiere, R. (1980). *Life Cycles of Groups*. New York: Human Sciences Press.

Schwartz, H. (1990). *Narcissistic Process and Corporate Decay. The Theory of the Organisation Ideal*. New York: New York University Press.

Stoltenberg, C.D. and Delworth, U. (1987) *Supervising Counselors and Therapists. A Developmental Approach*. San Francisco: Jossey-Bass.

Tuckman, B.W. (1965) Developmental sequences of small groups. *Psychological Bulletin*, 63 (6): 384–99.

Yalom, I.D. (1970) *The Theory and Practice of Group Psychotherapy*. New York: Basic Books.

6 Training for Multi-Cultural Supervision

Hardin L.K. Coleman

Clinical supervision is the process through which an accomplished or experienced member of a profession oversees the work of a junior member of that profession as he or she develops competence in the core functions of the profession. Ideally supervisors facilitate the supervisee's acquisition of competence within a structured relationship. Holloway (1995) suggested that the process of this relationship includes specific tasks and functions. The goal of this chapter is to describe ways in which these tasks and functions can be used to develop the multi-cultural counselling competence of the supervisee within the supervision process. Several steps will be taken to achieve this goal. The first will be to present some of the core assumptions underlying theories of multi-cultural counselling competence, with particular attention paid to the different perspectives as to how that construct can be defined. The second is to give an overview of the challenges facing supervisors in facilitating multi-cultural counselling competence in the supervisee. The third will be to articulate techniques that can be used in supervision to facilitate this competence and that address not only contextual issues surrounding the supervisory relationship but also the tasks and functions within the supervision process.

Perpectives in multi-cultural counselling

As Tyler, Brome, and Williams (1991) have suggested, theories of multi-cultural counselling tend to reflect one of three perspectives. The first perspective, the universalist, assumes that issues of culture are secondary to issues of individual personality. The universalist believes that the process of development is common across all cultures and that the individual's psychological development is the primary focus of counselling. The universalist assumes that the focus of counselling is on an essential human nature that all clients share. Treatment, therefore, needs to focus on the particular disorder of the client and whether or not the counsellor has the requisite skills to implement that treatment (for example, play therapy or systematic desensitization). Cultural factors such as race, gender or class, are not perceived as relevant concerns. If addressed, they come into counselling as presented and interpreted by the client.

Particularist is the label that Tyler, Brome and Williams (1991) give to the second perspective. The particularist assumes that the primary predictor of a client's worldview and sense of self will be dominated by a particular cultural factor (for example ethnicity or gender). In counselling, therefore, a primary focus will be to gain an understanding of how that cultural factor has led to the development of the disorder and is part of the how the disorder will be remediated. A significant amount of the counselling that is done from the particularist perspective has a strong psycho-educational component. For example, Bass and Coleman (1997), in a school-based intervention for under-achieving adolescents of African descent, spent most of their intervention teaching the participants how their cultural history affects both the problems they encounter and the solutions that are available to them. Specifically, the intervention involves teaching the participants certain Afrocentric principles and then helping the participants apply those principles in their daily living. What makes this a particularist approach is that it assumes that both the source and resolution of the client's problem primarily exist within their cultural rather than personal being.

One core assumption of the third perspective, the transcendentalist, is that both the client and counsellor have vast cultural experiences that deeply influence their worldviews and behaviour. Another core assumption is that it is the individual who has to make sense of and interpret those experiences. The transcendent or multi-cultural perspective suggests there are normative assumptions that can be made about individuals based on cultural factors such as race, gender and class, but that it is just as important to understand how these normative assumptions become reality through the idiosyncratic choices made by individual members of a group. For example, from the transcendent perspective it is equally important to understand how cultural expectations concerning body image affect the development of an eating disorder, as it is to understand the eating disordered client's family relations or his or her personal drive for control. These personal, familial and cultural factors are not perceived as independent contributors to the disorder but represent a complex interaction of factors that facilitate the expression of the disorder. The focus of treatment, therefore, has to include the client's interpretation of these factors as well as psycho-educational work on the role contextual factors have in the aetiology and maintenance of the disorder.

Sue, Ivey and Pedersen (1996) have articulated six assumptions that they believe are core issues in multi-cultural counselling which reflect the essence of the transcendent perspective. These assumptions are summarized as follows:

Assumption 1: Theories of counselling are cultural artifacts and, therefore, represent cultural worldviews. To be applicable, a counselling theory needs to articulate with the worldview of the client and counsellor.

Assumption 2: The counsellor's and client's identities reflect the totality of their experiences across multiple relationships and contexts.

Assumption 3: Cultural identity is a major determinant of the counsellor's and client's attitudes toward self and others.

Assumption 4: Effective counselling needs to be consistent with the life experiences and cultural values of the client.

Assumption 5: Effective interventions must address the context of the client's life and the counsellor be willing to involve helping relationships beyond the individual therapist (for example, community leaders or traditional/indigenous healers).

Assumption 6: The liberation of consciousness is a basic goal of multi-cultural counselling as it emphasizes the importance of expanding the client's understanding of his or her relationship to self, family, community and multiple cultures.

What is evident from these assumptions is that the cultural contexts of both the client and counsellor are active and important aspects of what happens in counselling and, therefore, the supervision relationship. It is within the supervisory relationship that the counsellor in training can receive guidance and support to integrate what he or she knows about cultural factors into effective counselling practice. To facilitate this integration, the supervisor needs to have (a) a theory of how cultural factors affect the counselling process; (b) a willingness to listen for how the supervisee does or does not address cultural factors in counselling; and (c) the ability to provide guidance, feedback and instruction to the supervisee on how to integrate ideas about cultural factors into counselling practice. As Tyler, Brome and Williams (1991) have categorized these theories of multi-cultural counselling, it is different from identifying one's preferred method of counselling (for example, psychodynamic or interpersonal process), as multicultural counselling involves articulating how and when one addresses issues of culture within the counselling process. Is culture secondary as with the universalist, is it central as with the particularist, or is it part of the warp and woof of the counselling as with the transcendentalist? To the question asked that way, the socially appropriate answer may seem obvious. How many of us, however, ask our supervisees about cultural factors when the counselling relationship (or the counselling and supervisory relationship) appears to be homogeneous across obvious cultural factors? Do we encourage our supervisees to help the client explore issues of cultural identity when both the counsellor and client are white, or just when the relationship is cross-raced? Do we encourage the exploration of gender issues when both the client and counsellor are male and the issue is not gender-identifiable (for example, workaholism, domestic abuse or violence)?

My experience as a supervisor in both school and community mental health settings suggests that issues of culture are most frequently raised when they are creating a problem in the assessment or treatment of the presenting problem. If the cross-cultural or cross-gender differences in language or interpretation inhibit the supervisee's ability to feel that he or she understands the client, then there is a willingness to explore cultural factors. When these issues are not obvious, they are too often considered irrelevant. A disturbingly common response among supervisees when asked about the client's ethnicity, if it was not offered, is a look of surprise and a query as to the question's relevance. Even more common is the extreme discomfort that comes when I ask a supervisee to make an educated assessment concerning the class of a client, especially if that client is a member of a dominant ethnic group. Even less common are assessments of cultural factors in the larger context in which the counselling relationship exists. Recently, when supervising counsellors who were in local placements, many of the supervisees did not know the dominant employer in the area in which they were working.

Given the general emphasis towards a universalist perspective in counselling training programmes it is not surprising that counsellors and supervisors tend to address issues of culture only when they are problematic. In order to facilitate the development of multi-cultural counselling competence in counsellors, it is necessary for supervisors to develop an explicit and structured approach to this aspect of their supervision (Leong and Wagner, 1994). The supervisor needs to be able to articulate at all levels of the supervision, how he or she is helping supervisees to integrate this competence into their professional identity. A universalist, particularist and transcendentalist, will do this in different ways. In the rest of this chapter, I want to present the process of developing multi-cultural counselling competence that can be used in supervision from a transcendent perspective. This process addresses institutional factors, issues concerning the tasks and functions of supervision, as well as the relationship between the supervisor and supervisee.

Institutional factors affecting the acquisition of multi-cultural counselling competence

To facilitate the acquisition of multi-cultural counselling competence, the process needs to start at the institutional level. In clinical training programmes, this can be achieved by integrating issues of culture throughout the programme (Coleman and Wampold, 1993; LaFromboise and Foster, 1992). The ability to work with a culturally diverse clientele needs to be understood as a core counselling competence rather than a specialization. This can be achieved in several ways. One is to identify experience of working with culturally diverse populations as part of the admissions criteria (along with traditional criteria such as academic competence and counselling experience) for both students and faculty. Another is to include this priority in all materials that describe the programme. It is also vital to have significant representation from various cultural groups within a training programme to provide trainees with the opportunity to expand their awareness and knowledge of cultural diversity within a challenging and supportive environment. A fourth institutional factor is the inclusion of a course that focuses on multi-cultural counselling very early in the training cycle. At the practice level, however, there are two institutional factors that are particularly important in facilitating multi-cultural counselling competence, placement and evaluation.

Placement issues

An extremely effective stimulus for developing competence in working with the manner in which cultural factors affect the aetiology and treatment of psychological distress is to work with clients who have different cultural characteristics from the counsellor (for example, race or gender) and represent groups that are not members of a dominant cultural group. That is obvious but cannot be underestimated. In choosing placement sites for trainees, it is important for supervisors to have an understanding of the range of cultural issues with which a trainee will work. If the trainee has a caseload that is at least 30 per cent diverse along cultural factors, then the trainee will have consistent and obvious opportunities to explore the manner in which these factors affect the counselling process. If the trainee only sees a culturally different client sporadically, then he or she will be allowed to see multi-cultural counselling competence as a specialized skill that is only applicable in certain cases. This will also allow the trainee to become comfortable with referring such clients to 'a clinician who has the skills to work with such a population'. Within the particularist tradition, this would be an appropriate response. Within the transcendent tradition, such an action can be interpreted as resisting the acquisition of a core counselling competence comparable to resisting becoming involved in group or family counselling. In this tradition, the reason to refer would be based on explicit problems that come up within a particular relationship or in response to the client's particular level of cultural identity development (Coleman, 1996).

Case example

Bob is a 13-year-old African descendant who has been placed out of his home since he was 9 years old. He was removed from his home because his younger sister alleged he had been sexually inappropriate with her (the exact nature of the behaviour was never ascertained). The case file suggests that

> Bob, himself, was a victim of sexual abuse, but the details of that assertion are also unclear. The major reason he has stayed out of the home is that his mother has not complied with any of the treatment recommendations. Bob's mother has a history of being fairly straightforward with counsellors and caseworkers about her disdain for their interventions, her belief that Bob should just be sent home so that she can take care of him, and her resentment at having to be called to meetings to discuss the behaviour of a child in settings over which she has no control. In school and in the foster home (with African descended foster parents) Bob's behaviour can be described as oppositional-defiant. Whenever he feels threatened, which is often, he responds by verbally attacking the perceived offender. If the 'offender' challenges his attack, Bob will escalate his attack to include shouting, cursing, and, if possible, running away. He will continue to escalate until he is removed from the situation whether that be a classroom, counsellor's office or the foster home. When attacking, Bob will often use the race of the 'offender' as a reason for their not understanding him or for wanting to hurt him. Bob does not have a history of positive peer or adult relationships and has never had a consistent relationship with an adult male of any race.

There are several clinical challenges within this case. There are the issues associated with the disorder of oppositional-defiance, with sexual predation and victimization, with family dynamics, and with ethnicity (most caseworkers and school personnel on the case are European descended). A universalist would attempt to address these issues from a coherent intrapsychic perspective. A particularist would see each of these issues as calling for specialized intervention (for example, for sexual predation, cultural identity, or oppositional-defiance). A transcendent approach would call for an integrated system of care that could address these issues coherently from both an intrapsychic and contextual perspective. To that end assessments would be made to determine the relative importance of the sexual issues and oppositional-defiance. Assessments would also address the relative importance of focusing on family dynamics, school behaviour, or cultural identity development. An effective treatment plan would include a consideration of who would be the best person or programme to respond to each of Bob's needs. Such a programme might include individual therapy that addressed the intrapsychic issues as well as a psycho-educational group experience that dealt with the development of Bob's African descended cultural identity. The governing principle is that such a treatment programme would be co-ordinated, not just created on the basis of available referrals. The ethnicity of the care providers would be a part of that conscious decision-making and not an avoidant response to Bob's race-based attacks.

If this was a trainee's only experience with African descended adolescents, it would be extremely hard for him or her to develop a useful perspective. Given the difficulty of the case, it would be possible for a trainee to feel he or she was incompetent to work with adolescents, issues of sexual predation, oppositional-defiance, individuals of African descent, or any combination of these clinical factors. It is only when a trainee is also working with a depressed African descended client, a suicidal Hmong client, and a West Indian client with an adjustment disorder, that he or she can learn to discriminate the relative effect of cultural and intrapsychic factors on the aetiology of the disorder, the formation of the treatment plan, and evaluation of his or her behaviour within the counselling process. To facilitate the acquisition of this perspective, training programmes need to address the institutional factor of placement as it affects the range and type of culturally diverse clients a trainee will have on his or her caseload. Certainly, we do not suggest a counsellor is competent to work with depressed clients, if they are in a placement where they see only one or two clients with depression!

Supervisors in the training programme and in the placement site need to attend to this institutional factor. They need both to learn to expect the trainee to be competent to assess and intervene within a culturally relevant framework, and to be prepared to make institutional interventions to facilitate the acquisition of this competence. For the programme supervisor this entails not only tracking the demographics of the clients a trainee is seeing, but tracking and commenting on the degree to which the trainee includes contextual factors within her formulation, treatment plan and clinical process. If the trainee is not seeing enough culturally diverse clients to practise these skills, then the supervisor needs to be prepared to address these issues with the site supervisor. It helps if this expectation has been made clear at the beginning of the placement.

For the on-site supervisor, her responsibility is in ensuring the effective treatment of the client more than the skill development of the trainee. It is her focus, therefore, to address issues of professional competence. As she becomes aware of deficits in the trainee that are a function of his training, then the supervisor needs to intervene through giving timely and accurate feedback concerning this pattern of deficit to the training programme. It is, of course, just as important to give timely and accurate feedback when there is a pattern of competence in this area!

Evaluation tasks

As I have suggested, there are several ways in which training programmes can institutionally demonstrate their belief that multi-cultural counselling competence is a core clinical competence. A programme can include it in its admissions criteria, it can integrate these issues into the curriculum, and it can make having access to culturally diverse clientele a central characteristic of acceptable training sites. An equally important method for institutionally validating the importance and stimulating the acquisition of multi-cultural counselling competence is to make the acquisition of that competence a criterion for graduation or successful programme completion, in the same manner in which individual or group counselling is used within summative evaluation criteria. When such a criterion is expected of all students within a programme, it accomplishes several goals. It highlights the value of multi-cultural counselling as a core skill. It provides accurate and useful feedback to trainees and supervisors as to how well this skill has been integrated into the professional identity of the supervisee. Such an evaluation criterion can act as a mechanism for stimulating discussion concerning the supervisee's understanding and skills in multi-cultural counselling. At an institutional level, it allows training programmes and sites to collect information on how well, or poorly, they are preparing counsellors to work in a culturally diverse society.

As with all evaluations, there needs to be a way to assess a supervisee's multi-cultural counselling competence in both a formative and summative manner. The formative approach needs to be integrated into the process of supervision. It can be a part of the weekly dialogue and the regular summary of progress that is an essential part of all supervision. The summative evaluation should be designed to capture, at a point in time, the level and quality of competence that a supervisee has acquired. This evaluation can be used as a gateway to increasingly demanding levels of training. The evaluation criteria, therefore, must be able to recognize the interaction between a trainee's experience and expected level of competence. In other words, an experienced counsellor should be able to demonstrate higher and more sophisticated levels of competence than a counsellor who is just finishing his or her initial coursework.

Elsewhere (Coleman, 1995) I have proposed using a system of portfolio evaluation to both stimulate and evaluate the acquisition of multi-cultural counselling competence. A portfolio has some unique advantages in that it can be used throughout a counsellor's career to demonstrate his or her constantly evolving competence (Skovholt and Rønnestad, 1992). A portfolio is much more than a collection of the clinical work that a counsellor performs. In fact, the primary focus of a portfolio is to capture the counsellor's reflection about his or her work. It is that reflection that facilitates the integration of a particular skill into the counsellor's professional identity (Tuescher, 1997). My colleagues Kimberly Tuescher, Dianne Morris, Shoshana Hellman, Amy James and Catherine McConnell, and I have developed a process for the preparation of a portfolio that can be used within supervision to stimulate the acquisition of multi-cultural counselling competence at the formative level and the evaluation of that competence at the summative level. A core focus of the supervision and evaluation of the counsellors we train involves the creation of a portfolio that serves to institutionalize the value we place on multi-cultural counselling competence. In Appendix A are the specific directions we have developed for creating a portfolio, that we provide for our supervisees.

Process factors in the acquisition of multi-cultural counselling competence

Having established portfolios as a mechanism to stimulate the integration of multi-cultural counselling competence into supervisees' work and to evaluate the development of that competence, the supervisor needs to find a way to integrate this focus into the on-going process of supervision. One effective way to achieve that integration is to schedule meetings to discuss the progression of the portfolio across the domains, modalities and settings in which the competence can be demonstrated. There are several valuable outcomes of establishing regular sessions to address this particular competence. The first is that it reinforces the core nature of the competence. The second is that it facilitates the supervisee's focus on issues of culture and how they interact with his or her clinical work. The third is that it serves to focus the supervisor on these concerns, particularly when the clientele being served by the supervisee does not represent obvious cultural diversity. Since few practising supervisors received this type of training or supervision in the early stages of their careers, this formal scheduling helps avoid regression to the universalist traditions into which they were professionally acculturated.

Another effective way to stimulate this integration is to identify and explore the manner in which the supervisee is addressing, or not addressing, issues of culture within his or her clinical work on a regular basis. This is a particularly useful approach when the supervisee is working in a culturally diverse setting. In such a setting, clinicians can become desensitized to issues of culture since they are a natural part of each interaction. In my work with a cultural-specific programme that addresses the needs of African descended families in which almost all the staff is African descended, we often find that we do not remain conscious of cultural factors because we assume we know our client's worldview and how it affects them because we share it. It is the same trap that captures same-gender or same-class relationships. We become focused on the intrapsychic or diagnostic issues and cease to raise the issues as to how race, gender or class influence the problems of the client or the nature of our therapeutic relationship. Within the transcendent perspective, it is the responsibility of the supervisor constantly to reintroduce the contextual factors into the conversation.

To be effective at this process, the supervisor must have an articulated theory as to how cultural factors interact with all aspects of the counselling relationship and use that theory to guide the type of questions and directions he or she shares with the supervisee. For example, in creating case formulations, I focus on three areas: the core concerns of the client, the source of those concerns, and the strategies a client uses to manage those concerns. I hypothesize that cultural factors are most often present in the source of the concern and what a client perceives as possible strategies they can use to cope with those concerns.

Case example of a working formulation

Brenda is a 14-year-old girl of African and European descent who has significant trouble controlling her behaviour in situations of interpersonal conflict. Brenda experiences high levels of anxiety as a result of her not feeling supported by adults in her environment and she does not have a secure base from which to meet the demands of the world. Brenda copes with this anxiety by withdrawing from or evading demanding situations. When this is not possible, she responds by pushing others away from her through the use of assaultive and abusive behaviour. Unfortunately, this is her primary method for managing interpersonal conflict and her anxieties.

If a supervisee presents the above formulation, I would want to know how Brenda's bi-racial status affects her perceived level of adult support and how her movement between aggressive and passive strategies for coping with her anxiety reflects the manner in which she might be attempting to emulate contradictory cultural standards of behaviour. There is clearly no right answer to these questions. Multi-cultural counselling competence is the willingness to consider these concerns and find ways to integrate them into the assessment and treatment of clients. A supervisor, therefore, needs to be prepared to address these concerns in the supervision and find ways to make them an integrated part of the training process. One way to facilitate this process is for a supervisor to develop his or her own portfolio of multi-cultural competence in supervision.

Relationship factors in the acquisition of multi-cultural counselling competence

As Holloway (1995) has indicated, the tasks and functions of supervision are effectively accomplished within the framework of a positive working relationship between the supervisor and supervisee. Cultural factors having a significant effect on this relationship need to be assessed and addressed within the relationship in an explicit manner. Claymore-Lahammer and Yutrzenka (1997) have found that supervisees' satisfaction with and sense of multicultural counselling competence are directly related to the level of discussion of cultural factors within supervision. As with many aspects of counselling, the degree to which a supervisor is able to assess and address cultural issues within the relationship will be affected by the degree to which the supervisor has examined his or her own cultural assumptions, expectations and worldview. In terms of one of the major constructs within the field of multi-cultural counselling, the supervisor needs to understand the stage or state of his or her own cultural identity.

Cultural identity

Cultural identity is the sense that an individual has as a cultural being. For each of us, this sense is dominated by two perspectives. The first is the perspective we have of ourselves as a cultural being. The second is the cultural being to which others in our context respond. Our cultural identity becomes an integration of these internal and external perspectives. For example, I tend to think of myself as African descended in terms of my cultural sense of self. In the environment in which I work, however, others tend to respond to me as a function of my gender or class background. This incongruence can be a source of misperception and miscommunication. It is only as I am able to integrate these perceptions into my own sense of cultural identity that I can become more effective in my interpersonal relations. When my mostly female supervisees see me as a male authority figure with power, and I am thinking of myself as a member of a disenfranchised group, there is bound to be a misinterpretation of our interactions. It is only as I am able to integrate the supervisees' framework for interpreting my behaviour that I am able to establish an effective working relationship.

Case example

An African American supervisee was working in a school setting that was culturally diverse but with a staff that was predominantly of European descent. Part way through the placement I was getting feedback from his on-site supervisors concerning behaviour that they perceived as unprofessional, mostly surrounding notifying them about his plans and, most often, change of plans. Although he had discussed these issues with his on-site supervisors in terms of shared expectations, both parties felt unresolved about the issues. After some discussion it became clear that the supervisee felt that the on-

> site supervisors had a lower level of trust of his competence due to his gender and race. Furthermore, he did not want to bring up 'problems' with me because it was important to him that I maintained a positive evaluation of him based on our shared racial background. Given these racial issues, he was having a hard time using supervision for either its educative or evaluative functions. This served to interfere with his learning curve and led to repeated mistakes. Once we identified the racial expectations and stereotypes, we were able to focus on how those factors facilitated and constrained his growth, and we were able to focus more clearly on the information I needed from him to be an effective supervisor. Articulating these issues allowed us to deepen our mutual trust and significantly improved the quality of our relationship.

Strategies for coping with cultural diversity

There are various resolutions of this situation. If I was more oriented towards a Black Separatist ideology, we could have addressed this issue with the on-site supervisors as a function of their cultural imperialism. If I was more interested in assimilating into the dominant culture, I might have invalidated this supervisee's concerns by focusing on his needs to become more like his supervisors and encouraged him to internalize their time orientation. I could have done so by making 'improvement' in this area of professional conduct a central focus of his evaluation. The supervisee's strategies for coping with cultural diversity would also have a significant impact on the resolution of this problem (Coleman, 1995, 1996). Central to the resolution of conflict in multi-cultural relations are the strategies individuals use to cope with cultural diversity. Some of us manage our relationship with the dominant culture by trying to become like members of that culture (acculturation). Some of us manage diversity by removing ourselves from contact (separation). Others work to develop competence in the second culture while maintaining significant and powerful relations with our culture of origin (alternation) while yet others attempt to create environments where multiple cultural perspectives are known and respected (integration). Each one of these strategies has value for particular individuals within particular contexts. Within supervision, however, the congruence of strategies between supervisees and supervisors will have a significant impact on the working alliance.

In American K-12 education schools the primary educational goal is to prepare students to develop skills that will allow them to become successful in the dominant society. To that end, counsellors are often asked to help children to learn how to 'fit in' to the system. Often, fitting in requires that students learn how to assimilate into the dominant strategy. Several authors (Coleman, 1995, 1996; LaFromboise, Coleman and Gerton, 1993) have described the manner in which the assimilation strategy has not been effective for ethnic minorities. If a supervisee, however, believes that this is an effective strategy and the supervisor does not, this will lead to conflict and/or ineffective interventions. Given the potential for conflict within the relationship, a supervisor needs to be aware of his or her own strategy, be able to assess the strategy of the supervisee, and institute a developmental plan into the supervisory process that effectively addresses how these strategies affect the supervisee's counselling effectiveness and the relationship with the supervisor.

Case example: strategies with clients

Barbara is a middle-class European descendant who is working in a school that has a small group of African descended students who are mostly poor, a large group of European descended upper middle class, and a large group of European descended students who live on working farms. Many of the African descended students are referred to her when they are having trouble academically and are violating 'social norms' as defined by the European descended teachers. These social norms usually include issues of time orientation, time spent on homework, and noise level. At the start of the supervisory relationship, it is evident that the supervisee knows very little about African American culture and has no social relations with members of that ethnic group. In discussing the challenges facing these students, it is evident that she believes that they would be best served if they could learn how to match the expectations of the teachers in terms of time orientation, homework, and noise level. She is considering starting a group with these students that focuses on the acquisition of these skills. The supervisor believes that not only does this supervisee use the separation strategy in her own life, but advocates the assimilation strategy for ethnic minority students. The supervisor believes that this latter strategy is a very ineffective one for ethnic minority students and, when presented to such students, is often met with disdain for and rejection of the counsellor. If the supervisor points this out, the probable response from the supervisee might be disbelief, argument, or, worse, foreclosure on discussing issues of culture with the supervisor. A more effective and developmental intervention would be to recommend that the supervisor spend time interviewing the students to understand their perspective on the problem. This would facilitate the supervisee's acquisition of awareness and knowledge about the students' culture which may serve to contradict her personal strategy of separation. If the supervisee can be helped to appreciate the students' perspective (integration or alternation) she can be helped to develop an intervention that honours the students' cultural perspective while facilitating the acquisition of skills that are useful in this school environment (alternation). Such an approach to the supervision allows the supervisee to acquire a different response set that is appropriate to the cultural needs of her students and serves to expand her repertoire of professional and personal skills.

Case example: strategies with supervisees

Joy is an African descendant working in a similar school to Barbara's. Joy's on-site and university supervisors are all European descended. Joy is very comfortable with that arrangement. Even though she went to an historically black college, most of her peer relations are with European descended individuals. Joy is often willing to share her beliefs about the needs of African descended individuals but her university supervisor has been surprised that she is often resistant to considering the role of race or other cultural factors in the aetiology and resolution of the problems her clients were reporting to her. Early in her placement, a male African descended adolescent sought her out to discuss issues he was having with truancy, his mother, and, as the counselling progressed, his relationships with girls. Through supervision, Joy was able to see the elements of this relationship that were affected by her gender (i.e., transferential issues around the client's mother) but consistently denied the racial aspects of

> the relationship even though the client regularly made references to their shared racial background. This was a case in which the cross-raced nature of the supervision was extremely helpful in expanding the multi-cultural competence of the supervisee. Given the supervisor's race, Joy's assimilation strategy was not directly challenged the way it might be in a same-raced relationship. Using humour, the supervisor consistently noted that it was interesting that she, 'the white girl', picked up on issues that Joy seemed to miss. Over time, this process allowed Joy to disclose and address issues related to race that affected her counselling competence. The supervisor, through her work and training in feminist therapy, had developed the use of an integration strategy in her personal and professional life which enabled her to accept Joy's universalistic approach to cultural factors in counselling, while simultaneously challenging her to consider alternative perspectives. A supervisor who promoted an assimilation strategy would have found great comfort in working with Joy as there would be low levels of conflict on how to interpret cultural factors in counselling. The opposite would have been true for a supervisor who used a separation strategy. In such a case, cultural factors would have been the framework for both formulating this client's concerns and implementing a treatment plan, but may have led to conflict with Joy, if not foreclosure of discussion.

In both of these cases, a supervisor who is unable to approach the strategies the supervisee uses to cope with cultural diversity from a developmental perspective is one who puts the working alliance with the supervisee at risk. Certainly, discrepancy between the supervisor's and supervisee's perspectives is a natural part of the supervision process. How those discrepancies are managed, however, will be predictive of the relationship's quality and how the supervisee can use that relationship to integrate multi-cultural counselling competence into his or her professional identity. In the first case, the supervisor used an experiential/cognitive strategy to encourage the supervisee to explore cultural factors. The supervisor assumed that by becoming more immersed in the students' interpretations of their cultural world, the supervisee would expand her range and choice of strategy. The assumption was that she would 'figure it out' as she became more responsible for working within the students' frame of reference. This strategy was appropriate for increasing the supervisee's level of awareness and knowledge. In the second case, the supervisor determined that Joy had the awareness and knowledge but was, at one level, 'choosing' not to integrate those competencies into her practice. The supervisor chose an interpersonal process approach to helping the supervisee examine her resistance to integrating her understanding of cultural factors into her practice. By having Joy examine these issues within the framework of their relationship, this facilitated Joy's examination of these factors in her personal and professional roles.

These examples of how the strategies a counsellor uses to cope with cultural diversity will affect how he or she chooses to deliver clinical services are also examples of the multiple ways in which these issues can be addressed within the supervisory relationship. In neither case would it be possible to define the right approach for the counsellor. What the supervisor in both cases was willing to do was to examine the supervisee's behaviour within a cultural framework and choose interventions that were appropriate to the supervisee's current level of multi-cultural counselling competence. Needless to say, these individual instances did not lead to wholesale change in the supervisee. These concerns needed to be raised repeatedly in order to have them integrated into the supervisee's professional identity.

Openness to cultural factors

A key element in using supervision to facilitate the acquisition of multi-cultural counselling competence is the supervisor's openness to examining the role of cultural factors in counselling on an on-going basis. This is not something that can be effectively achieved by assigning a particular week to considering cultural factors. Nor will it be effective if cultural factors come to dominate the discussion of the psychological issues facing the client and supervisee. The parallel issue in counselling is concerns about ethical behaviour. Not every counselling interaction stimulates a concern about ethical behaviour, but an understanding of ethical behaviour should guide all counselling interactions. Competent supervisors listen to every counselling interaction to make sure ethical guidelines are followed and regularly require supervisees to consider the ethical implications of their attitudes, beliefs and behaviour. To do so effectively, the supervisor must be open to ethical considerations. The same is true for multi-cultural counselling competence. Two issues need to be considered in a supervisor's openness to multi-cultural counselling competence – experience and feelings.

Supervisor's experience with cultural factors

One of the awkward moments in supervision comes when a supervisee presents a case that represents a problem with which I have little experience. One of the best moments comes when a case represents a problem with which I have worked repeatedly and about which I have immersed myself in the relevant literature on its aetiology and treatment. My personal experience of working with ethnic minorities and working within predominantly white institutions contributes to my ability to help supervisees of all races address cultural issues with their clients. It is a perspective that I could not bring to work if my supervisees were working with thought-disordered clients. To be effective in this type of supervision, I would need to take certain steps. Initially, I would have to familiarize myself with the current thinking on thought disorders. I would then need to work with several such clients under supervision. At this point, I would be better qualified to supervise others in this work. For a supervisor to be effective in helping supervisees integrate multi-cultural counselling competence into their professional identity, it is useful for the supervisor to have done so. The most effective way to achieve this integration is through supervised practice.

Supervisor's feelings about cultural factors

As important as knowledge and skills are in the practice of multicultural counselling, issues of trust tend to determine the difference between being effective and ineffective with clients (Nickerson, Helms and Terrell, 1994). Many ethnic minorities enter counselling with personal and cultural issues concerning the degree to which the counsellor will respect them as an individual and as a cultural being. The former is certainly shared by all cultures, but the latter gets exacerbated within both cross- and same-culture counselling relationships. These feelings are powerful in the client and draw powerful feelings from the counsellor. The more a counsellor is aware of his or her cultural being, the better able he or she is to manage those feelings and use them to benefit the counselling relationship. Supervisors also need to understand how they define and feel about their cultural being in order to address those feelings effectively in the supervisory relationship. Whenever I work with African descended supervisees I need to be constantly aware and responsive to two aspects of my own internalized racism. On the one hand, I need to resist my urges to protect other African descendants from discrimination and feelings of isolation. When I feel that urge to protect, I start working very hard at being accepting of the supervisee and emphasizing their strengths. In turn, this allows me not to confront them around the areas in which they need to gain greater competence. I am afraid that they will feel bad, that it will have a negative effect on their racial self-esteem, or that they will think I am rejecting them because of their race. This urge seems to be dominated by my own feelings about being African descended in a predominantly white profession, and not about the professional needs of my supervisees.

On the other hand, my internalized racism can lead to a hypercritical stance in evaluating the work of African descended students. This stance can lead me to be less perceptive concerning the quality of their work and more likely to devalue their work as coming from a stigmatized source. This gets expressed in expecting less of them and giving less feedback than I do with European descended students. In both these reactions, my feelings lead me to treat the supervisee as a member of a race rather than as an individual who has a race. When I act out of these feelings, I fail to create the positive working alliance that is based on mutual and accurate respect.

It is only through examining these uncomfortable feelings that I can gain control of them. It is when I can control them that they can become a useful part of my supervision. When I am in touch with those feelings, I am better able to respond to the positive and negative projections of my supervisees. I am also better able to work through these issues and concerns in my own life.

Conclusion

From a transcendent perspective, there is no one way to view the effect of cultural factors in counselling or supervision, but there is an imperative to explore the ways in which these factors are part of the warp and woof of counselling and supervision. In this chapter, I have attempted to describe various ways in which cultural factors can be addressed within supervision to facilitate the acquisition of multi-cultural counselling competence among supervisees. It is important to recognize that this competence can most effectively be acquired if it is addressed at the institutional and process levels of counsellor training and supervision. It is also important to recognize that this is a dynamic and ever changing process. It is the supervisor's responsibility to develop a systematic method for understanding the effect of cultural factors in his or her work and to communicate that method with supervisees and colleagues.

Appendix A: Multiculturally focused portfolios

During this semester, the portfolio will be used as a means of focusing training and learning on the area of multicultural counseling competence. Thus, you will be focusing on multicultural issues as you develop your portfolio. The term 'multicultural' is to be interpreted inclusively and will thus reflect a broad concept of diversity (i.e. age, gender, sexual orientation, physical (dis)ability, socio-economic status, race and ethnicity). Appropriate material for the portfolio would include anything that reflects your own multicultural awareness, knowledge and skills. At the end of this manual are a number of resources that may help you reach these objectives.

GUIDE TO PORTFOLIOS

A portfolio is:

> [A] purposeful, interrelated collection of student work that shows [his or her] efforts, progress or achievements in one or more areas. The collection includes evidence of [the students'] self-reflection, and their participation in setting the focus, selecting the contents, and judging merit. Activities are guided by performance standards. A portfolio ***communicates what is learned*** and ***why it is important*** (Paulson, Paulson and Meyer, 1991, p. 62, bold and italics added).

A portfolio may be used by a counselor trainee to demonstrate his or her competence in one or more areas of counseling (awareness, knowledge and skills). The development of a portfolio is guided by its **purpose** (why it is being developed), its **goals** (what will be demonstrated), and the **context** in which it is created. A portfolio consists of (a) exhibits (work selected for inclusion), and (b) reflections about the selected work.

Each portfolio is the unique creation of its developer, and no two portfolios are exactly the same. Guidelines, rather than specific dictates, are provided to aid in the development of the portfolio. Material can be selected and 'deselected' for the portfolio at any time during its development, and the final decision regarding what goes into the portfolio is made by each individual trainee.

PURPOSE OF A PORTFOLIO

Portfolios generally serve one (or both) of two functions:

1. **Pedagogical** (where the focus is on instruction and learning)
2. **Assessment** (where the focus is on formative and summative evaluation)

a. *Formative assessment* – the ongoing assessment of the trainee's progress

b. *Summative assessment* – the final, or end-point assessment of the trainee's status compared to an external, professional standard of excellence

The purpose of the portfolio will guide its development and the types of material selected to be included. At this time, there is greater empirical support for the use of portfolios in instruction and learning than in assessment.

GOALS

The portfolio should provide concrete evidence of your awareness, knowledge and skill in counseling – it will reflect what you know and are able to do. The portfolio assembled this semester might be used to demonstrate:

(a) Your current level of multicultural counseling knowledge, awareness, and skill
(b) Your particular strengths and identify areas in which you need more experience
(c) The progress you have made over the course of the semester

A key component of any portfolio is the **self-reflections** that are required at each step of portfolio development. Self-reflections are documented in brief **'captions'** that accompany each 'exhibit' selected for inclusion in the portfolio, as well as in a **'competence statement'** completed at the end of the semester summarizing your efforts and learning. 'Caption' forms are provided with this manual to help guide the self-reflection process.

As you review your portfolio over the course of the semester, it will provide the basis for ongoing (formative) self-evaluation, which may be helpful in guiding your future efforts.

STEPS IN DEVELOPING A PORTFOLIO

1. **Determine the function/purpose of the portfolio** – As part of your training, your portfolio will be used as a strategy for instruction and learning. It will also be used as a form of assessment of your competence in this area.
2. **Establish learning goals** – what you will demonstrate through the portfolio exhibits
3. **Development of the portfolio**
   a. ***Table of Contents*** – a 'working' exhibit which is open to modification and revision as exhibits are selected (and deselected). At the end of the semester, a final table of contents should be included in the front of the completed portfolio.
   b. ***Competence statement*** – also a 'working' exhibit during the semester, completed in final form at the end of the semester. The competence statement should include:
      i. Your goals for the portfolio
      ii. What you learned (strengths and areas where there is room for change, growth or improvement)
      iii. The personal meaning of what was learned
   c. ***Portfolio exhibits/selections*** may be drawn directly from class assignments
   d. Each selection should be accompanied by a ***brief caption*** with the following information:
      i. Title of the exhibit
      ii. Date and context in which the item was produced
      iii. Brief description of the selection
      iv. Statement as to why the item was selected
      v. What competence you feel the selection demonstrates
4. **Organization of the Portfolio** – The portfolio should be organized so that a third person, unfamiliar with your work, can understand and evaluate the material.
5. **Establish a Time-line for the Development of the Portfolio** including the date for submission of the completed project.

CONFIDENTIALITY

In developing counseling portfolios, steps must be taken to ensure confidentiality of the materials selected for inclusion.

1. Remove any information that identifies individuals or institutions (unless the portfolio is being used only within the institution).
2. If identifying information cannot be removed (i.e. videotape), the individuals whose material is being used must give their informed consent. A copy of that written consent must be included in the portfolio.

Appendix B: Issues in multicultural counseling competence

LEARNING OBJECTIVES for Multicultural Training (Ridley, Mendoza and Kanitz, 1994). Culturally competent counselors should demonstrate:

1. Culturally responsive behaviors (i.e. appropriate cultural factors reflected in *observable* behaviors, that are *beneficial* to the client (or other persons in the professional setting)
2. Ethical knowledge and practice pertaining to multicultural counseling and training issues
3. Cultural empathy (reflected through (a) identification of culturally relevant applications of traditional counseling skills, (b) modification of traditional counseling skills/ techniques to make them culturally relevant, and (c) creating new skills/techniques when necessary to address the needs of culturally different clients)
4. The ability to critique existing counseling theories for cultural relevance
5. Development of an individualized theoretical orientation that is culturally relevant
6. Knowledge of normative characteristics of cultural groups
7. Cultural self-awareness (i.e. cultural heritage, values, assumptions, world view)
8. Knowledge of within-group differences (i.e. level of acculturation, age, individual expression of cultural values, cultural identity)
9. Knowledge of multicultural counseling concepts and issues
10. Respect for cultural differences

CAPTION SHEET

Title (of the exhibit) ______________________________

Date ______________________________

Brief description of the selection

____

____

____

____

____

What competence do you feel the exhibit demonstrates?

____

____

____

____

____

Why was the exhibit selected (why is this exhibit important to you)?

____

____

____

____

____

What did you learn as a result of producing this exhibit?

____

____

____

____

____

DIMENSIONS OF PERSONAL IDENTITY
(Arredondo et al., 1996) Characteristics that contribute to each individual's identity. Different characteristics will be more or less important, depending on the individual.

- **Dimension 'A'** – Characteristics that are innate, or basically 'fixed' and, therefore, less changeable:

  Age, culture, ethnicity, gender, language, physical disability, race, sexual orientation, social class
- **Dimension 'B'** – Characteristics which often reflect the consequences of the first and last dimensions ('A' and 'C' noted above and below):

  Educational background, geographic location, income, marital status, religion, work experience, citizenship status, military experience, hobbies/recreational interests
- **Dimension 'C'** – Characteristics of the individual's historical, political, sociocultural, and economic environments (contexts). Events over which the individual has little or no control:

  Historical moments or events, eras (i.e. Vietnam War), relationship between the United States and an individual's country of origin, periods of oppression or disenfranchisement

QUESTIONS TO GUIDE THE EXPLORATION OF MULTICULTURAL ISSUES

The following questions may be used to raise your awareness of multicultural issues.

1a. What are the main demographic variables that make up my own cultural identity and that of my client (i.e. age, gender, sexual orientation, socioeconomic status, race/ethnicity)?
1b. What worldviews (e.g. assumptions, values) do I bring to the counseling relationships based on my cultural identity?
2a. What value systems, based on my demographic identities, are inherent in my approach to counseling?
2b. What value systems, based on my demographic identities, underlie the strategies and techniques I use in counseling?
3a. What knowledge do I possess about the worldview of my client (who may have different cultural identities from me)?
3b. What skills do I possess for working with clients who have different cultural identities from me? What other skills would be helpful to learn?
4a. What are some of my concerns and/or challenges in working with clients who are culturally different from me?
4b. How are these issues best resolved?
5. How might I improve my ability to work with culturally diverse clients?

Table 6.1 *Summary of multicultural counseling competencies and standards*

	Counselor awareness of own assumptions, values and biases	Understanding the worldview of the culturally different client	Developing appropriate strategies and techniques
Beliefs/ attitudes	1. Is culturally self-aware; values and respects differences 2. Is aware of how his or her own cultural background and experiences, attitudes, and values and biases influence psychological processes 3. Recognizes limits of his or her own competence and expertise 4. Is comfortable with differences between self and client	1. Is aware of his or her own negative emotional reactions towards culturally different clients and the potentially negative impact they might have on the client in counseling 2. Is aware of personal stereotypes and preconceived notions regarding those who differ from him or herself	1. Respects clients' religious and spiritual beliefs and values (including those regarding physical and/or mental functioning) 2. Respects indigenous helping practices and minority community help-giving networks 3. Values bilingualism and does not consider another language a hindrance in counseling
Knowledge	1. Knows own racial and cultural heritage and how it affects perceptions of normality and abnormality and of counseling 2. Knows how oppression, racism, discrimination, and stereotyping affect oneself and one's work – this allows counselors to acknowledge their own racism 3. Understands the social impact he or she may have on others. Is knowledgeable about different styles of communication and how his or her own style may help or hinder communication with a culturally different client	1. Knows about the life experiences, cultural heritage, and historical background of his or her clients 2. Understands how race, culture, and ethnicity may affect development of personality, vocational choices, psychological disorders, help seeking behaviors, and the (in)appropriateness of counseling approaches 3. Knows about and understands the sociopolitical influences in the lives of racial/ethnic minorities (i.e. integration, poverty, racism, stereotyping, powerlessness)	1. Knows and understands how generic counseling (culture bound, class bound and monolingual) may conflict with minority cultural values 2. Knows how institutional barriers prevent minorities from using mental health services 3. Knows about bias in assessment tools; considers clients' cultural and linguistic characteristics when selecting procedures and interpreting findings 4. Is familiar with minority family structures, hierarchies, values and beliefs as well as with community and family resources 5. Recognizes discriminatory practices operating in client's environment and

			how they affect psychological functioning
Skills	1. Seeks out continuing education, consultation, and training to expand understanding and effectiveness in working with culturally different populations; recognizes personal limits of competence and consults, refers, and/or seeks more training when appropriate 2. Constantly tries to understand self as a racial/cultural being and to develop a nonracist identity	1. Is familiar with relevant research and findings regarding mental health issues of culturally different groups – constantly seeks to develop cross-cultural knowledge, understanding and skills 2. Becomes involved with minorities outside of counseling setting so that perspective is more than academic (community events, social/political functions, celebrations, friendships)	1. Is able to send and receive (accurately and appropriately) a variety of verbal and nonverbal messages. Uses a variety of approaches to avoid culture bound and inappropriate services. 2. Initiates institutional interventions on client's behalf; identifies problems due to racism and/or bias to prevent clients from inappropriately blaming themselves 3. Seeks consultation with traditional healers or spiritual leaders when appropriate 4. Interacts in language preferred by client (seeks appropriate translator or refers to bilingual counselor when necessary) 5. Is trained in (and is familiar with cultural limitations of) assessment and testing procedures 6. Is sensitive to issues of oppression, sexism and racism and works to eliminate biases, prejudices, and discriminatory practices. Is aware of sociopolitical contexts in conducting evaluations and providing services 7. Educates client in processes of psychological intervention (i.e. goals, expectations, legal rights, counselor's theoretical orientation)

Table 6.2 *Multicultural counseling competence within specific treatment modalities and across treatment settings*

The following are suggestions of how multicultural counseling competence may be demonstrated within specific treatment modalities and treatment settings (Sue et al., 1992)

	Awareness	Knowledge	Skills	Relationship
Self	Is fully aware of what it means to be a member of his/her own culture	Has examined and understands his/her stage of racial identity	Can manage non-verbal cues to facilitate communication with a culturally different client	Is aware of social customs and culturally mitigated styles of interaction; is aware of the effect of racial identity on inter-personal relationships
Modalities				
Individual	Can recognize a cultural concern	Can describe the cultural etiology of a pattern of behavior	Can address a cultural concern within counseling (e.g. recovery skills)	Is aware of implications of gender differences within a cultural context
Group	Includes culturally relevant materials in handouts	Can design a culturally relevant intervention	Can resolve a within-group conflict that is cultural in its etiology	Is sensitive to group dynamics and communication styles that may be related to cultural differences
Family	Is aware that parental role is different in each culture	Knows the parental role within particular cultures	Adjusts interventions to be culturally relevant	Is cognizant of cultural differences in family structure, and of relationships among members of the 'family' (culturally defined)
Consultation	Can identify culture norms within an organization	Knows how different cultures react to different organizational styles	Can facilitate a discussion about cultural norms in culturally diverse and homogeneous organizations	Is sensitive to and (where appropriate) actively enlists the aid of culturally sanctioned helpers (e.g.

				members of the client's religious community; shaman)
Case Manager	Aware that context can influence help-seeking behavior	Knows what type of interventions are culturally appropriate	Adjusts interventions to fit the cultural norms of clients	Is aware of, and when possible, facilitates, the relationships the client must negotiate to resolve his/her issues, taking into account the role of cultural differences
Settings				
School	Is aware that guidance activities need to include culturally diverse materials	Can design guidance activities that are culturally relevant	Has equivalent success with minority and majority students	Understands how the client's culture may affect relationships with peers
Hospital	Is aware of the relationship between culture and health beliefs	Can design programs that maximize access to treatment by culturally diverse clients	Has successfully implemented such a program	Is aware of power differentials within the hospital community and is cognizant of racism/ discrimination that may interfere with appropriate delivery of health care
Community	Is aware of the relationship between culture and help-seeking behavior	Can design programs that maximize access to treatment by culturally diverse clients	Has successfully implemented such a program	Understands the relationships among and between cultural groups in the client's community

References

Arredondo, P., Toporek, R., Brown, S.P., Jones, J., Locke, D.C., Sanchez, J. and Stadler, H. (1996) Operationalization of the multicultural counseling competencies. *Journal of Multicultural Counseling and Development*, 24: 42–78.

Bass, C.K. and Coleman, H.L.K. (1997) Enhancing the cultural identity of early adolescent male African Americans. *Professional School Counselor*, 1: 48–51.

Bernard, J.M. and Goodyear, R.K. (1992) *Fundamentals of Clinical Supervision*. Boston: Allyn & Bacon.

Claymore-Lahammer, V. and Yutrzenka, B.A. (1997) Influence of ethnicity and multicultural discussions within supervision on supervisees. Paper presented at the 105th Annual Convention of the American Psychological Association. Chicago, IL.

Coleman, H.L.K. (1995) Strategies for coping with cultural diversity. *The Counseling Psychologist*, 23: 722–40.

Coleman, H.L.K. (1995, August) Conflict in multicultural counseling relationships: source and resolution. Paper presented at the meeting of the American Psychological Association. New York City.

Coleman, H.L.K. (1996, August) Heuristics for choosing cultural specific treatment. Paper presented at the meeting of the American Psychological Association. Toronto, Canada.

Coleman, H.L.K. and Wampold, B.E. (1993, August) An integrated curriculum: course examples. Paper presented at the meeting of the American Psychological Association. Toronto, Canada.

Constantine, M.G. (1997) Facilitating multicultural competency in counseling supervision. In D.B. Pope-Davis and H.L.K. Coleman (eds), *Multicultural Counseling Competencies: Assessment, Education and Training, and Supervision* (pp. 310–24). Thousand Oaks, CA: Sage.

Holloway, E.L. (1995) *Clinical Supervision: A Systems Approach*. Thousand Oaks, CA: Sage.

LaFromboise, T.D. and Foster, S.L. (1992) Cross-cultural training: scientist-practitioner model and methods. *Counseling Psychologist*, 20: 472–89.

LaFromboise, T.D., Coleman, H.L.K. and Gerton, J. (1993) Psychological impact of biculturalism: evidence and theory. *Psychological Bulletin*, 114: 395–412.

Leong, F.T. and Wagner, N.S. (1994) Cross-cultural counseling supervision: what do we know? What do we need to know? *Counselor Education and Supervision*, 34: 117–31.

Nickerson, K.J., Helms, J.E. and Terrell, F. (1994) Cultural mistrust, opinions about mental illness, and Black students' attitudes toward seeking psychological help from White counselors. *Journal of Counseling Psychology*, 41: 378–85.

Paulson, F.L., Paulson, P.P. and Meyer, C.A. (1991) What Makes a Portfolio a Portfolio? *Educational Leadership*, 48: 60–3.

Pope-Davis, D.B. and Coleman, H.L.K. (eds) (1997) *Multicultural Counseling Competencies: Assessment, Education and Training, and Supervision*. Thousand Oaks, CA: Sage.

Ridley, C.R., Mendoza, D.W. and Kanitz, B.E. (1994) Multicultural training: reexamination, operationalization, and integration. *The Counseling Psychologist*, 22: 227–89.

Skovholt, T.M. and Rønnestad, M.H. (1992) *The Evolving Professional Self: Stages and Themes in Therapist and Counselor Development*. New York: Wiley.

Sue, D.W., Arredondo, P. and McDavis, R.J. (1992) Multicultural counseling competencies and standards: a call to the profession. *Journal of Counseling and Development*, 70: 477–86.

Sue, D.W., Ivey, A.E. and Pedersen, P.B. (1996) *A Theory of Multicultural Counseling and Therapy.* Pacific Grove, CA: Brooks/Cole Publishing.

Tuescher, K.D. (1997) *The Effect of Portfolios on Self-reflection in Counseling Students.* Unpublished dissertation, University of Wisconsin-Madison.

Tyler, F.B., Brome, D.R. and Williams, J.E. (1991) *Ethnic Validity, Ecology, and Psychotherapy: A Psychosocial Competence Model*. New York: Plenum Press.

7 Training for Supervision Evaluation

Maria Gilbert and Charlotte Sills

Introduction

We conceptualize the task of evaluation in supervision as assessing answers to the following questions: What is the aim of supervision? Is that aim being achieved?

This chapter focuses on training supervisors in the evaluation of their supervision. Supervisors generally agree that the goal of supervision is to enhance the quality of the service to the client and towards this end to develop the competence of the practitioner. Given this focus, in thinking about training for evaluation, we consider it important for the supervisor to reflect on what evaluation might mean in their own particular context and within their own theoretical orientation. The specific answers to the above questions, the details of what constitutes an enhancement of service and what particular skills are relevant in the repertoire of the supervisee, will be influenced by (a) the person's orientation; (b) the context in which they work; and (c) their individual style and preferences.

For example, the person-centred supervisor might see the exercise of the 'core conditions' as central to the practitioner's work and therefore shape his interventions in such a way that congruence and empathy are modelled. In an analytic framework, on the other hand, where interpretive skill and self-analysis might be deemed to be more important, the supervisor will place a high emphasis on the explication of intrapsychic dynamics. Similarly, the supervisor of a practitioner who is working in a setting where the intervention for the client is limited to six sessions will be focusing in supervision on what can be realistically achieved in that time frame. A supervisor who ignores this critical time dimension will not be offering an appropriate or effective service to the supervisee.

All supervisors, in defining their task and goals in the supervision process, will need to answer for themselves such questions as:

What factors do I believe represent an effective service to the client? (This starts to include a definition of therapy and its goals.)
What does the client consider to be an effective service?
What constitutes safe and ethical practice?
What skills and competence do I believe are effective in a therapist?
How would such skills be learned in supervision?
What is the supervisor's contribution to the achievement of the desired outcomes?

The specific answers to these questions will influence supervisors' style and methodology of supervision. The training of supervisors in evaluation should therefore involve inviting them to think about what evaluation would uniquely mean to them given their particular orientation and circumstances. Given these differences there are, however, certain elements common to the evaluation of supervision which span orientations and contexts, and these will be our focus in this chapter.

Different methods of evaluation

Evaluation of supervision can be approached in any or all of the four ways described below:

Self-evaluation of the process of supervision

This can be achieved by the supervisor reflecting on her own responses and the reactions of the supervisee to her interventions in the supervisory dialogue. This would mean assessing in an ongoing way whether you as a supervisor are attuned to the supervisee and are responding accurately to the supervisee's needs of supervision. For example, a supervisor may sometimes give feedback in an overly critical manner that leads the supervisee to feel shamed and so avoid bringing crucial issues to supervision in the future. Alternatively, the supervisor might reflect after the session on an audiotaped recording of the process, using a technique such as Interpersonal Process Recall (Kagan, 1980).

Self-evaluation of the outcome of supervision

This may involve questions such as: Did I as supervisor meet the supervisory contract? Does the supervisee feel 'helped' by having a clearer idea of the way forward? This is particularly helpful in situations where the supervision may be flowing along 'too smoothly' or may have settled into a comfortable routine and the supervisor questions whether he is missing critical elements in the supervisee's process or is being induced in some subtle way to avoid certain difficult areas.

Other-evaluation

This may involve evaluation by peers or of a supervising supervisor/consultant. It can be evaluation of micro-skills, of a sessional outcome or outcomes over time. The advantage of this type of evaluation is that a person outside the process is able, for example, to spot parallel processes, or whether an effective contract has been made and fulfilled. A supervisor is as susceptible as a counsellor or psychotherapist to entering into confluence with or becoming enmeshed in the supervisee's process, where an uninvolved outsider's view can be invaluable.

Evaluation by consumers

In this case the consumers are the practitioners receiving supervision who can either be asked for direct verbal feedback in a supervision review or requested to give feedback in a questionnaire. In this way, supervisors can gain valuable information both on style and on the effectiveness of what they are delivering. Contrary to popular belief, research suggests that it is not the overly careful and 'nice' supervisor who is valued, but the one who provides both support and evaluation in an open honest manner (Austin and Altekruse, 1972; Dodenhoff, 1981; Henry et al., 1993; Holloway and Neufeldt, 1995; Holloway and Poulin, 1995; Leddick and Dye, 1987).

We regard feedback as integral to the evaluation process. Carifio and Hess (1987) report in some detail the results of a study by Freeman (1985) in which are outlined important considerations for the supervisor delivering feedback. Since giving feedback is the essential component of any evaluation, we summarize these findings here to serve as a guide for the supervisor in his evaluative task, whether within a session, at the end of a session or at the end of a period of supervision. Effective feedback, according to Freeman (1985), possesses the following characteristics:

1 It is systematic (objective, accurate, consistent and reliable, minimally influenced by subjective variables).
2 It is timely (delivered soon after the event).
3 It is clearly understood (both positive and negative feedback are based on explicit and specific performance criteria).
4 It is reciprocal (feedback is provided in two-way interactions in which suggestions are made, not as the only way to approach a problem, but as only one of a number of potentially useful alternatives).

These findings suggest that the supervisor's feedback will be most effective if it is directly related to aspects of performance, for example, to a detailed analysis of interventions of a particular piece of work with a client. For this reason, we find that using audio or videotaped segments of a session as the basis for supervision provides both the therapist and the supervisor with specific material for discussion and evaluation. A particular intervention or series of interventions can then be reviewed from the perspective of the outcomes that followed and how these did or did not relate to the therapeutic goals. Such micro-skills analysis helps the supervisee to develop internalized criteria for judging for herself whether an intervention is effective or not, which is one of the most important goals of supervision.

We will now proceed to discuss the model we have developed for conceptualizing supervision evaluation. In this model (Figure 7.1), we offer a variety of lenses through which to evaluate supervision from the micro-skills level through to outcomes over time. Each of the four methods discussed above can be used at each level. Examples and suggestions are offered throughout the discussion which follows the diagram.

Depending on your learning style, you may wish to use this diagram from the top down or from the bottom up! We will start with the broad overview of supervision outcomes over time

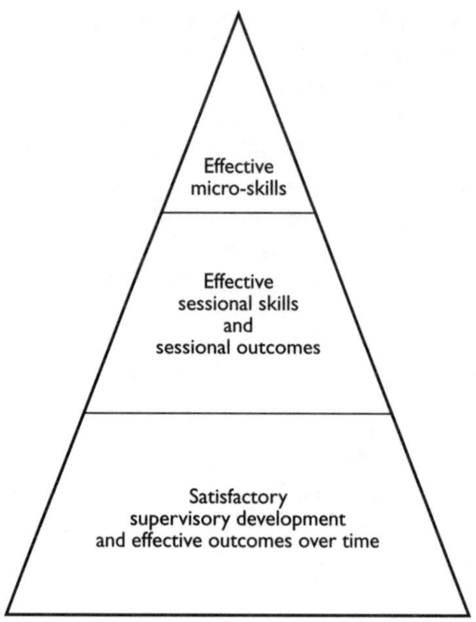

Figure 7.1 *Lenses for evaluation*

(listed at the bottom of the diagram) and then narrow down to the moment-by-moment skills (at the top).

Satisfactory supervisor development (outcomes over time)

An obvious external measure of supervisors' skills is the successful performance of their supervisees in their work with clients. A supervisee who is working effectively reflects on the competence of the supervisor. The clearest measure of this is when the supervisees are in training and will be submitting themselves to examination or accreditation processes. These processes provide an objective and external measure of effectiveness which reflects directly on the supervisor's work. We are taking into account that some students are better suited to the profession than others and no supervisor can realistically expect a 100 per cent success rate! However, we do believe that examination successes are related to the effectiveness of both training courses and the competence of supervisors involved in the process, because they provide an external measure of effective outcomes.

This facet of supervisor evaluation does of course introduce the dilemma of the supervisor's ego-involvement in the supervisee's success. This tension can create serious difficulty in the supervision relationship. A supervisor may put undue pressure on a student by suggestions that sound more like demands for perfection. If the student's assessment achieves a less than glowing result, the supervisor, fearing adverse judgement himself, may be unsupportive in his disappointment. This can turn the assessment process into a shaming experience for the student. In the supervision of their own supervision, we consider this a particularly important focus for supervisors.

Not all supervisees, of course, are in training and other evaluative measures of the supervisor's performance are called for that are more directly based on the supervision relationship. These will provide a general measure of satisfactory outcomes over time and can be applied to both training and consultative supervision.

Supervisors will regularly be evaluating the effectiveness of their supervision over varying periods of time, for example at the end of a year's contract with supervisees. To aid us in this section we have drawn on some of the outcome research into supervision. From this research which reflects the needs of 'consumers' of supervision, we have sought those factors that have been rated by supervisees as measures of effective supervision over time. Since this research was conducted almost exclusively with students in therapy or counselling training, it may reflect more heavily the needs of therapists in training rather than the needs of qualified practitioners in search of consultative supervision. We decided, however, that the variables that emerged are, in our experience, of sufficient interest and relevance to supervision in general to form the basis of two scales that can be used to evaluate outcomes in supervision. (One of these scales can be found in the following section since it is aimed at assessing the outcome of an individual supervision session.) The first one (Figure 7.2) looks at desired outcomes over time.

This list can be used in the context of group or individual evaluation sessions with supervisees by which means supervisors get feedback on their own effectiveness. It also lends itself very well to use in an on-going training context where peer supervisors in a training group can be taught to evaluate one another's progress and development over time in terms of these criteria.

Relationship dimensions: The Supervisor

1. Communicates respect for differences in values and experiences as well as respect for personal privacy.
2. Values independence of supervisee.
3. Respects the supervisee as a person.
4. Uses humour in supervision.
5. Avoids conducting psychotherapy during supervision.
6. Provides consultation in dealing with supervisee's emotions.
7. Helps supervisees to realize that new skills seem awkward at first.
8. Discloses her own experience as this is directly related to supervisee learning needs.

Professional Role: The Supervisor

1. Agrees mutual goals which are renegotiated at regular intervals.
2. Monitors sessions either by video or audiotape.
3. Provides direct training in intervening with clients.
4. Provides direct training in conceptualizing cases.
5. Gives feedback on supervisee's therapy style.
6. Balances the facilitation of supervisee's self-understanding with a focus on client dynamics and how to help the client.
7. Focuses on strengths and growth areas instead of concentrating on weaknesses.
8. Helps supervisees assess their own weaknesses.
9. Uses supervision relationship to demonstrate principles of therapy.
10. Provides conceptual frameworks for understanding client processes.
11. Encourages supervisee to experiment with novel strategies.
12. Provides modelling of relevant skills.

Figure 7.2 *Assessment of supervision outcomes over time (derived from Leddick and Dye, 1987; Carifio and Hess, 1987)*

Effective performance along these dimensions will be a good indicator that the supervisor is ready for accreditation.

Feedback along these dimensions can also regularly be sought from the supervisee in the course of a routine supervision review in order to discover how far the supervision is perceived to be meeting the supervisee's needs. This information provides an on-going evaluation of the supervisor's performance. Inskipp and Proctor (1993) describe the importance of regular reviews in supervision and suggest at least one a year. Such a review has several purposes. One obvious one is to agree a goal for the coming period and to assess how far the previous goals have been met. However, it is also an opportunity for supervisor and supervisee (as well as group members if the supervision takes place in a group context) to give each other feedback about their work in

Client work
How is my work with individual clients going? With groups?
How do I rate my effectiveness?
How is the balance of my caseload? Are there changes I wish to make?
Is my case-recording adequate and appropriate for me?

Use of supervision
What have I learned from this supervisor?
How do I work differently as a result?
Is my preparation appropriate?
Do I present in a way that serves my purposes and is helpful to my supervisor?
Am I using the sessions well – to explore – to understand better – to practise more effectively?

Development as a psychotherapist
How far have I met the goals I have set myself?
What skills, understanding, personal qualities do I now want support and challenge in developing?
Do I need other professional development (training, the opportunity to present workshops etc.)?

Effectiveness of the working alliance
What has been enjoyable for me? What have I not enjoyed?
What would I like more of? Less of?
What balance of normative, formative and restorative work? Of support and challenge?
How safe do I feel in this relationship? In this group? How empowered do I feel?
What would I most like to hear from the supervisor?
What would I least like to hear?
What do I most want to say to my supervisor?
What do I least want to say?
What feedback do I have for the other individuals in the group?

Changes to the contract
In the light of this review what changes to the contract do you want to negotiate?

Figure 7.3 *Supervision review (based on Inskipp and Proctor, 1993)*

Short Supervision Review
What was our contract and have we met it?
What have you found most useful from your supervisor?
What do you want more of from your supervisor?
What do you want less of from your supervisor?
What is the next developmental edge for you?

Figure 7.4 *Short supervision review form*

the group and to remind themselves of their rights and responsibilities. All this can be a useful part of evaluating the supervisor's effectiveness and is best viewed as a collaborative process. In such an evaluation process, the supervisor may grow to realize that her style of supervision suits some supervisees better than others and can be challenged to extend and deepen her repertoire. Inskipp and Proctor include a detailed suggestion for conducting a supervision review. With their permission, we reproduce it here (Figure 7.3) with very little amendment. This review is conducted by the supervisor and the supervisee jointly at regular intervals. The material can subsequently form the basis of a further review of the supervisor's learning goals in the context of the supervision of their supervision.

We also include a short supervision review form (Figure 7.4) which has fewer questions and can therefore be done more quickly and thus perhaps more frequently than the full one. It nevertheless provides a powerful tool for monitoring the effectiveness of supervision. This shorter review can provide a rapid assessment of the on-going supervision contract.

Successful Sessional Outcomes

The following is a list of sessional skills (Figure 7.5) valued in a supervisor (based on Carifio and Hess, 1987; and Leddick and Dye, 1987) which research has revealed to be the consumers' perceived needs of supervision. Although several of these items refer to specific categories of supervisor skills, we have included them in this section because they relate more to an evaluation of the overall sessional outcome of supervision. This list provides the supervisor with valuable information about the effectiveness of supervisor performance in a particular session. We consider that it may be used as an occasional check on how the supervisor is progressing with particular individuals, where there is doubt about the effectiveness of service to an individual supervisee and in the training of supervisors where much of the training is based on evaluating single supervision sessions.

Following reflection on the research findings and drawing on our own experience as supervisors, we find that there are three main elements which are generally thought to contribute to a successful sessional outcome:

- effective completion of agreed tasks;
- the development and maintenance of an effective supervisory relationship;
- the creation of a safe learning environment which includes both challenge and support.

These three areas are covered in the twenty statements in Figure 7.5 below and in our view constitute the essence of a satisfactory sessional outcome. Supervisors are encouraged to check back with the supervisee that the contract has been met and that the supervisee has experienced the session as facilitative of their client

1. The supervisor negotiated specific objectives, explicit and measurable goals.
2. Goals were mutually arrived at by supervisor and supervisee.
3. Goals appropriately addressed the supervisee's concerns, e.g. treatment issues, therapist skills in relation to client characteristics, diagnoses, ethical or dynamic issues.
4. There was identification and discussion of expectations.
5. Supervision was structured towards task efficiency.
6. Evaluation was specific, concrete and clear.
7. The session allowed for an honest, open exchange.
8. The supervisor gave direct suggestions rather than using exclusively Socratic style questioning.
9. The supervisor provided both support and evaluation.
10. The supervisor framed feedback in terms of whether interventions either did or did not facilitate therapy objectives (rather than in terms of 'right' or 'wrong').
11. The supervisor encouraged the supervisee to experiment with a new technique(s) to discover their own styles and develop self-confidence as therapists.
12. The supervisor gave feedback about supervisee's positive and non-facilitative behaviours with clients.
13. The supervisor was actively empathic, genuine, warm, flexible and non-restrictive.
14. The supervisor aimed to manage rather than eliminate tension in supervision to enable supervisee to reduce performance anxiety while stimulating motivation to learn.
15. The supervisor dealt directly with supervisee defensiveness.
16. The supervisee benefited from a mix of modalities, e.g. didactic presentations, feedback and evaluation, etc.
17. Supervisory feedback was specific and related to therapy goals.
18. Supervision was highly active, providing large amounts of observation, feedback and instruction.
19. The supervisor demonstrated a wide range of interpersonal skills.
20. The supervisor showed patience!

Figure 7.5 *Assessment of a successful sessional outcome*

work. It is likewise important for the supervisor to reflect on the session in terms of these three dimensions.

We find that a focus on the tasks (or different 'roles') required of a supervisor can assist the supervisor in assessing the delivery of supervision in relation to the three areas summarized above. Michael Carroll (1996) offers a particularly useful overview of the tasks of supervision which can be used as a format for evaluating a session (or assessing the process of supervision over time). The seven tasks he identifies encompass much of the material discussed above and provide a way of focusing on the different facets of the supervisor's role. Following his model, the following evaluation can be done by the supervisor or by observers (in a group or training context).

In this particular session which of the following tasks has the supervisor performed effectively?

- setting up a learning relationship
- monitoring administrative aspects
- consulting
- counselling
- monitoring professional or ethical issues
- evaluating
- teaching

An assessment of the tasks within a session will allow the supervisor to reflect on the initial contract and whether it has been satisfactorily completed. The supervisor will also be accumulating information about herself and her supervisory style which will contribute to her long-term evaluation of her competence. For example, the supervisor who finds that most of her sessions are taken up by teaching, or for that matter by counselling, may wish to develop skills in some of the other tasks. This method is very helpful for monitoring rigidity and flexibility in style since as supervisors we may easily settle into a preferred style and so not be challenged to broaden our repertoire (Holloway and Wolleat, 1981).

One of the supervisor's primary tasks in any session is to identify the central concern or issue that the supervisee is bringing to the session, whether consciously or unconsciously. This challenging task will inform the supervisor's choice of focus, whether that is a more profound understanding of the client's presenting problem or an exploration of the therapist's counter-transference. Hawkins and Shohet (1989) and Clarkson and Gilbert (1991) provide two useful frameworks for conceptualizing the supervisor's options. However, the choosing of priorities in a supervision session is a task that is learned over time as the supervisor becomes progressively attuned to the finer nuances of the supervisory process in relation to the supervisee's level of development as a practitioner. The frameworks mentioned above can provide a teaching and learning tool in this challenging process.

We include here an example of a sessional process evaluation that occurred in the context of a longer supervision session.

> Margaret has been observed in a training session doing a piece of supervision with a fellow trainee. The observer noticed that she established a safe relationship in which her supervisee clearly felt able and willing to explore and learn. She negotiated a goal for the supervision which she returned to regularly. However, her interventions were almost exclusively restricted to reflective listening and to commenting on the supervisee's process in the room. She drew attention to the supervisee's language, she mirrored his gestures and bodily postures and she shared the response that they evoked in her. At the end of the supervision, it became clear that Margaret had had several hypotheses about what might be going on for the client as well as between the client and the therapist (her supervisee). However, she had not spoken them out loud. Neither had she thought to explore the context of the work. When she reflected on the process she realized also that she had a specific recommendation for the supervisee concerning an aspect of the therapy. She realized that her desire to be 'person-centred' had limited her from taking her authority in the situation. Her growing edge was formulated as identifying (and carrying out) the appropriate use of clear feedback and direction.

Effective micro-skills

We have been examining the skills and tasks involved in the supervisor's role as identified by an evaluation over time, of sessional outcomes and of the sessional process. It is important at this point therefore to address our attention to the specifics of the supervisor's interventions. What skills are needed to accomplish the desired effect? Clearly, the supervisor needs to have a range of interventions which will support, instruct and challenge the supervisee and which will also invite her to develop her thinking, her intuition and her observational skills.

Various writers offer us ways of deconstructing the dialogue and categorizing types of intervention. Heron (1989) offers six categories broadly separated into two groups of 'Authoritative' and 'Facilitative'. Berne (1966) describes eight 'therapeutic operations' designed to increase the awareness of the client (or in this case supervisee), broaden understanding and facilitate change and development.

We believe that it can be misleading to categorize interventions according to type without relating them to their purpose. For example, giving information to a supervisee may be seen as supportive, reassuring, challenging or directive depending on what its intention is and what effect it achieves. The evaluation of interventions must therefore be seen in this light. It can be useful however, to use a general framework for types of intervention and then in terms of this to analyse the moment-by-moment process of the supervision in order to develop awareness of the supervisor's range of interventions and ensure that her scope is not limited by such factors as habit or anxiety.

We have identified the following categories of intervention, all of which have a part to play in successful supervision. We have drawn on and adapted the work of Berne (1966) and integrated this with our own experience.

Inquiry

Phenomenological inquiry involves careful exploration of the supervisee's experience. The supervisor gathers information, listens and invites the supervisee to reflect on the issue brought to supervision. Socratic or circular questioning which deepens the person's understanding can be combined with the use of 'continuation responses' which encourage the supervisee to speak freely.

Specification

Specification was the word chosen by Berne (1966) to describe the style of intervention which underlines or highlights some central aspect of the narrative. Specification includes reflective listening, summarizing and paraphrasing. As this process can be strongly confrontative, careful empathic attunement is essential.

Challenge

Challenge involves commenting on discrepancies between two or more previously specified pieces of material. It also includes offering feedback on skills levels, making observations on body signals or the use of words and commenting on dynamics in the therapeutic relationship, for instance unrecognized counter-transference responses.

Explanation

Intervening with explanation includes giving information, offering a particular view or relating material to a theoretical framework. The function of explanation is often an extension of training as it broadens and deepens the supervisee's knowledge base. It is appropriate to offer explanation where there is an obvious gap in knowledge but the supervisor needs to be alert to avoid thinking for the supervisee instead of alongside him.

Confirmation

In the process of confirmation the supervisor draws together themes which have previously emerged and been specified in the course of the supervision in order to highlight important issues in the work. In this way, the supervisor invites the supervisee to notice recurring patterns in interpersonal dynamics that affect the therapeutic relationship or the intrapsychic world of the client.

Illustration

Sometimes the supervisor will illustrate her point by sharing her own experiences or relating relevant examples from the clinical literature. She might also use or invite the use of metaphor or imagery in order to expand the supervisee's range of understanding of unconscious processes. This might include moving from the purely intellectual to the intuitive, or from empathic to observational functioning.

Interpretation

The supervisor may choose to invite the supervisee to explore various interpretations of the clinical material. The dynamics of a relationship or the possible meaning of the client's words or actions may be explored in terms of theoretical concepts (or 'hunches'!) which may illuminate the therapeutic narrative.

Crystallization

Crystallization means summing up succinctly the essence of a situation, issue or theme in such a way that the central dilemma is highlighted. In this process the supervisor does not seek to offer answers but rather to focus a spotlight on what may be the emergent core issue. Offering such clarity enables the supervisee to reflect not only on the direction but also on the significant impact on the client of the process of change.

In addition to his therapeutic operations, Berne also adds what he calls 'parental operations' (1966: 248) although, speaking to the therapist, he advises against them. However, one of the significant differences between the role of the supervisor and that of the therapist or counsellor, is that the supervisor is required not only to assist the supervisee to develop her own thinking but to monitor, to evaluate and to guide. For this reason, it is appropriate to include them in the list of supervisor interventions.

Support

Part of the supervisor's role is to offer appropriate support to the supervisee who is often under pressure in working in a setting where it is rare and usually inappropriate for a client to offer feedback or praise to his therapist. As a consequence of this a practitioner might feel isolated and uncertain of his own skills. Supervision may be the main place in which he can receive support and encouragement, even reassurance or sympathy. The supervisor needs to avoid empty palliatives but be prepared to fulfil the 'restorative' role in supervision (Proctor, 1986).

Exhortation

While normally the supervisor will seek to model an empathic facilitative process, there may be occasions when the supervisor decides that it is important to interrupt the direction of the clinical work and recommend or even instruct the supervisee to follow a particular course of action. This might take the form of encouraging a supervisee to have the confidence of his convictions but more usually it will have to do with the therapist's greater awareness of ethical or professional considerations which may be involved.

From the above list we have drawn up a checklist (Figure 7.6) which can be used by the supervisor using a tape-recording or transcript and/or by the observers and tutor watching a piece of live supervision. Supervisors receive concrete feedback about their tendencies towards one or another type of intervention. Gaps in the range are usually significant. Common amongst new supervisors is an avoidance of those interventions which require them to take their authority as a supervisor. Others, perhaps through anxiety at the responsibility, find that they are using far more 'parental interventions' than are effective for the development of the supervisee. Even experienced supervisors can benefit from this sort of analysis, as habits develop of which they are not aware.

An alternative way of looking at the moment-by-moment process of supervision is to use the Interpersonal Process Recall method described by Kagan (1980). The IPR is a way of developing a person's own capacity to self-supervise, to develop his curiosity and awareness of his own process. It was originally designed for use by practitioners, but it is equally useful for supervisors and can therefore form part of an evaluation of supervision. Although it is a tool for self-examination, it is best used with the help of an 'Inquirer' who facilitates by structuring the process. Normally it requires a video or tape-recording of a session, although it can be adapted to be used following an observed piece of live supervision if necessary.

The tape of the session is played by the supervisor and her inquirer. The supervisor is in charge of the process and stops the tape from time to time, at any point which seems interesting to her – a choice point, a moment of anxiety, doubt or confusion, and so on. The advantage of this method is that the supervisor remains 'in charge' of the process since he can decide when to stop the tape and initiate the process. The inquirer then facilitates an

Tick each time the intervention is used.

- ☐ Inquiry
- ☐ Listening (silently or with 'paraverbals')
- ☐ Socratic questioning
- ☐ Reflecting
- ☐ Summarizing/paraphrasing
- ☐ Expressing empathy
- ☐ Commenting on discrepancies
- ☐ Offering feedback (positive)
- ☐ Offering feedback (constructive/negative)
- ☐ Noticing process (body signals, use of words, etc.)
- ☐ Naming themes/patterns
- ☐ Sharing own experiences/telling anecdotes
- ☐ Suggesting avenue of exploration (e.g., encouraging imagery)
- ☐ Commenting on dynamics (in here or out there)
- ☐ Offering hunches
- ☐ Making theoretical interpretations
- ☐ Highlighting key issue
- ☐ Suggesting a course of action
- ☐ Recommending/instructing
- ☐ Supporting, encouraging, etc.

Figure 7.6 *Micro-skills checklist*

exploration of the supervisor's recalled process by such questions as:

1. What were you feeling?
2. What were you thinking?
3. What were you feeling in your body?
4. What did you do?
5. What could you have done or said instead?
6. What would have been the risks for you in doing or saying this?
7. What do you think the supervisee might have experienced?
8. Do you have any images, association from other situations?
9. Do you remember anything else about that moment?

An example of the Interpersonal Process Recall method in supervision is contained in the following transcript from a supervision session.

> John is listening to the tape of his supervision. His supervisee is describing how she confronted her client about apologizing for having 'rabbited on' in the previous session. She says that she pointed out to her client that what he had been talking about was very important and that he had been 'discounting' with his remark. She went on to list three important areas that he had

identified and suggests that they address them in order. John replies 'Mm'. He stops the tape:

Inquirer: What were you feeling?

John: I was feeling uncomfortable and a little sorry for the client.

Inquirer: What were you thinking?

John: I was thinking that she was being a little . . . well . . . business-like with a very sensitive subject.

Inquirer: And feeling in your body?

John: I don't know. Uncomfortable really.

Inquirer: What could you have said?

John: Well, thinking about it now, I could have said something like 'I wonder what your client felt like when you said that to him', or 'Why do you suppose he said that?'

Inquirer: What do you think stopped you from saying something like that?

John: I think it was that at the time I couldn't think of any tactful way to put it. Actually I think I was feeling a bit appalled. I wanted to say 'For heavens sake, that poor guy needs you to really empathize with him.' Then her face would have fallen and I would have hurt her. But she was dealing with the client as if he was a kettle to be mended and seemed to be missing the importance of the issue for the client. Oh! That's interesting, there's some sort of parallel there. Either minimizing the importance or smacking someone in the face with it. I need to model something different. [*Pause to reflect*] I think I'll go on now.

Use of this IPR method combined with the micro-skills checklist can be an extemely powerful way of developing understanding of the supervisor's use of self, and what lies behind her choice of intervention.

The formal evaluation of supervisees: writing reports

A task that often falls to the supervisor is to provide a written evaluation of a supervisee's competence. In this process a supervisor can use any of the tools or approaches to assessment that we have already discussed. We find it useful to devise a set of criteria against which to assess the supervisee, and we find the following list (Carroll, 1998: personal communication) to be a comprehensive overview of the relevant areas to be reviewed. It can, of course, be easily adapted for supervisor evaluation.

1. **The counselling/therapeutic relationship**
   Is the practitioner able to establish an effective therapeutic relationship?
   Does the practitioner engage appropriately with the client?
   Does the practitioner use power appropriately in the therapeutic context?
2. **Self-awareness**
   Is the practitioner aware of himself/herself and his/her own strengths and limitations?
   Is the practitioner able to reflect on his/her practice?
3. **Skills/competence**
   Does the practitioner demonstrate the following skills?
   Self-presentation
   Listening and responding empathically
   Effective challenge
   Range of effective interventions
4. **Understanding the therapeutic process**
   Does the practitioner understand what is happening between self and client?
   Is the practitioner aware of the stages of the therapeutic process?
5. **Diagnosis/assessment**
   Has the practitioner a method of assessing/diagnosing clients?
   Is the practitioner able to make clear and accurate diagnoses?
6. **Contextual issues**
   Is the practitioner aware of relevant contextual issues?
   Is the practitioner aware of individual differences and their significance?
7. **Ethics/professionalism**
   Does the supervisee subscribe to a clear code of ethics?
   Is the supervisee ethically sensitive to what happens in the therapeutic context?
8. **Theory**
   Does the practitioner have a coherent theoretical orientation guiding the work?
   Is the practitioner congruent in theory and practice?
   Does the practitioner have sufficient knowledge to back up practice?
9. **Attitudes, beliefs, values**
   Is the practitioner flexible?
   Is the practitioner tolerant and able to stay with painful issues?
   Is the practitioner able to learn from supervision?
   Does the practitioner deal positively with feedback?

Figure 7.7 *Formal evaluation of supervisee progress*

A final word: troubleshooting

As regards troubleshooting, we think that some of the issues that we face as trainers training in the area of evaluation involve personal issues or sensitive areas on the part of both supervisor and supervisee.

Most people have emerged from such a shame-based educational process that any feedback which is in any way critical seems to 'devastate' the person, so that as trainers and supervisors we can become disempowered by this process. We may end up avoiding giving necessary feedback and confrontation of a trainee supervisor in order to spare their feelings while condoning ineffective work in this process. The experience of shame is undermining for the person in the learning context since it leads to people hiding their perceived weaknesses and faults so that they do not get the input that would most help them to develop effective assessment processes for their own work. Part of teaching evaluation becomes the healing of the wounds that people have incurred in previous learning situations where being assessed has led them to conclude that they are 'stupid', 'ineffectual' or even 'bad'.

This is often exacerbated by the person's extremely critical 'internal supervisor' (Casement, 1985) which requires perfection and is satisfied with nothing less; any feedback is interpreted as a fall from perfection ('I should have known that') which stands in the way of developing effective internalized standards. What underpins an attitude of this kind is the assumption that there are 'wrong' and 'right' interventions in supervision and that somewhere there is a blueprint that people must get to know, rather than that it is a process of learning and shaping one's responses to suit the individual's needs and learning style in order to meet an agreed contract. So in a sense a large part of the training is involved in working with these two related issues (shame in the Child and the power of the internalized critic in the Parent) until gradually people can develop criteria for evaluation that are realistic and accept that everyone is going to be making mistakes and is on a learning curve at any point in their developmental process.

Another of the particular 'troubleshooting' issues is that trainee supervisors may collude in group exercises by not giving each other any negative feedback so as to avoid receiving any in return.

This process then leaves the trainer in the unenviable position of having to assume the role of critic in the group while all the other members remain overly supportive. The supervisor will need to challenge this process and teach people ways of giving feedback in line with the guidelines given in this chapter so that everyone can gradually become more robust around the evaluation process. In addition, for some people evaluation is seen to conflict with humanistic values such as 'unconditional positive regard' so that they do not wish to involve themselves in a process that they perceive as 'power-based'.

Dealing with the supervisor's issues around taking their own authority becomes figural here. This is often the most difficult aspect for beginning supervisors. In addition to this is the issue of the fair and appropriate exercise of power in the evaluative processes. We cannot avoid the fact that we are evaluating people's performance and that this is a crucial aspect of any training process. What is vital here is that the criteria are clearly expressed and understood so that trainee supervisors are able to assess their own work and that of others in terms of very specific criteria. Many of the tools we have included in this chapter are designed to be used in this way. An open process in which both the trainer and the trainee-supervisors understand what is being assessed and looked for in the evaluation task is the goal in teaching this most challenging area in supervision training.

References

Austin, B. and Altekruse, M.D. (1972) The effect of group supervision roles on practising students' interview behavior. *Counselor Education and Supervision*, 12: 63–8.

Berne, E. (1966) *Principles of Group Treatment*. New York: Oxford University Press.

Carifio, M.S. and Hess, A.K. (1987) Who is the ideal supervisor? *Professional Psychology: Research and Practice*, 18: (3): 244–50.

Carroll, M. (1996) *Counselling Supervision: Theory, Skills and Practice*. London: Cassell.

Casement, P. (1985) *On Learning from the Patient*. London: Routledge.

Clarkson, P. and Gilbert, M. (1991) The training of counsellor trainers and supervisors. In W. Dryden and B. Thorne (eds), *Training and Supervision for Counselling in Action*. London: Sage.

Dodenhoff, J.T. (1981) Interpersonal attraction and direct-indirect supervisor influence as predictors of counselor trainee effectiveness. *Journal of Counseling Psychology*, 28: 47–62.

Freeman, E. (1985) The importance of feedback in clinical supervision: implications for direct practice. *The Clinical Supervisor,* 3 (1): 5–26.

Hawkins, P. and Shohet, R. (1989) *Supervision in the Helping Professions.* Milton Keynes: Open University Press.

Henry, W.P., Schacht, T.E., Strupp, H.H., Butler, S.F. and Binder, J.L. (1993) Effects of training in time-limited dynamic psychotherapy: mediators of therapists' responses to training. *Journal of Consulting and Clinical Psychology,* 61: 441–7.

Heron, J. (1989) *The Facilitator's Handbook.* London: Kogan Page.

Holloway, E.L. and Neufeldt, S.A. (1995) Supervision: Contributors to treatment efficacy. *Journal of Consulting and Clinical Psychology,* 63 (2): 207–13.

Holloway, E.L. and Poulin, K. (1995) Discourse in supervision. In J. Siegfried (ed.), *Therapeutic and Everyday Discourse as Behavior Change: Towards a Micro-analysis in Psychotherapy Process Research.* New York: Ablex.

Holloway, E.L. and Wolleat, P.L. (1981) Style differences of beginning supervisors: an interactional analysis. *Journal of Counseling Psychology,* 28: 373–6.

Inskipp, F. and Proctor, B. (1993) *Making the Most of Supervision,* Part I. Twickenham: Cascade.

Kagan, N. (1980) *Influencing human interaction – eighteen years with IPR.* In A.K. Hess (ed.) *Psychotherapy Supervision.* New York: Wiley.

Leddick, G.R. and Dye, H.A. (1987) Effective supervision as portrayed by trainee expectations and preferences. *Counselor Education and Supervision.* 27, 2: 139–54.

Proctor, B. (1986) Supervision: a co-operative exercise in accountability. In M. Marken and M. Payne (eds), *Enabling and Ensuring: Supervision in Practice.* Leicester: National Youth Bureau.

8 Training Supervisees to Use Supervision

Francesca Inskipp

Introduction

I was originally trained in supervision in the late 1960s by Joan Tash (1967) who wrote one of the early books published on supervision. This was a course for supervising Youth and Community workers where I was involved in training at that time. Joan Tash came from social work with some interest in counselling, and my training contained elements of both. In 1973 I moved into training counsellors and supervising their work, and was not aware of any training for supervising counsellors at that time, or of any literature on supervision, apart from some American papers. My supervision, like that of most of my colleagues, was based on how I had been supervised and it was not until the 1980s that, driven by the British Association for Counselling, supervision became mandatory for all counsellors belonging to that association. At that stage BAC began to set up a process for recognizing supervisors and I was fortunate in taking part in the working group.

From this, courses for training supervisors began to spring up, and, with a colleague, Brigid Proctor, who was a very experienced supervisor, we decided to produce some audiotapes to elucidate and demonstrate supervision. As we began to think about what we wanted to say we came upon the then novel idea that we wanted first to train supervisees on how to use supervision. Thus our first project was 'Skills for Supervisees', including one audiotape with a booklet of exercises and some theory. It was an interesting project and stirred up a lot of thinking about power, responsibility, self-managed and reflective learning and the importance of contracting in supervision. We followed this by two audiotapes on 'Skills for Supervisors', with a booklet. Both sets have sold well to a variety of the helping professions.

We then began to design and run supervision courses and were influenced in our thinking by the books and articles which began to appear – particularly Hawkins and Shohet (1989), Carroll (1995, 1996), and workshops run by Elizabeth Holloway, subsequently published (1995). We wanted to make our training available to a wider audience so have written and published a training resource or open learning course, 'The Art, Craft and Tasks of Supervision': Part 1, 'Making the Most of Supervision'; and Part 2, 'Becoming a Supervisor'. Part 1 continues our thinking on training for supervision and I hope to expand on that in this chapter. Our next project is to make some demonstration videos of experiential exercises and supervision sessions which could be used for supervisor training courses, particularly training for group supervision.

I am currently involved in a group that is setting up and running a new BAC Accreditation Scheme for Supervisors, and also in helping with the design of National Vocational Qualifications in supervision. Both these stimulate me to explore and read some of the literature on supervision which now pours out of the presses. I hope this chapter will perhaps add something to encourage further exploration, and provide even better ways to develop reflective practitioners, who can give their best possible service to their clients.

Why train supervisees in the use of supervision?

I suggest there are three main reasons:

1. It is empowering for the supervisee. If the supervisee has a clear idea of what is expected of her in supervision and what she may expect and require, this changes the power base. I believe that if supervision is seen as primarily a sharing of responsibility for the supervisee's professional development and for protection of the client, this enhances the learning possibilities. It also provides a model for work with clients.
2. The supervisor can only supervise on what the supervisee brings, and I believe it is the supervisee's task to find ways to make her work and herself increasingly visible both to herself and to her supervisor. To do this she needs to feel safe to

expose herself and her work; training how to make a clear contract to set up a working alliance can aid this, and can help her feel confident to ask for what she needs. Some research has shown that there is a correlation between the quality of the working alliance, as experienced by the supervisee, and the extent of the self-disclosure in supervision (Webb, 1997).

3. The supervision alliance is a facilitative relationship which requires active and intentional participation by both parties. The working alliance is a particular set of role relationships. The boundaries of the roles, rights and responsibilities of both parties need to be clearly defined, understood, and agreed between supervisor and supervisee in an explicit working agreement.

All this requires special skills, knowledge and attitudes, so a supervisee needs to be able to:

- understand the tasks, roles and boundaries of supervision;
- negotiate a contract and build and maintain a working alliance with her supervisor;
- record her work with clients and reflect on it;
- develop awareness of her internal processes, thoughts, emotions, bodily sensations, fantasies, images and be able to describe them to herself and to a supervisor;
- develop awareness of the moment-to-moment interaction between herself and her client and the conscious and unconscious processes involved, and be able to articulate this awareness in supervision;
- present her work economically – prioritize, select, use words, images, metaphors;
- bring her work and share it freely and accessibly and be clear about her needs from supervision – and the boundaries between counselling and supervision;
- negotiate with her supervisor how she will present – verbally, in writing, by audiotape, whether every client every time, which clients, organizational or ethical issues, her developmental needs, her learning style;
- be open to feedback and be prepared to monitor her practice in the light of it;
- define her own developmental learning needs and use the available supervision time to the best advantage for developing her counselling and for helping clients;
- monitor and review her use of supervision and take responsibility for giving feedback to her supervisor about its usefulness for her and her clients;

- engage with her supervisor with increasing integrity, courage, clear intention and openness in order to best serve her clients;
- search for and select an appropriate supervisor (if given the opportunity).

I believe training is the most economical way of developing these competencies.

Context in which this approach is relevant

The following contexts seem appropriate places for training supervisees:

First, As part of a professional initial training course when students are learning how to work with clients/patients. Students need to learn how to record and reflect on their work, how to develop their own learning plan, and this can be extended to how to present in supervision. This is an opportunity for them to learn how to use supervision, what are their rights and responsibilities, how they can contract to use supervision for their support and learning – and, if appropriate, how to find and choose a supervisor.

Second, supervisor training courses provide an opportunity for new supervisors to learn how to make the most of their own supervision. I have found this has sometimes been an enlightening experience for supervisors to explore and examine their use of supervision. They often seem to find they are not really getting the supervision they want and this may be due to no clear contracts, no opportunities for review sessions or for feedback to and from their supervisor. There can be some very useful learning from this.

Third, some professions, for example health and education services, which had hitherto only used managerial supervision are now beginning to provide non-managerial supervision – opportunities to reflect on their work, to be accountable for their work with patients or pupils, and to get support for the emotional and physical stresses which they encounter. These workers are often suspicious of supervision and have differing expectations; they could make much better use of what is on offer if they have some training in what to expect and how to use it.

Fourthly, for supervisees who have had no specific training, supervisors can provide some material for new individual and group supervisees. I ask my new supervisees, before we start and during our work together, to use Open Learning materials – *Skills for Supervising and Being Supervised* (Inskipp and Proctor, 1989) for non-counsellors, and for counsellors, *Making the Most of Supervision* (Inskipp and Proctor, 1993). Carroll (1996) is also useful reading for counsellor supervisees. He suggests for supervisees, 'This book may help them articulate their supervisory needs and put them in a stronger position when they go in search of a supervisor who will negotiate with them' (p. 4).

Finally, some workers, especially those in nursing and related health services, are required to produce portfolios as evidence of continuing professional development. Training for using supervision, especially recording, reflecting and identifying their ongoing learning needs, helps to produce proactive learners and can be a useful lead into self-managed learning and portfolio work.

Theoretical underpinnings of the approach, and relevance to supervisory action research

There is a still a scarcity of research into supervision, and especially into exploring how supervisors and supervisees might be educated into providing and making the best use of supervision. Some studies highlight the importance of educating supervisees how to use supervision. One study by Byrne (1995) investigated the supervision experience and perspectives of a number of trainee counsellors in voluntary sector clinical practice, in particular their preparedness and preparation for supervision. The survey comprised thirty-three voluntary counsellors from two voluntary counselling organizations and represented a minimum of thirteen different counsellor training courses. Byrne (1995) found that '49% of participants had received no formal preparation for supervision and 91% believed that counsellor training courses should prepare trainees for the supervisee role'.

Kaberry (1995), researching on abuse in supervision, suggests one way of avoiding abuse in supervision is for 'supervisees [to be] prepared so that they know what to expect from supervision and can be assertive about poor supervision' (quoted in Carroll (1996): 156). Carroll's research (1996: 4) indicates that 'there is some evidence that even after two years of being supervised regularly supervisees are still uncertain about what to expect from supervision.

Webb (1995: 186), in research on how honest counsellors dare to be in the supervisory relationship, used an anonymous questionnaire with 216 counsellors, all from the psychodynamic tradition. The research conclusions state: 'The inhibition of counsellors to explore sensitive areas in supervision under certain conditions, is of serious concern . . . the shocked reactions implicit in a proportion of participants at even being asked about such issues suggest that further attention to supervisees' abilities to use supervision is needed.'

These studies highlight the importance of preparing supervisees – not only trainees but experienced counsellors – for supervision, and more studies are needed into which methods might be most efficacious.

Training suggestions

As an example of possible training, I outline below an instructional module/unit to include in the initial training for counsellors – Diploma or Masters Course. This could be set up before and during the early stages of starting work with clients and starting supervision. Much of this training will probably already be part of course work, especially preparing students to work with clients, but it could be useful to tie it up with preparing for and using supervision. I have set this out in time units but courses could pick and mix items to fit in with their own syllabus. Eight units of 1.5–2 hours are suggested, spread out over two to three months. Exercises and handouts can be found in the Appendix to this chapter.

Aim

To develop counsellors who are intentional learners, who can reflect on their work, can use supervision to integrate theory with practice and so develop into competent, confident and ethical practitioners who give good service to clients.

Teaching/learning goals

To understand the purposes, tasks and boundaries of supervision.
To develop motivation to make the best use of supervision.
To develop skills of:

- negotiating a supervision contract;
- sharing in the building and maintenance of a working alliance;
- recording and reflecting on client work;
- preparing for and presenting in supervision;
- developing ability to prioritize and use time well;
- using feedback and monitoring the use of supervision;
- giving feedback to the supervisor;
- defining learning needs and learning style.

Programme and methods

UNIT 1 – INTRODUCTION TO SUPERVISION

Content: Definition, purposes, tasks and roles of supervision; responsibilities of supervisor and supervisee; ethics of supervision.

Method: Teaching session with handouts.

Content: Contracting; setting up a supervision contract; understanding what contracts exist between the training course and supervisors either within or external to the course; also any contracts with agencies providing placements for students.

Method: Discussion on how external contracts may affect individual contracts with supervisors.
Brainstorm items for an individual contract, or group contract.
Experiential Exercise 1 'Wants' and 'oughts' in supervision (see p. 194).
Add any items which arise from this exercise.

Content: Negotiating skills – 'active listening' skills + purpose and preference stating.

Method: Audiotape or live demonstration of contracting session, students watch and define negotiating skills used.
Students work in threes: supervisor and supervisee

negotiate and set up a contract; observer gives feedback on skills and content.

Content: Building a working alliance.

Method: Discuss in threes: What will help to build a good alliance, what may hinder? What skills are needed? What qualities? What issues of power exist? How will assessment or accountability affect the relationship? Compare with counselling relationship – similarities and differences, especially boundaries. What difficulties might arise, and how might they be dealt with?
Share in large group.

UNIT 2 – PREPARING FOR THE SUPERVISION SESSION. PART I: RECORDING

Content: Client records – methods, systems; legal and ethical requirements; course – or agency-specific requirement; keeping a supervision notebook.

Methods: Teaching session with group discussion – handouts, from flip-chart or OHP.
What to record – content and process.
Teach four-focus method of recording from *Handout 1: Recording content and process* (p. 202).
Watch video or listen to audio recording of part of a counselling session with accompanying handout of example of content and process written record.
Work in pairs. Students do ten-minute session, one counsellor, one client. Spend fifteen minutes recording content and process. Reverse the process. Hand in records to tutor for feedback.

UNIT 3 – PREPARING FOR THE SUPERVISION SESSION. PART II: REFLECTING

Content: Developing physical, emotional and cognitive awareness and of the interpersonal process – the internal supervisor.

Method: Set up and teach Interpersonal Process Recall (*Exercise* 2), using *Handouts 2 and 3* (pp. 203–5).

Homework: Do exercise on *'What to bring to supervision' (Handout 4: 205–6)* and bring to next session.

UNIT 4 – PRESENTING IN SUPERVISION

Content: Specific requirements of the course, for example case study or process recording sent in advance, or other possible ways of presenting; learning to ask for specific 'wants' from the presentation; recording learning from supervision.

Method: Teach with handouts, demonstrate live or with audiotape.
Students practise presenting in threes using material from homework above. Observer gives feedback on clarity.

UNIT 5 – FOCUSING IN SUPERVISION

Content: Seven ways of focusing in supervision.

Method: Teach 'seven-eyed supervisor' with *Handouts 5 and 6* (pp. 206–8).
Set up exercise on identifying different foci – either demonstrate a live supervision session or show video or audiotape, students identify and note different foci used by the supervisor or supervisee, and compare after in threes.

UNIT 6 – DIFFICULT ISSUES IN SUPERVISION

Content: Self-disclosure in supervision.

Method: Give out *Handout 7: Self-disclosure in Supervision* (p. 209), students fill in for themselves, then discuss in threes and finally explore in large group.

Content: Oppression and difference in supervision.

Method: Use *Exercise 3: Oppression in supervision* (pp. 199–200).

UNIT 7 – REVIEWING AND LEARNING, DEALING WITH ASSESSMENT AND REPORTS (This unit might come after some months' experience in supervision.)

Content: Links with Learning Journal (if kept); how to use reviews; self and supervisor assessment; working with the supervisor to produce reports; balance of support and challenge; ending a supervisory relationship.

Method: Teaching with handouts and discussion.

UNIT 8 (IF RELEVANT) GROUP SUPERVISION

Content: Responsibilities of being a supervisee in a group;

skills of working in a group – developing relationships and responding to others' presentations; awareness and use of group process.

Method: Teaching with handouts.
Practising skills of *Empathic responding (Exercise 4)* (pp. 200–1).
Revision of challenging skills.
Observe video of group supervision session or listen to audiotape.

Conclusions

In the course outline I have endeavoured to cover most of the important areas for supervisee training and have included some exercises and handouts which we have found particularly useful, in the Appendix. Further information, exercises and illustrations can be found in the publications quoted above, developed by my colleague and myself. *The Art, Craft and Tasks of Supervision*, Part I, *Making the Most of Supervision* and Part II, *Becoming a Supervisor*, have been written as Open Learning Courses and include audiotapes of examples. Besides being useful for individual learning, the materials are used by many trainers for their own courses.

In counsellor training courses it takes many hours of course time to cover all these suggested areas. Tutors already struggle to decide what is essential for counsellor training, but I would suggest much of this could enhance the other work of the course. Courses which have set up this specific training find it is sometimes in conflict with supervision external to the course. Some courses offer training to external supervisors and this can be very successful in melding the supervision with the general work of the course. Difficulties in finding client placements for students mean courses may have little power to influence supervisors, and students may have supervisors with different counselling theoretical orientations from that taught on the course. I have not included this specifically in the training for supervisees, but they certainly need help with this, especially if the supervisor is strongly boundaried by their orientation. Experienced counsellors often gain from a supervisor with a different orientation, but also may need some training in how to use this, especially in a group of several different orientations. There is a move to develop this in some supervisor training, and it could be included in supervisee training.

The British Association for Counselling depends on supervision for monitoring the profession, but there is some criticism that there is no research backing to show that supervision is successful in doing this. It is hard to show that clients really are protected and helped by supervision, but I believe that the more supervison becomes a joint responsibility, with supervisees taking an active part in their own development, the more chance there is for clients to get the service they need. I hope this book will further that cause.

APPENDIX

List of Exercises and Handouts

Exercise 1 'Wants' and 'oughts' in supervision

Objectives

- To help participants become aware of the unspoken hopes, fears and expectations which they bring to the roles of supervisee and supervisor.
- To demystify 'the supervision experience' by playing with these hopes, fears and expectations.

It helps if the facilitator/s demonstrate very briefly what is meant by 'hamming up'.

STAGE 1 (10 minutes)
The objectives of the exercise are explained and the participants are told they will not, in this exercise, be required to supervise or be supervised. Participants divide into groups of three and opt for the role of supervisor, supervisee or observer.

STAGE 2 (3 minutes)
The supervisee tells the supervisor all the things he would really like from his supervisor, but might not usually acknowledge (for example, tell me all you know, think I'm a very good counsellor, never disapprove of me, teach but let me think I know it already, etc.). (In TA jargon he talks out of his Free Child state.) The supervisor does not reply at this stage.

(3 minutes)
The supervisor then hams up all the things she might really want from the supervisee and not acknowledge (for example, think I'm wonderful, tell all your colleagues how good I am, bring me amazing cases, etc.) (again Free Child). The supervisee does not reply.

(3 minutes)
The supervisee then tells the supervisor all the things he feels and thinks he *ought* to do and be as a supervisee (for example, I ought to prepare very well, to listen respectfully, do as you say, etc.). (In TA talk he comes from his Parent/Adapted Child ego-state.) No reply from the supervisor

(3 minutes)
The supervisor tells the supervisee what she *ought* to do and be as a supervisor (for example, ought to teach you all I know, not interfere with your way of doing things, protect your clients, etc.).

The observer takes responsibility for time, but also has the role of keeping each of the others to the task. It is quite hard for some participants to stay with their 'wants' and ham up the Child hopes and fears. It can also be hard for some to acknowledge the demanding and conflicting 'oughts' they have of themselves and others, and to take permission to be their most inconsistent selves.

It is the observer's task to encourage and facilitate them to play with the task.

STAGE 3 (7 minutes)
Supervisor and supervisee together negotiate on the basis of the information they have given themselves and each other, the realistic demands they have of each other in order to realize their realistic expectations. The task of the observer at this stage is to facilitate the negotiation.

STAGE 4 (10 minutes)
Participants de-role within their triads, and give feedback to each other about the experience.

STAGE 5 (10 minutes)
The group reconvene and share experiences and any thinking and reflecting that has been going on as a result of the experience.

(Exercise from Proctor, 1989)

Exercise 2 Workshop for developing awareness of 'process' in the counselling and the supervision sessions

One of the most difficult skills for counsellors to learn seems to be the ability to use their inner awareness in interaction with the client or the supervisor, and to communicate this appropriately. It often feels risky and against the norms of usual interaction so needs plenty of practice of both the awareness and the communication skills.

I have found one of the best ways of training for this is **Interpersonal Process Recall** – a training technique which can help supervisees develop:

- a way of taking responsibility for their own learning;
- internal awareness – what is happening inside them in interactions;
- awareness of what is happening between them and a client in the relationship (transference and counter-transference);
- skills to express this awareness appropriately to the client;
- an internal supervisor;
- a monitoring process to help them use supervision;

- an awareness of when they feel real and genuine in a situation and when they feel false – and the difficulties of expressing this.

Interpersonal Process Recall is a training method developed by Norman Kagan (1975) at Michigan State University, not specifically for counselling but for interpersonal work in the helping professions. It is fairly widely used in training but all its possibilities are not always exploited. From my early work with Kagan I developed a workshop which extends and adapts his ideas – and improvises when conditions, time and resources are not ideal.

The workshop

Resources: One room to hold all the students and sufficient spaces where pairs of students can use a tape-recorder without overhearing another pair – often difficult but all sorts of spaces can be used.

Arrange beforehand for students to have at least one tape-recorder between two, making sure it will work on battery – or that there are electric plugs available and the tape-recorders have the necessary adaptors and one audiotape each.

Prepare handouts for

(a) explaining the recall process (*Handout 2*, pp. 203–4);
(b) the role of inquirer and questions to use (*Handout 3*, p. 204).

Prepare a brief counselling session of yourself on audio or videotape, with a client which you can use to demonstrate the method.

Session

- Introduce the method and explain the structure for the day. They will be using their own material as clients, and hearing each other's tapes, so confidentiality is important throughout the day and after.
- Start with an awareness exercise – scanning the body (can lead this by going round the body identifying all the parts outside and in), relaxing, watching breathing, watching thoughts, watching emotions, visualizing a beautiful place to go to, using all the senses to experience it, going back to watching

thoughts, breathing, and back to the room. Talk to a partner about the experience.
Encourage the use of this exercise during the day – and regularly, in part or whole. I have found this exercise increases the learning from the day.

- Teach the recall process and the inquirer role by demonstration, using the taped session and having another trainer play the inquirer role. If no other trainer, teach inquirer role first and ask a student to volunteer to work with you – or get a student to make the counselling session beforehand and do the recall with you as inquirer. Or show a video or audiotape of the process.
- Give out handouts of the recall process, the inquirer role and inquirer questions (*Handout's 2 and 3*, pp. 203–4). Allow time for questions and clarification.
- Write up on flip chart and explain the logistics of the recall process and get co-operation from the group to keep to time and return to the main room punctually between rounds.

Round 1	A's are counsellors. B's are clients for a 15/30-minute counselling session, recorded.
Round 2	A's will do the recall. B's become inquirers but for another counsellor (20/40 minutes).
Round 3	B's are counsellors. A's are clients and in a different pair from Round 1 (15/30 minutes).
Round 4	B's do the recall. A's become inquirers for another counsellor (20/40 minutes) (put in times depending the length of the workshop).

You will work in four different pairs and must return here to change over.

- Set up the pairs. I usually ask the students to stand in two circles, A's on the inside, facing a partner, barn-dance fashion. That is the first pair. They return to this formation each time and one circle moves on so that they change partners for each round.

Remind them to check tape-recorders before starting – and it is their responsibility to erase tapes at the end of the day.
- Between Rounds 2 and 3 it is useful to bring the group together to see if there are any queries and to get comments how the process is going, what is being learnt.
- After Round 4 bring the group back together; give an opportunity for students to write down some of their learning, share it with yet another partner, consider how they will continue this learning and how they will use it in their counselling and supervision. Then have some exchange in the big group. Summarize the learning if this is useful – or your style!
- Ask for feedback on you and on the workshop and end.

If time and space preclude students making tapes during the workshop, require them to bring a taped session made with a client – a colleague or real client if permission is given.

When the students have learnt and practised the method they can set up sessions for themselves, using actual client material. This is a good build up to supervision and can be an addition to supervision during the course. It can also be used as part of supervision at times, either in group or individual supervision. A student brings a tape, or part of a tape and the supervisor changes role and acts as inquirer.

The inquirer role needs careful teaching to stay neutral, not to get involved in the 'case', and not to use counselling skills, but by questions help the counsellor deepen her awareness. I used to train inquirers to sit with their back to the video or try and not listen too hard to the audio tape, so that their focus was on the counsellor and what she was wanting from the recall.

Workshop adapted from Inskipp (1996).

Exercise 3 Oppression in supervision

Objective: To raise awareness of possibilities for power and oppression in supervision.

- Ask the participants to work in groups of three, each group with a large sheet of paper and marker.
- Ask them to divide the sheet into two halves each headed

    Ways the supervisor can oppress the supervisee
    Ways the supervisee can oppress the supervisor

In ten minutes discuss and record as many items as possible on the sheet.
- Display the sheets, read and discuss in the large group.
- Explore with the group how gender, race, culture, class, age, counselling orientation, and any other differences might lead to oppression in supervision, recognized or unrecognized.

(Good references and further work for this can be found in 'Working cross-culturally and with difference', Bubble 3, in Inskipp and Proctor (1995).)

Exercise 4 Empathic responding in a group

This exercise is useful for helping supervisees in a group learn to listen to each other and respond, without giving advice but helping the presenter do the work. I often use this with a new group of supervisees.

You need a supervisee willing to present a client or an issue, and a manager of the process. If you are lucky enough to have a co-trainer, it is useful for trainers to take both roles. If not, do both roles yourself or ask for a volunteer supervisee willing to present. The volunteer supervisee needs to be assertive enough, and sensitive enough to 'feel' the level of the responses. If you take both roles yourself you will have to come out of the role of presenter to teach and manage, but it can be done.

If the students are not clear what a basic empathy response is, demonstrate it before you start the exercise – either live or have an audio or videotape.

Setting up the exercise

- Ask for six volunteer supervisees to sit in a circle, with six coaches sitting behind them.
- The supervisee will present the issue, talking for about three or four minutes. The supervisees listen, each one then in turn making a basic empathic response to the presenter, if possible not repeating each other. Supervisees may pass or ask their coach for help.
- The presenter responds non-verbally to each response, showing whether it felt empathic or not. (My co-trainer calls the good response 'getting the noddy-jackpot'.) If they do not get

it right they have another go, with the help of the coach if they choose. The manager may point out, or get the group to recognize why some responses do not get the jackpot. This helps students identify the subtleties of 'good' and 'poor' responses.

- The presenter then chooses one response and goes on talking. She can ask for the first responses to be repeated if necessary.
- The supervisees respond as before. If the presenter's response has been very brief they may not be able to find six different responses but they can try, and the process is repeated as above.

The exercise can go on until it is clear everybody in the group can make very accurate empathic responses – the coaches can become the counsellors at some point.

The presenter may respond to two or more of the accurate responses in any round, showing how different responses may lead to different paths of exploration and this can be discussed in the group. The idea of coaching can help to build confidence and reinforce the norm of students helping each other learn. The presenter often finds a good supervision session comes from this exercise.

Handout 1 Recording content and process

Content and process

One structure for reflecting on your work is a content and process model described in the diagram below:

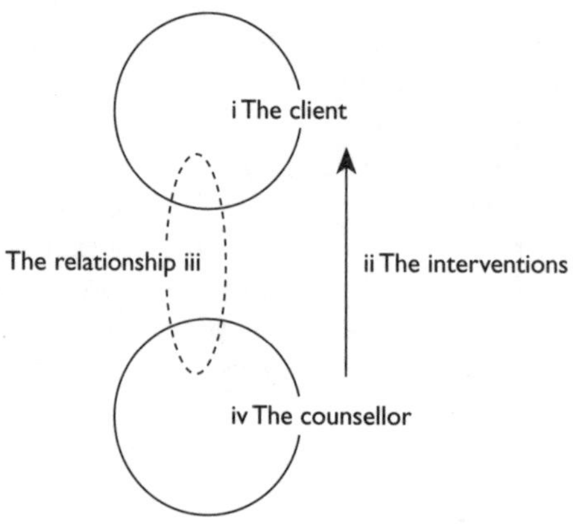

Content of the session

i. The client – history etc.
ii. The interventions – what the counsellor did, techniques

Process of the session

iii. The interaction and relationship between them
iv. The internal processes of the counsellor

(We define Process as 'the communication which happens in one second within and between people which moves them into the next second'.)

Diagram from Inskipp and Proctor (1993: 59).

Handout 2 Interpersonal Process Recall: A method of individual self-learning, a self-discovery process

In any interaction we pick up many cues from the other person, of most of which we are only half-aware. Feelings, thoughts and bodily reactions flash through us at great speed. Some we suppress, some puzzle us, some we communicate to the other person, but we are probably only half-conscious of most of what is going on inside us. All of it is potentially useful.

Awareness of your senses, body sensations, thought patterns, images, fantasies, self-talk (your inner conversations) – and the ability to explore these – is best developed by having the opportunity to learn to monitor your internal processing in an atmosphere free of external judgement, for example by a supervisor, and with increasing internal self-acceptance.

IPR was developed by Norman Kagan at Michigan State University in the early days of video. Professors who had been videoed asked to see their 'performance' and Kagan, who was only a respectful onlooker, noticed how much of their internal processes they remembered and remarked upon. From this he developed the IPR method, videoing sessions and inviting the counsellor to replay it in the presence of another person. The counsellor decided when she stopped the tape and what she recalled. Kagan developed the role of the inquirer, a neutral person who asked helpful questions when the counsellor was recalling, to help to deepen the counsellor's awareness of the processes.

Recalling using an audio or videotape of a session: The fair witness

One of the important skills of self-monitoring is to be able to develop in yourself a 'fair witness' who can stand back and look in on your work without judging or criticizing. The greatest hindrance to good self-monitoring is our eternal critic who sits on our shoulders (often with parental voice) and judges our thoughts, feelings, actions – and even our fantasies. We need to be able to suspend this critic and explore ourselves with unconditional positive regard and empathy. Assessment can come later!

You are in charge of stopping and starting the tape.

Before you start the tape there may be many thoughts, feelings, images as you enter the interaction with this person and it is often useful to start by recalling these. Then start the tape and stop it whenever there are internal stirrings – physical, emotional, cognitive, images – express them and trust your inquirer is not judging you; notice any of your own judgements. Your inquirer will ask some questions to help you deepen your exploration of the *process*, not the *content*. You may find you use only a few minutes of the tape in a 20\30-minute recall.

From Inskipp and Proctor (1993).

Handout 3 Inquirer role and inquirer questions for IPR

The inquirer is not concerned with the *content* of the session but is there to help the counsellor explore the *process*.

When the counsellor stops the tape and comments, use any of the following questions that seem appropriate to help her deepen her exploration.

What were you feeling?
Do you remember where in your body you felt that?
What were you thinking?
What do you think/imagine the other person was feeling/thinking?
How did you want the other person to feel about you?
Were you aware of wanting to do something?
Were you having any fantasies/images at that moment?
Did you have any plans where you wanted the session to go?
Was there anything you wanted to say but could not find the appropriate words?
Were there any risks involved?
Did you feel he/she had any expectations of you at that point?
Was she/he giving you any clues as to how s/he was feeling?
What kind of image were you aware of projecting? Is that what you wanted?
Did you have any goals at this point in the session?
Did s/he remind you of anyone else in your life? What effect did that have on you?

At the end of the recall:

Was there anything you did that pleased you?
Was there anything you did that was ordinarily difficult for you?
What enabled you to do it this time?

What things did you learn from the recall?
If you did the session again what, if anything, would you do differently?

From Inskipp and Proctor (1993).

Handout 4 What to bring to supervision – a reflective exercise

Have your notebook beside you. Relax, take some deep breaths and allow yourself to concentrate on your breathing for a minute or two. Then let your mind drift back over your work with clients in the last week/s.

What surfaces for you immediately? Notice it and let it go. Let your mind wander over the following questions:

What interactions/sessions/clients/interventions were you pleased with?
What was difficult for you?
What were you, are you, uncertain about?
What are you looking forward to in your next working session?
Are there any anxieties about the way you are working with a particular client?
Are there some anxieties about your relationship with any clients?
Are there are some doubts/anxieties just 'out of view' which you'd rather remained out of view? Identify the feelings not the items.
Which interactions have you enjoyed most? What were the feelings?

Now jot down a list of what has surfaced for you as a result of this reverie.

Scan through your records, do any further points stand out for you which you might like/need to talk about? Add them to your list.

Imagine you are replaying a video of one session (or part of one), are there ideas or feelings which come up for you which you might, or might not, like to bring to your supervisor? Note them.

Read through your list. Mark with an N any items which do not seem significant enough to take, mark with a P any items you feel reluctant to talk about, would rather postpone (there may not be any). Make a tentative priority of the other items by numbering 1, 2, 3, etc.

If you have marked some P items, gently explore with yourself what are the risks to you, or to your relationship with your supervisor were you to bring these up. (The exercise on self-disclosure in supervision may help you here). What might you gain/learn if you did? Leave these to simmer and go back to your list of priorities.

Think about what you want to learn and how you might present your material – and yourself.

This may not be what you talk about when you go to supervision – other priorities may arise – but you will have given yourself and your clients an airing!
(From Inskipp Proctor (1989).

Handout 5 FOCUSING – the seven-eyed supervisor

Peter Hawkins's concept of the Process Model of Supervision (Hawkins and Shohet, 1989) is an extremely useful framework for the possibilities of focus. At one time he named it the six-eyed supervisor model. We have added a seventh focus, *the systems*, and so have renamed it the seven-eyed supervisor.

It is our observation that supervisors and supervisees can become quite routine in their focusing – both *where* and *how* they direct their attention. It is likely that we will discover habitual phenomena to focus on, according to our training, that pay good dividends in most cases. However, we believe that should be because we have explored other possibilities and find our habitual focus universally useful.

Factors affecting what may be most useful to focus on at any one time

- the contract
- the developmental stage of the supervisee
- the theoretical orientation
- identified learning needs from the previous session/s
- tie up with current learning

- the stage of the work of the client
- time constraints
- the mood of the moment
- 'outside' elements affecting the work

What are the possibilities?

Key:

1. The client's life and experience
2. The counsellor's interventions and techniques
3. The process and relationship between client and counsellor
4. The internal experience of the counsellor
5. The here-and-now relationship and process between counsellor and supervisor
6. The internal experience of the supervisor
7. The systems which may affect any of the others above

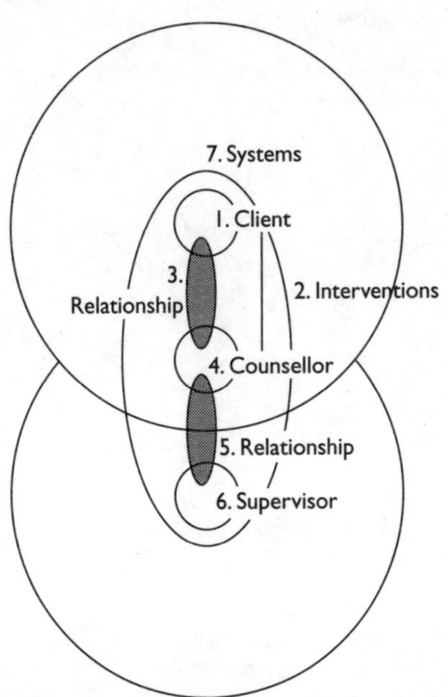

It is worth remembering that the decision where to focus may be portrayed as a *continuum* – supervisor chooses focus . . . supervisor offers option of focus . . . supervisor helps counsellor review options . . . counsellor chooses focus.

Handout 6 Focusing in supervision – an expansion of the seven possible foci

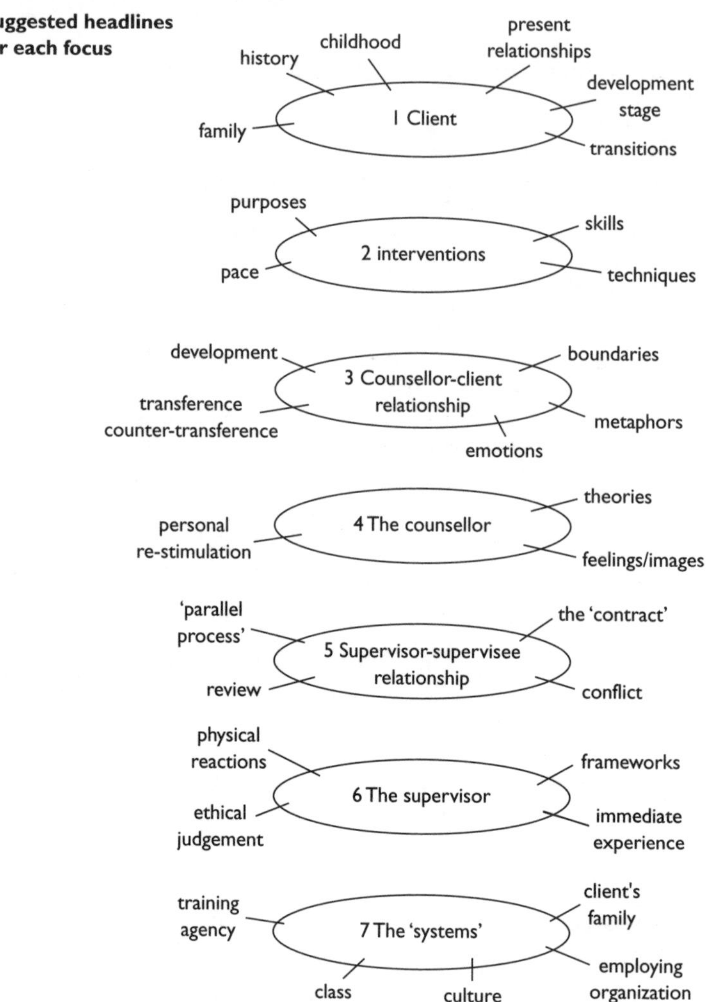

Diagram from Inskipp and Proctor (1995: 61).

Handout 7 Thinking about self-disclosure in supervision

Here are some of the feelings/thoughts/experiences that counsellors can find it hard to talk about and share:

A	B
Telling my supervisor an instance of when I was	Sharing with my supervisor when I am

hopeful/cheerful
afraid
feeling guilty/ashamed
feeling appreciated/admired
critical/impatient/disliking
admiring/loving
envious of another's qualities, possessions
jealous of attention given to another
feeling proud
feeling ignorant/incompetent
feeling humiliated
feeling competent
despairing, depressed
frustrated, angry

Score yourself on the A side and on the B side using for a scale:

very hard to do (h)
risky (r)
perhaps (p)
no problem (n)

You may then go on to note those feelings/experiences which you would like to feel more free to disclose in a safe enough situation.

What are some of the factors that you need to weigh up when you consider:

- the risks of self-disclosing and
- the gains of self-disclosing?

What might your supervisor do to help you disclose appropriately? Would it be useful to give this feedback?
(From Inskipp and Proctor (1989).

References

Byrne, E. (1995) *Preparedness for Supervision: Trainee Counsellors in Voluntary Sector Clinical Practice.* M.Sc. Dissertation, City University, London.

Carroll, M. (1995) *The Generic Tasks of Supervision: An Analysis of Supervisee Expectations, Supervisor Interviews and Supervisory Audio-taped Sessions,* Ph.D. Thesis, University of Surrey.

Carroll, M. (1996) *Counselling Supervision: Theory, Skills and Practice.* London: Cassell.

Hawkins, P. and Shohet, R. (1989) *Supervision in the Helping Professions.* Milton Keynes: Open University Press.

Holloway, E.L. (1995) *Clinical Supervision: A Systems Approach.* Thousand Oaks, CA: Sage.

Inskipp, F. (1996) *Skills Training for Counselling.* London: Cassell.

Inskipp, F. and Proctor, B. (1993) *The Art, Craft and Tasks of Counselling Supervision. Part 1: Making the most of Supervision.* Twickenham: Cascade

Inskipp, F. and Proctor, B. (1989) *Skills for Supervising and Being Supervised,* Principles of Counselling audiotape series. St Leonards-on-Sea: Alexia Publications.

Inskipp, F. and Proctor, B. (1995) *The Art, Craft and Tasks of Counselling Supervision. Part 2: Becoming a Supervisor.* Twickenham: Cascade.

Kaberry, S.E. (1995) *Abuse in Supervision.* M.Ed. Thesis, University of Birmingham.

Kagan, N. (1975) Influencing human interaction, – eleven years with IPR. *The Canadian Counselor,* 9: 74–97.

Proctor, B. (1989) *Supervision: A Working Alliance.* Videotape and manual (out of print).

Tash, J. (1967, 1984) *Supervision in Youth Work.* London: National Council of Social Services, YMCA.

Webb, A. (1995) *How Honest do Counsellors Dare to be in the Supervisory Relationship? An Exploratory Study.* M.Sc. Dissertation. University of Birmingham.

Webb, A. (1997), How honest do counsellors dare to be in the supervisory relationship? An Explanatory study, *Counselling,* 8, 3: 186.

9 The Portfolio: A Method of Reflective Development

Shoshana Hellman

For the last twenty years, I have been a supervisor for school counsellors in Israel. Being born in Israel, even before the country came into being and carrying the cultural heritage of my family who settled in Israel long before the declaration of the State of Israel, has shaped the way I work as a counsellor and supervisor. Although educated in Europe and the United States in linguistics, guidance and counselling, and counselling psychology, I feel our work as counsellors and supervisors in Israel is unique. Living in a country that is continually on alert affects the daily life and needs of all the people. It also puts an emphasis on counselling supervision which plays a central role in maintaining the psychological health and well-being of our school counsellors. The schools, as in any industrialized nation, are a part of local community activity and reflect the socio-political climate of the country. As a result, they also have become a primary resource for response to crises in the nation and the stresses of our children growing up in this environment. As such, the role of the school counsellor is central to responding to the fears and anxieties of students in times of uncertainty and insecurity.

Recognition of schools as a vital resource to families and children, and of school counsellors as mental health professionals in times of crisis, prompted the Ministry of Education and the department of psychological and counselling services to set up a comprehensive system for the supervision of school counsellors. The primary goals were to assist the school counsellor in the delivery of effective services within the schools and to provide guidance and support in their professional development as counsellors. In 1965, there were only a few hundred counsellors in the schools; in 1998 there were about 2,500 counsellors. Each of these counsellors, regardless of level of experience, is supervised through a network of supervisors across the nation. The system implemented thirty years ago has given birth to a vital and active group of professional supervisors.

As a counsellor educator, I have been involved in the development of a supervision training for school counsellors in Israel as they progress from their role as experienced counsellor to that of supervisor. Over the last two years, I have initiated the use of a portfolio system as a tool to enhance and refine the competencies of these supervisors. In this chapter I will outline the purpose of the portfolio project, its application in training settings, and an illustration of its use.

Supervision of school counsellors in Israel

Counselling in Israel is prevalent in the school system (see Figure 9.1 for a representation of school supervision organization). School counsellors are employed by the Ministry of Education which is also responsible for their professional development and supervision. There are about 25 consulting supervisors appointed

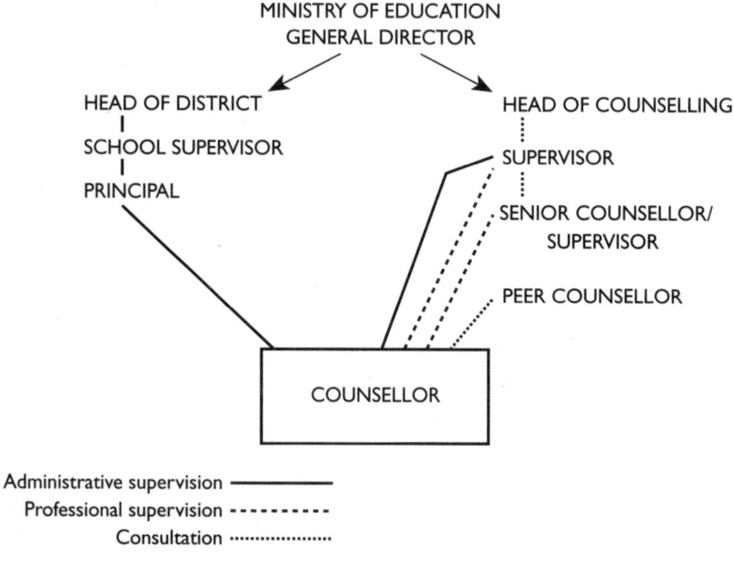

Figure 9.1 *Supervision network and roles in Israel*

by the Ministry of Education to provide supervision for all counsellors in the country and about 100 supervisors who are senior counsellors trained to deliver supervision mostly to entry-level counsellors in their first and second year of work. The supervisors have advanced degrees and have taken a two-year university course organized by the Ministry of Education. Supervisory assignments are made for two years. The supervisor is expected to provide individual and group supervision. Supervision is given usually in the office or home of the supervisor, while the consulting supervisor meets the counsellor usually at the school. In recent years the counsellor has been able to choose his/her supervisor, and supervision models have become more dynamic and flexible. After the completion of the initial two-year assignment, the counsellor primarily receives group supervision and in-service training usually by the consulting supervisor or by other supervisors assigned by the consulting supervisor.

School counsellor roles and competencies

The role of the supervisor in Israel includes both clinical and administrative functions, similar to those defined by the Association for Counselor Education and Supervision in the United States (ACES, 1995). Administrative supervision refers to those supervisory activities which increase the efficiency of the delivery of counselling services – for example, assisting the counsellor in time-management, staff relationships, and contact with school administrative personnel. On the other hand, clinical supervision includes the supportive and educative activities of the counsellor designed to improve the application of counselling theory and technique directly to clients. Roberts and Borders (1994) include clinical knowledge and skill working with students in individual or group counselling sessions and in consultation with parents and teachers, as specific competencies for the school counsellor. Other models for supervision of school counselling have referred to supervision focused on programme development, implementation and co-ordination of classroom guidance activities (Barret and Schmidt, 1986; Schmidt, 1990).

The Ministry of Education has defined the major roles of counsellors in all settings. These roles require various competencies and skills: individual and group counselling; classroom guidance; consultation with management, teachers, parents and other professionals; working with an inter-disciplinary team; working with the school as an organization; and programme planning and evaluation. At each stage of professional development the counsellor is requested to demonstrate additional competencies, depending on the setting he or she is working in and the needs of clients. In addition, because of the socio-political situation of the country, one of the major roles of the school counsellor is centred on crisis intervention and coping strategies for stress. The school counsellor is functioning for all practical purposes as a mental health practitioner in a school setting. The constant high stress and emotional demands placed on the school counsellor make professional burn-out an all too familiar event. As in supervision contexts in general, the roles and competencies of the school counsellor necessarily influence the role, competencies and context of the supervisor's work. The supervisor is crucial for the professional care of the counsellor particularly in the containing of work-related stress. Thus, the supervisor has to be trained in the competencies demanded of crisis work and community disasters in order to help to guide the counsellor in these respects as well as to provide professional support and prevent professional burn-out. In this context, it is important that supervision be viewed as an opportunity to consult, receive guidance, and share the daily experience of working in a highly volatile and unpredictable situation.

Because it is not desirable or possible for the supervisor to be immediately available even in times of crisis, the goals of self-reflection, self-evaluation, and self-instruction are particularly important. The first goal of the supervisor is to encourage professional reflection which will help the counsellor increase his or her competence by learning strategies for self-evaluation (Skovholt and Rønnestad, 1992). The second major goal is the facilitation and enhancement of the counsellor's personal and professional development. The third is promotion of accountable counselling and guidance services and programmes (Boyd, 1978; Roberts and Borders, 1994).

Training course for supervisors

Because in Israel supervision is provided not only to student counsellors, but to professional counsellors also, a supervision system is required that can be responsive to the learning needs both of the novice and of advanced counsellors. Thus, the consultant supervisors appointed by the Ministry of Education are helped by senior counsellors working in the field who provide supervision to novice counsellors (see Figure 9.1). Instruction for these supervisors is through university courses in supervision supported by the Counselling and Psychological Services in the Ministry of Education. Courses are for two years, one full day a week. At the end of the course supervisors get a certificate as school counselling supervisors. The course consists of a theoretical component, covering theories and models of supervision, different orientations to supervision and discussion of articles on supervision. The other component consists of teaching various techniques and skills in counselling and supervision.

The main task during the course is for the supervisor to provide individual supervision to a novice counsellor in the first year, and in the second year group supervision to a group of counsellors. The senior counsellors on the course receive supervision of their supervisory practice with the novice counsellors. Unfortunately, because of financial and organizational limitations, it is impossible to provide each of the supervisors on the course with on-going individual supervision on his/her supervision. In lieu of individual supervision we decided to use the self-instructional method of the portfolio.

The portfolio is an instructional technique frequently used in educational settings. It has proved very useful in helping students integrate the knowledge that they have learned in applied settings that demand complex thinking and action. The portfolio, as we developed it, was used by supervisors to document the process of their supervision and their learning in general for the duration of the course. The remainder of this chapter will describe and illustrate the use of the portfolio as a training and supervision tool.

The use of the portfolio as a self-instructional tool

Portfolios in counsellor education programmes have been used for a number of years in the United States (Carney, Cobia and Shannon, 1996). The portfolio has had two primary purposes: (a) documentation of the student's professional work and growth, and (b) a tool for assessing the quality of the student's work.

Because the portfolio is essentially a qualitative tool, educators have found it challenging to use as an assessment instrument. Several educators (Collins, 1992; Messick, 1994; Navarrete, 1990) have identified the issues of reliability and validity in the evaluative process as a major stumbling block to effective use of the portfolio. It is difficult to get consistent data over time and adequate coder reliability, especially with a portfolio rating system. The costs in time and resources are very high for developing and assessing portfolios. I have been involved in projects that have developed a system for evaluating a school counsellor portfolio rating system (Coleman, James, Tuescher and Hellman, 1996), but the complexity and labour demands involved make it impractical for our situation in Israel. In our experience with supervisors, therefore, the portfolio has been used mostly as an instructional tool to sharpen various competencies of the supervisor. As an instructional tool, supervisors are able to use it to encourage and enhance a detailed and critical review of their work and reflect on their individual development as supervisors. With this approach the portfolio has proved to be a critical vehicle for self-evaluation and professional growth.

Components of the portfolio

A portfolio can be described as a purposeful collection of a learner's work that tells the story of their efforts, progress and achievements. The portfolio requires several skills: documentation of a process in various ways, assuming responsibility for assembling the evidence of change, reflecting upon the process, engaging in self-assessment, and emphasizing and understanding the developmental process. The collection of materials and decision on their inclusion involves a thoughtful decision-making process for the learner. S/he must consider the guidelines for selection, the criteria for judging merit, and the evidence therein to attest to a reflective process of integration (Arter and Spandel, 1992). In our supervision course, we identified five major purposes for the portfolio: self-reflection, self-evaluation, learning progression, individual active learning, and peer collaboration.

The use of portfolios was found to stimulate *self-reflection*. Self-reflection is defined as the process of observing one's actions in a given event, then interpreting these actions with a broad understanding for the purpose of developing and acting on new cognitive structures which are based on the integration of new and old cognition (Tuescher, 1997). Alschuler (1996) and Coleman (1996) have suggested that one of the main outcomes of portfolios is a higher level of self-reflection.

Authentic self-evaluation in counselling and supervision is a complex task. Many writers have emphasized the importance of school counsellors being involved in the process of demonstrating accountability and performing evaluations (Housley, McDaniel and Underwood, 1990; Vacc, Rhyne-Winkler, and Poidevant, 1993). A common approach to evaluating counsellor and supervisor performance is to collect participant evaluations such as attitude surveys, direct observations, case studies, goal-attainment scaling and follow-up studies (Borders and Drury, 1992; Holloway, 1995). The portfolio can include all these approaches and at the same time demonstrate a progression of learning. Portfolios have the potential to be authentic assessments of a professional's work because they call for demonstrations of competence rather than only scores on tests that are designed to measure the skills one needs to perform in a given situation. (Wiggins, 1989; 1991).

The fact that the preparation and development of the portfolio is a learning process, helps the supervisor to document the *learning progression* and to see himself/herself in different stages of his professional development. The portfolio of a first-year supervisor will be different from that of a more senior supervisor. The demonstration of supervision skills and theory-based interventions can be chronicled over time in various formats. By using the portfolio there is a longitudinal month-to-month, year-to-year record keeping and data collection. Longitudinal samples of supervisors' work can be assessed by comparing acquired skills over time.

By developing a portfolio and choosing the evidence to reflect the competencies of the supervisor, the supervisor becomes an *active learner*. It is his or her responsibility to inform and demonstrate to other people the learning that has occurred through the evidence presented in the portfolio. It can also be done in different ways (not necessarily verbal) which allow him/her to demonstrate their learning style. The choice of the materials presented in the portfolio and their demonstration are the personal choice and responsibility of each supervisor. At the same time it offers a multi-dimensional view of learning. The portfolio allows the supervisor to demonstrate skills within the context of certain situations, whether by videotape, by describing situations verbally on audiotape, or in any other creative manner. This choice by the supervisor is in contrast to the dominant position held by many counsellor educators of utilizing audio or videotape recordings as the preferred method to train counsellors and supervisors (Hum, Calder and Zingle, 1981).

The portfolio can be a tool to promote *dialogue and collaborative learning* among peer supervisors on relevant issues. Because the portfolio involves peer evaluation, and is a process, the supervisor, while developing it, will not only evaluate himself but will interact with his peers about issues in the portfolio. It will also involve an on-going dialogue with the trainers on the course as to the content and competencies presented in the portfolio.

In developing portfolios there are *ethical considerations* such as ensuring confidentiality of the materials selected for inclusion. If identifying information cannot be removed in cases of videotapes etc., informed consent must be given. This informed consent should include what materials would be used, how they would be used and who would have access to the materials. This can pose problems, especially if written consent is required.

Trainers must consider carefully the validity, reliability and psychometric limitations of the portfolio before using it as the sole means of summative evaluation. Flexibility and individualization are sometimes contrary to the ethical requirement of having standardization in assessment. Thus the use of portfolios in decisions such as termination or extension of training of counsellors or supervisors is inadvisable unless used in conjunction with other methods (Herman and Winters, 1994; Trustees' Colloquy, 1995). In our context in teaching the supervision course, the prime value is the process of development and self-inquiry that results from this activity.

The process of developing the portfolio

Before developing a portfolio for a specific teaching-learning context, there are several questions that should be addressed. What is the purpose of the portfolio? Who is it designed for? What are the components of the portfolio? Its content? How will the portfolio be reviewed (criteria for evaluation, who will evaluate, when)?

Since in the literature one of the important aspects in developing the portfolio is that it is the responsibility of its owner, we felt that the above questions would be answered most relevantly by the supervisors themselves. We chose two focus groups, both consisting of supervisors, with the task of deciding on the components and the criteria for evaluation of the portfolio. The supervisors were asked what made a good supervisor and to give examples of competence in supervision. The main points made by the group were that a good supervisor

- can apply theory to practice;
- can assess the needs of the counsellor, and the contextual setting;
- can guide the counsellor through the goals that they define together;
- knows how to raise questions and not necessarily solutions;
- has the ability for self-evaluation and feedback;
- encourages the counsellor to think reflectively;
- is open to new ideas, keeps being updated and develops him or herself;
- is ethical, knows how far to go (boundaries, limits in supervision);
- possesses good interpersonal communication skills and gives support.

To conclude, the group decided to divide the competencies into three basic categories: (a) *organizational skills*: contract between supervisor and supervisee, common definition of goals, needs assessment; (b) *personal characteristics*: flexible, open, clear professional identity, supportive; and (c) *knowledge*: cognitive skills and knowledge of various techniques; knowledge of supervision and counselling theories and programmes.

It was decided that the purpose of the portfolio would be to sharpen the competencies of the supervisors in their practice. Supervisors and trainers would collaborate in its development through the duration of the course. Organization of the contents of the portfolio followed the Systems Approach to Supervision (SAS) (Holloway, 1995) because the model is flexible enough to accommodate different field and cultural settings while also providing an organized scheme for analysing supervisory interaction. Thus, all supervisors were trained in the SAS model as a part of the work of the course. To promote a collaborative learning style in the course, it was decided that the portfolio would be reviewed by a peer supervisor on the course. This collaboration would promote an on-going dialogue throughout the development of the portfolio, rather than leaving evaluation to the end when it would take on a more summative tone.

The portfolio consisted of five parts:

1. Theoretical basis: school counselling as a profession, statement of goals and philosophy, theories of supervision of school counselling, various relevant articles, class assignments in relation to theoretical readings and reflection on the process of learning and developing a professional identity.
2. Supervision sessions with the supervisee (counsellor) – sessions were described and analysed according to the model of supervision by Holloway (1995). In addition there were audiotapes of three sessions. Materials presented to the supervisee for use with students were also included. Every session was followed by self-reflection as to the competencies demonstrated in the session.
3. General self-assessment of the process of supervision. This section also included an assessment form filled in by the supervisee, major strengths and weaknesses as seen by the supervisor in the supervision process, and description of critical moments in supervision.
4. Dialogue with a peer supervisor during the process. Major points of professional development as presented in the portfolio. Competencies in various stages of the professional development of the supervisor as seen by the peer supervisor.
5. External evaluation of the two trainers on the course, given at three points during the year.

An elaboration of the second part of the portfolio follows, since it is the core of the work of the supervisor. This section of the portfolio was organized according to the seven dimensions in Holloway's systems approach to supervision (1995; see Figure 9.2).

Case example of the SAS supervision portfolio

As described in Holloway's (1995) model, the wings are of differing importance depending on the training case being analysed. In this section critical contextual factors of the relationship will be discussed, and the SAS matrix will be applied to demonstrate the supervisory intervention. (Names of supervisor and supervisee have been altered in order to protect identity of participants.) First, I will describe the contextual factors of supervisor, (trainee) supervisee, institution and client – abridged from the original portfolio materials because of limitations of space. The core factor of relationship is the most critical aspect of this training dilemma and is therefore presented in more detail. This was also the basis for the dialogue with the peer supervisor.

The supervisor

Professional experience: The supervisor, Aliza, has worked as a school counsellor for fourteen years.
Role in supervision: The supervisor has been involved in supervision informally for the previous three years. She is part of a (leading) counsellors' team developing specific counselling programmes for schools and is in charge of teaching those programmes to her colleagues.
Theoretical orientation: Masters degree in counselling. Aliza is trained in various approaches. She mainly uses a cognitive-behavioural approach in her counselling and supervision.
Cultural characteristics: Middle-aged woman. Married. Two adolescent sons. One daughter who is almost the age of the supervisee.
Self-presentation: The supervisor offers her knowledge in supervision and also her functioning as a consultant by being on the leading team of counsellors.

The supervisee

Professional experience: Batya, the counsellor, is working for the first time as a counsellor. She has worked for a short period as a schoolteacher.
Theoretical orientation: Batya is finishing her Masters degree in counselling. She is not clear as to a specific orientation in counselling.
Learning needs and style: She likes to collect data and information before acting. She can be described as a detail-oriented person.
Cultural characteristics: Young woman (27 years old), married with a baby. Israeli *Sabra* (born in Israel).
Self-presentation: A strong desire to be supervised and a need to learn more.

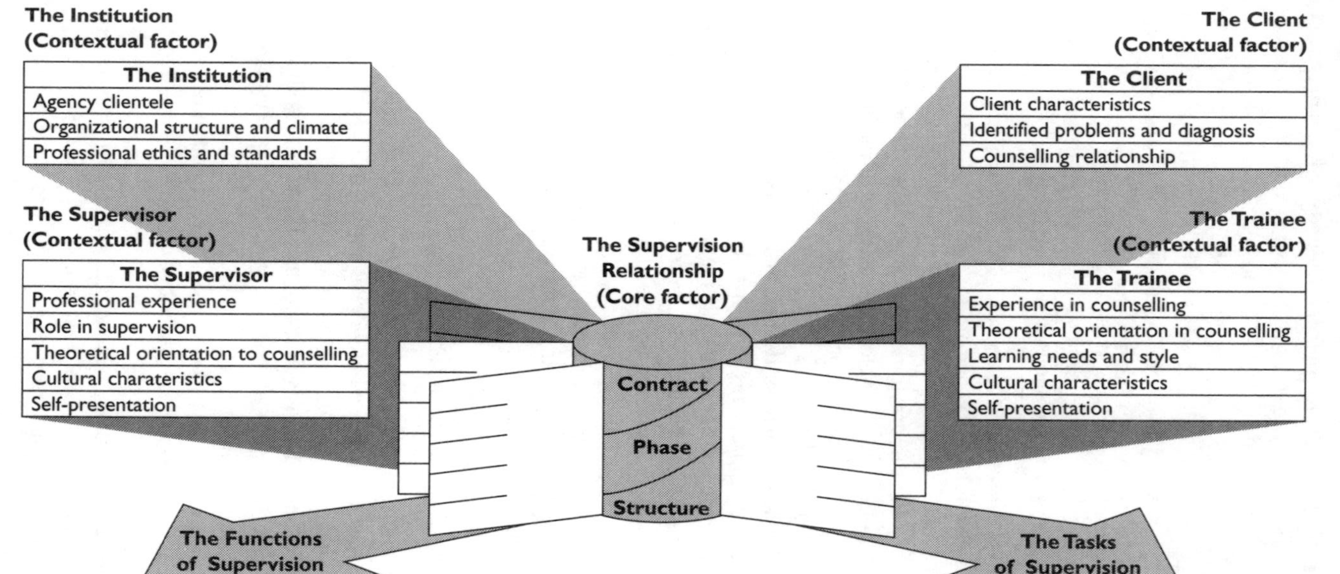

Figure 9.2 *Systems Approach to Supervision (Holloway, 1995; copyright by Sage Publications, Thousand Oaks, CA. Reprinted with permission of the author.)*

The institution

Agency clientele: Both supervisor and counsellor work in a school setting. Counsellor (supervisee) is offering counselling services not only to the students but also to teachers and management.
Organizational structure and climate: The principal of the school where the counsellor works is new and introduces a lot of changes in the school. The supervisee (counsellor) has taken the place of a senior counsellor who used to work in the school.
Ethical policies and procedures: Supervisor and supervisee work in the same district, while the consulting supervisor is responsible for the professional development of both. There are issues of confidentiality as to what information should be given to the consulting supervisor and to the principal of the supervisee.

The supervisory relationship: critical factors

There were three critical phases in the development of this supervisory relationship. Each phase is represented by the contextual factors of supervisor and supervisee, the core relationship, and the process matrix in Figures 9.3, 9.4 and 9.5. The remaining contextual factors, institution and client, are not depicted because they were not as prominent in the dynamics that ensued between the supervisor and supervisee. This is not meant to suggest that they were not considered in devising intervention strategies.

Phase one

The supervisor, Aliza, reflects in the portfolio about the supervision relationship. The supervision relationship at this early stage was accompanied with a lot of stress and tension, especially felt by the supervisor (also noticed by the supervisee as reflected in the taped supervision sessions). To help uncover the elements that might have been contributing to this interpersonal tension, Aliza and her peer supervisor engaged in a focused dialogue using the supervisee (trainee) elements of SAS (see Figure 9.2). By doing this, the underlying reasons contributing to her anxiety in this relationship became clear to Aliza, the supervisor. It was very hard for her to face the fact that the supervisee, Batya, was a young women who had almost finished her graduate studies in counselling, while she, the supervisor, as an older woman, struggled even to be accepted for graduate studies.

In the description of the first session (shown also on a videotape), Batya, the supervisee, brought her frustration to the session. She explained to the supervisor that she felt a need to satisfy the demands of the teachers in the school who tended to refer too many students to her. The teachers were hoping for immediate solutions to their students' problems. Batya felt completely overwhelmed by her counselling role and the teachers' demands, yet also thought that she must do something to justify her role as a school counsellor. Aliza, experiencing her supervisee's sense of urgency, responded by providing her with a series of short-term strategies to deal with the teachers' needs (Figure 9.3, matrix, advising and instructing with counselling skills).

In the portfolio, the supervisor reflected on the parallel process at this stage. She saw her own need to satisfy the supervisee and respond immediately by giving her prescriptions rather than engaging in a dialogue about Batya's anxiety around her role. It seemed to Aliza that she also was trying to justify her value as a supervisor (Figure 9.3, supervisor wing, professional experience). She noted that this first session was also devoted to express mutual expectations and goals for supervision (contracting).

This session was analysed according to the tasks and functions of supervision, following Holloway's model (1995; see Figure 9.3). The supervisor examined and reflected on the teaching tasks and functions she demonstrated during the session. One of the questions the supervisor asked the counsellor was why she chose to become a counsellor (matrix – professional role). Batya's response was that she needed to be in control and to satisfy the needs of other people. This response described the supervisee's primary interpersonal strategies or 'self-presentational style' (supervisee wing) and helped the supervisor to reflect on Batya's view of her professional role and on the role of interpersonal needs in the counselling and supervisory relationship (relationship-structure).

The dialogue of reflection with her peer supervisor led Aliza, the supervisor, to realize that the first phase of the supervisory relationship was characterized by tension and anxiety. In attending to her own sense of inadequacy in her professional achievement, Aliza recognized that she was threatened by Batya's high motivation on one hand, and her unrealistic expectations as to satisfying the needs of every one at school. In some ways it seemed to Aliza that she had taken on those same needs as a supervisor with Batya. She started to understand that the tension was related to her own sense of competitiveness with Batya's academic achievement. She acknowledged that she felt

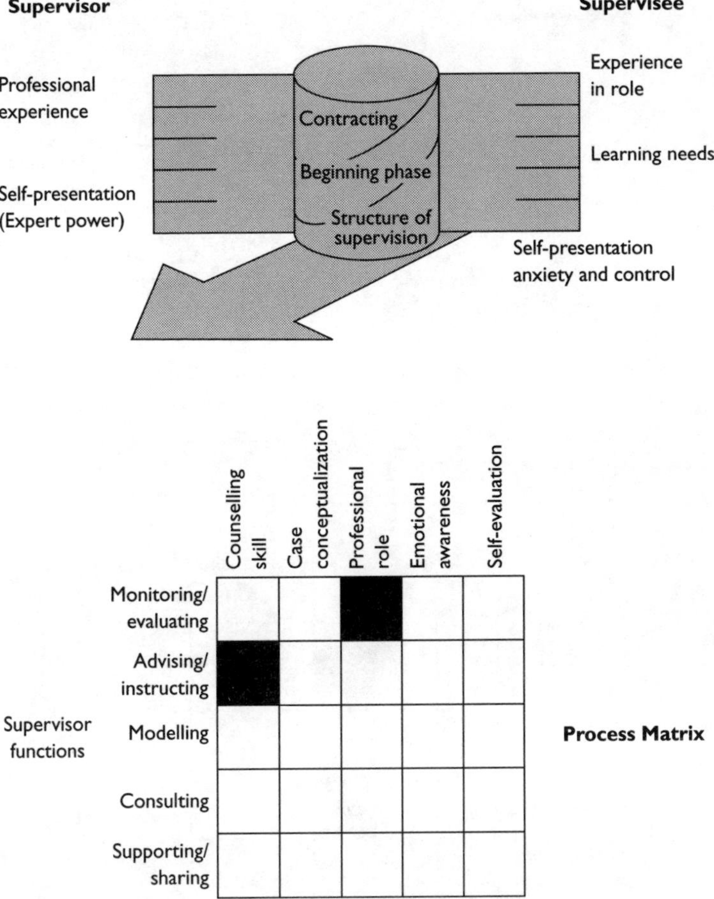

Figure 9.3 *Phase one of supervisory relationship (Holloway, 1995; copyright by Sage Publications, Thousand Oaks, CA. Reprinted with permission of the author.)*

unable to meet all of Batya's needs because of her sense of failure in relation to her own education and knowledge.

Phase two

The second phase (Figure 9.4) of the supervisory relationship is centred on the counsellor's response to a student whose brother was killed in an army attack in Lebanon. As soon as the school had been notified about it, the counsellor was involved

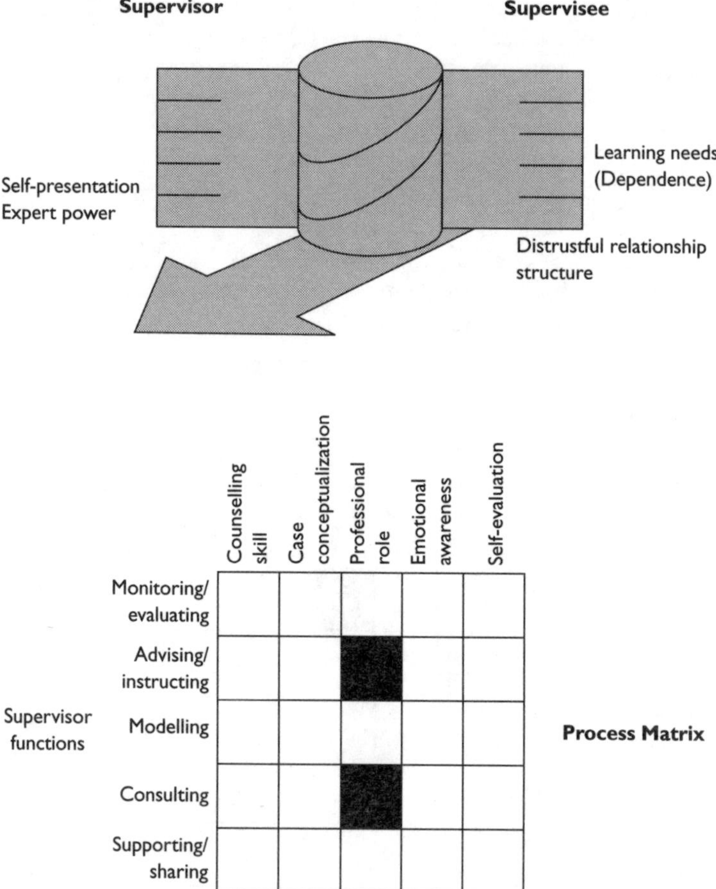

Figure 9.4 *Phase two of supervisory relationship (Holloway, 1995; copyright by Sage Publications, Thousand Oaks, CA. Reprinted with permission of the author.)*

in consulting teachers and talking to the students in the victim's sister's class. Some of the students also had brothers in the army and were overwhelmed with fear that their own brothers might be killed. This is not an unusual reaction and Batya, the counsellor, was able to provide them with individual counselling sessions around these issues. However, she felt helpless as to how to proceed with the teachers and other classmates. This was surprising to Aliza, the supervisor, because the constant potential of death from military activities in Israel means that there are very specific guidelines for handling such situations. The supervisor reflected on the fact that in the process of supervision at this point, she herself was mostly involved in consulting and instructing around the professional role of the counsellor, almost dictating to her a plan of action, while she really felt she should have been involved in uncovering Batya's feelings of being overwhelmed emotionally (supporting and emotional awareness) even though the supervisee was more likely to present it as not knowing what to do (learning needs and counselling experience).

In this second phase, the relationship, although not as tense and competitive, was characterized by the supervisee's dependence on being told what to do and her unwillingness to trust that the supervisor would be able to help her. Aliza found herself instructing and advising in order to be helpful, and yet she also reflected on how this approach made her feel superior to and more expert than the counsellor in spite of her inferior academic qualifications. She saw also how her sense of inadequacy was being communicated subtly to Batya, thus promoting Batya's distrust of her advice.

Phase three

The third phase (Figure 9.5) was a supervision session which was centred on the need of the counsellor to be involved in group work at school but, at the same time, she reported a sense of inadequacy in managing this task. She felt that she was disappointing the supervisor by not being prepared to do group work. Aliza, the supervisor, had spent most of the previous supervision session giving Batya ideas and instructions on how to proceed with the group, and on hearing Batya's report felt very guilty that she had not helped Batya. This time, instead of teaching more strategies, Aliza was able to support the counsellor by explaining the difficulties of working in groups, especially under the conditions that the counsellor described. The reflection of the supervisor moved from advising and instructing around the professional role, to supporting and sharing around Batya's emotional response to the group work and her need for more realistic self-evaluation. She taught her not to be so critical of her work hoping that it would free her to be more effective and accepting of where she was in her learning progression. In this third phase, the

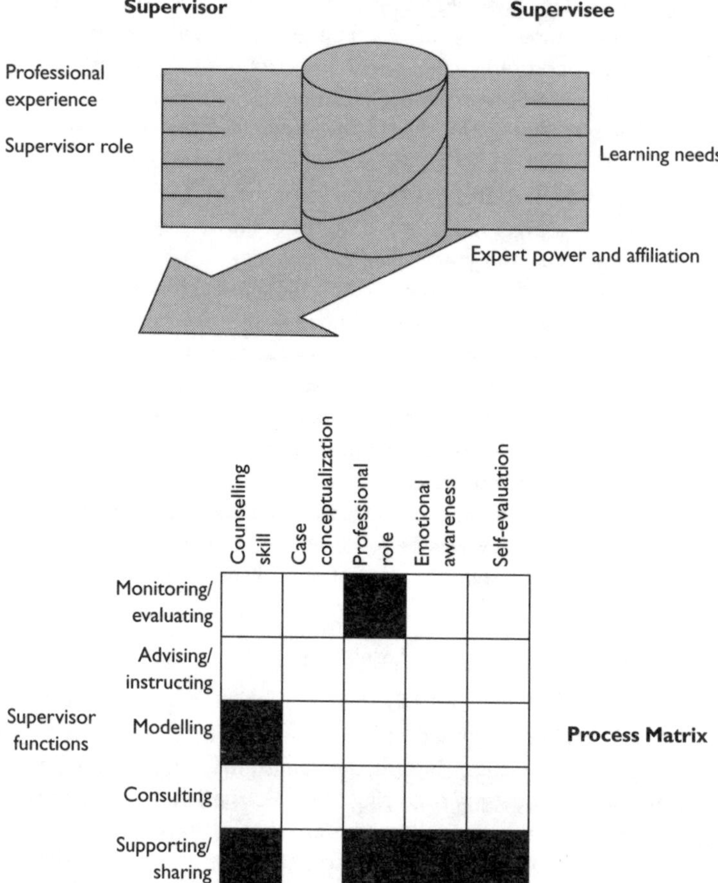

Figure 9.5 *Phase three of supervisory relationship (Holloway, 1995; copyright by Sage Publications, Thousand Oaks, CA. Reprinted with permission of the author.)*

counsellor showed more confidence, but there was still a big gap between her knowledge and understanding and her ability to apply it in practice. No longer experiencing competitiveness with Batya, the supervisor became more supportive and more involved in developing the supervisee's emotional awareness around her role as a counsellor. By being able authentically to offer encouragement and belief in the abilities of the counsellor, yet acknowledge her own shortcomings, Aliza was able to experience herself as a helpful supervisory guide.

The final reflection on this process of relationship development was reflected in the peer supervisor's notes:

> I can see the process of the counsellor moving from a dependent position and lacking self confidence to independence and a clear professional identity. In spite of the difficulties you encountered with the supervisee in your interpersonal relationship, I can see her using you as a support and a professional resource person. Your self-awareness, ability to apply your theoretical knowledge to practice, your use of various techniques and your professional modelling were obvious throughout this process.

The articulation of the phases of supervision became clear to the supervisor as she engaged in the portfolio process and reflected on her work with the peer supervisor. The SAS model (Holloway, 1995) as a basis of organizing the analysis of the process and having a common language to frame the events helped the supervisor to self-evaluate her own dynamic needs, her supervisor role, and understand how these factors influenced the process of teaching and learning in the relationship. To summarize, I would like to quote one of the supervisors in her portfolio:

> Developing a portfolio was a very complicated and controversial task. On one hand it involved a lot of time and thus did not appeal to me; on the other hand, you hear so much about portfolios in education that I was curious to be involved in it. There is no other way but to experience it yourself if you want to know what it is. The main contribution in developing the portfolio for me was the dialogue with my peer supervisor and my own self-reflection. There would not have been any other way to explore, understand and use my competencies as supervisor if I were not able to look into the process I went through with the help of the portfolio. For me it was one of the best learning tools I have experienced. In spite of the long process and hard work, I can only thank you for allowing me to know this tool.

References

ACES (Association for Counselor Education and Supervision) (1995) Ethical Guidelines for counseling supervisors. *Counselor Education and Supervision*, 36: 270–6.

Alschuler, A.S. (1996) The portfolio emperor has no clothes: he should stay naked: *Counselor Education and Supervision*, 36: 133–7.

Arter, J.A. and Spandel, V. (1992) Using portfolios of student work in instruction and assessment. *Educational Measurement*, 11: 36–44.

Barret, R.L. and Schmidt, J.J. (1986) School counselor certification and supervision: overlooked professional issues. *Counselor Education and Supervision*, 26: 50–5.

Borders, D.L. and Drury, S.M. (1992) Comprehensive school counseling programs: a review for policy makers and practitioners. *Journal of Counseling and Development*, 70: 487–98.

Boyd, J. (1978) *Counselor Supervision*. Indiana: Accelerated Development.

Carney, S.J., Cobia, D.C. and Shannon, D.M. (1996) The use of portfolios in clinical and comprehensive evaluations of counselors-in-training. *Counselor Education and Supervision*, 36: 122–32.

Coleman, H.L.K, (1996) Portfolio assessment of multicultural counseling competency. *The Counseling Psychologist*, 2: 216–29.

Coleman, H.L.K, James, A., Tuescher, K. and Hellman, S. (1996) Portfolio assessment of school counselor competence. Unpublished manuscript.

Collins, A. (1992) Portfolios for science education: issues in purpose, structure and authenticity. *Science Education*, 75: 451–63.

Herman, J.L. and Winters, L. (1994) Portfolio research: a slim collection. *Educational Leadership*, 52(2): 48–55.

Holloway, E.L. (1995) *Clinical Supervision: A Systems Approach*. Thousand Oaks, CA: Sage.

Housley, W.F., McDaniel, L.C. and Underwood, J.R. (1990) Mandated assessment of counselors in Mississippi. *The School Counselor*, 37: 294–302.

Hum, A., Calder, P. and Zingle, H.W. (1981) Language laboratory use and the development of self-instructional training tape programs in counsellor education. *Canadian Counsellor*, 15 (4): 185–92.

Messick, S. (1994) The interplay of evidence and consequences in the validation of performance assessments. *Educational Researcher*, 23: 13–23.

Navarrete, C. (1990) *Informal Assessment in Educational Evaluation: Implications for Bilingual Education Programs*. Washington, DC: Office of Bilingual Education and Minority Languages Affairs. National Clearing House for Bilingual Education.

Roberts, E.B. and Borders, L.W. (1994) Supervision of School Counselors: Administrative, Program and Counseling. *The School Counselor*, 41: 149–57.

Schmidt, J.J. (1990) Critical issues for the school counselor: performance appraisal and supervision. *The School Counselor*, 38: 86–95.

Skovholt, T.M. and Rønnestad M.H. (1992) *The Evolving Professional Self. Stages and Themes in Therapist and Counselor Development*. New York: Wiley & Sons.

Tuescher, K.D. (1997) *The Effect of Portfolios on Self-reflection in Counseling Students*. Unpublished dissertation, University of Wisconsin-Madison.

Trustees' Colloquy (1995) *Performance Assessment: Different Needs, Difficult Answers*. Princeton, NJ: Educational Testing Service.

Vacc, N.A., Rhyne-Winkler, M.C. and Poidevant, J.M. (1993) Evaluation and accountability of counseling services: possible implications for a midsize school district. *The School Counselor*, 40: 260–6.

Wiggins, G. (1989) A true test: toward more authentic and equitable assessment. *Phi Delta Kappan*, 70: 703–13.

Wiggins, G. (1991) Standards, not standardization: evoking quality student work. *Educational Leadership*, 47: 17–25.

Index